SEX, DEATH AND VIDEOTAPE

Fotopoulos stood behind Deidre and raised the camera, focusing it on a smiling Ramsey. He had told her she too would face a test that night. He ordered Deidre to shoot. She looked at him for a long, questioning moment, then raised the gun.

The slight cough of the small weapon was lost in the pine woods, but it was captured by Kosta's whirring video camera. Through the viewfinder, he saw the handsome blond teenager's leg jerk in pain. He heard him groan, then cry out to God. The small weapon in Deidre's slim hand sputtered yellow-blue flame twice more. Ramsey slumped against his bonds, his chin on his bloodied chest. The camera saw Deidre stride forward toward the boy. With a steady hand, she filled her fingers with his hair, pulled his head upward, and fired a fourth shot into his brain. Deidre was breathing hard. Her eyes blazed in wild, almost carnal triumph. Fotopoulos lowered the camera.

Upon their return to Lenox Avenue, Deidre and Kosta clawed away each other's clothing and made white-hot, hurting love. . . .

FEMMES FATALES

True Stories of the Most Vicious Women on Death Row

Tom Kuncl

First published in Great Britain in 1995 by
True Crime
an imprint of Virgin Publishing Ltd
332 Ladbroke Grove
London W10 5AH

First published in the USA by Pocket Books,
a division of Simon & Schuster Inc.

A catalogue record for this book is available from the British
Library.

ISBN 0 86369 873 5

Printed and bound in Great Britain by
Cox & Wyman Ltd, Reading, Berks

The author wishes to dedicate this work to the two little girls who are the sunrise that dawns each morning in his heart, the rainbows of sweet promise that subdue life's tears at each day's end, the fond custodians of warm memory he hopes one day they will recall, and the strong, proud, good persons he knows it is their destiny to become. Natalie, Nicole, my wondrous, precious daughters, you are always with me, even though we are apart.

Contents

Contents

Introduction

America remains one of only two major world nations in which the crime of murder may be punished by death. It is the only enlightened nation in recent history to execute a woman for a capital offense.

Since the Colonial era, nearly 18,500 persons have been put death by those in whom the law has vested the authority to take a life for a life. Among those legions of condemned, fewer than 500 have been women.

How wisely, humanely, and with what result that power has been employed in the course of our history has been a cloudy, divergent, emotional thesis among people of equal conscience.

You may choose from the opinions of numerous great minds to reach a personal conclusion as to the justice, the morality, the societal consequences, of exacting an eye for an eye when the hand fresh with mayhem's blood is found out.

"Every unpunished murderer takes away something from the security of every man's life," famed American statesman-orator Daniel Webster believed.

With icy cynicism, poet Alexander Pope passed his own judgment on the sentence of death:

The hungry judges soon the sentence sign,
And wretches hang that jurymen may dine.

On the bleak death rows of thirty-six states that impose execution as the punishment for heinous murder, more than 2,600 condemned slayers await their fate. Among them, at present, are thirty-two women.

The total number, comprising both men and women, varies from year to year owing to the carrying out of some death warrants—less than thirty in 1992—cases overturned on appeal, new death sentences decreed, some rescinded by commutation, and a few made moot through death by natural cause of some of the row's aging residents.

Since the resumption of capital punishment in 1976, only one woman on America's death row has been killed by the state. Arsenic poisoner Velma Barfield died at the hands of North Carolina's executioner on November 2, 1984. The current appeals process makes it unlikely another woman will die soon for the crimes of which she was adjudged guilty.

That women comprise little more than 1 percent of those under sentence of death in America seems to be specifically indicative of little more than unprovable, often novel hypothesis. Women are, by nature, less prone to violence, you may conjecture, yet more than 2,000 are charged with the crime of murder each year, the FBI reports. The murders committed by women are frequently crimes of reaction, not premeditation, one may presume with some justification. They are impulsive, a goaded or protective response to some brutal menace of a husband, a boyfriend. Yet the pages of this book overflow with acts of cruelty judged cold, heinous, and undeserving of mercy by juries that, in more than one agonizing instance, searched their souls to find some grounds to stay their hand from marking the death ballot.

To say that women who kill rise from some easily

defined social strata or condition denies the evidence. A minister's wife ruthlessly poisons numerous victims over the course of a small-town life above suspicion; a grandmother on a Missouri farm takes part in the cold-blooded slayings of young farm hands; the daughter of a respected Oklahoma family trades sex and drugs for the contract murder of her devoted husband; a freckle-faced angel from a broken home begins a life of drug abuse at ten and slaughters two victims with a bloody pickax at twenty-four—the lives of women who kill have no discernable or predictable weave.

Sincere people hold opposite views about imposing the death penalty. I believe it to be just. The adoption of more humane methods of execution, such as lethal injection, although cold comfort for those who must suffer it, has brought us to an era of compassion that has not always attended this grim necessity. From *The Book of Common Prayer* (1892), these terrible passages were read to men awaiting the fall of the gallows trap:

> Dearly beloved, it hath pleased Almighty God, in His justice, to bring you under the sentence and condemnation of the law. You are shortly to suffer death in such a manner that others, warned by your example, may be the more afraid to offend; and we pray God that you may make such use of your punishment in this world that your soul may be saved in the world to come. . . .

I choose to believe a more loving God withholds final judgment for each haunted inhabitant of America's death row, as He does for us all.

— Tom W. Kuncl
Singer Island, Riviera Beach, Florida
Christmas 1992

1

Maria Isa

ANOTHER DAY OF SEETHING, EXHAUSTING FAMILY UPHEAVAL had buffeted and torn at the heavy heart of Maria Isa. Behind the counter of her small grocery store on grimy Shaw Boulevard, Maria distractedly tried to focus her attention on friendly banter with her familiar black and Hispanic customers. She rang up their small purchases, bagged them, and waved an absent thank you as they exited back onto the street under a cloudy November St. Louis sky.

But there was no way to avoid hearing the endless rantings of her bearded husband, Zein, as he spewed an agitated stream of Arabic into the telephone. He had been making and receiving calls from family members and friends almost continuously. Each conversation boiled over with more red anger and black threats, all of them concerning what was to be done about the youngest of the Isas' four daughters, Palestina.

She would not call herself by that sacred name. Instead, the pretty sixteen-year-old insisted on answering only to Tina. Zein was furious with Tina, who had become dangerously seduced by sinful American

ways, who was turning her back on holy Islam, who
dared to defy her father's Muslim code, and who now
sneaked about seeing a twenty-year-old black man
against the family's outraged objections.

Maria Isa shuddered but made no protest as she
heard still another outburst of rage as Zein ranted on
the telephone about Tina to one of his other dutiful
daughters.

"You know, for me, this one has become a burned
woman, a black whore, and there is no way to cleanse
her except through the red color that cleanses her,"
the sixty-year-old father barked into the phone.

"There is no way, there is no way to teach her
manners. Teaching her has to take place in the hotel
underground. If God makes my wish, I'll put her in
the grave," Zein Isa said before hanging up the phone.

Forty-eight-year-old Maria Isa turned away from
her husband's glare. She quickly crossed herself to
bring God's protection on her warring family, a
simple supplication of faith she had learned reared as
a Roman Catholic in Brazil. She added a silent prayer
that God had been too busy to hear Zein's dreadful
petition.

Even as an acquiescent wife, Maria had been partly
a stranger in Zein's dim, secretive, volatile camp of
faith, family, and passionate politics. With her husband, Maria had four handsome daughters. The family had lived nomadically in the Mideast, Brazil,
Puerto Rico, and, finally, St. Louis, Missouri, where
they had settled in 1984, five years earlier. Zein
maintained close contact with events in the Middle
East. He seemed to know a great deal about the
activities of the Palestine Liberation Organization
(PLO). Although Zein had become a naturalized
American citizen and Maria had not, he angrily
disapproved of the moral emptiness he saw in life
here. But three of his daughters had grown to saintly

2

womanhood guided by his firm prophet's hand. So would Palestina, he vowed.

It was much easier for Maria Isa to understand what her bright, vivacious, fun-loving youngest daughter was going through. Tina was an eager, quick-to-adapt teenage girl who had lived in various blighted and chaotic corners of the world. Of course she wanted to explore and pass through all the new and wonderful doors life in America was opening to her. Maria Isa could imagine what different roads her own life might have taken if she'd had Tina's opportunities.

Zein Isa, his older daughters, and the closely knit congress of refugee Palestinians who had settled in St. Louis had no such tolerance for the alarming directions they believed Tina's young womanhood was taking. They saw Tina's every act, however innocent appearing, as a new, head-strong gauntlet of rejection and rebellion flung in the face of the family and their deeply rooted values.

Tina was becoming a scandal, her elder sisters said. Perhaps remembering their own regimented upbringing, they goaded their father to impose the same harsh standards on Tina that had worked so well to keep them true to the family faith and honor.

A year earlier, when it was discovered that Tina had disregarded her father's edict that she not attend a junior prom at Roosevelt High School, the sisters roared with their father to the school gym and physically forced a tearful and embarrassed Tina to leave with them and return home.

Maria Isa found herself almost constantly on painfully rocky family ground. Her three obedient daughters had begun to imply—sometimes straight to her face—that she had been far too sympathetic to Tina's erring ways, that she was not a proper mother to Tina or a faithful wife to their father because of her sympathy for their younger sister's impudence. The day was soon coming when she would have to decide just whose cause was right, they warned. A cold front settled between Maria Isa and her three daughters. Zein Isa openly berated his wife for her vacillation and laxity where Tina's spiritual welfare was concerned.

Maria Isa agonized over these damning accusations. She needed to examine her conscience. Was she wrongheadedly pitting herself against the honest concerns of her own family, relatives, and friends? Was Tina the sweet and innocent child she so desperately believed her to be? Or was there some truth to the dark suspicions of everyone else—that Tina constantly used deceitful ploys to remove herself from the family's watching eyes in order to secretly live a shameful life that would lead her to the worst depths of an infidel's hell?

When Tina said she wanted to play on her school's tennis team and the hockey squad, it had taken Maria's strong intervention—against Zein's objections—to allow her to play.

"Her place is working in the store after school. Her sisters did and she must, too," Zein commanded. "I think she is about the devil's business."

On other occasions, Maria had not so strongly taken up the girl's cause, and Zein and the family's iron-handed decisions prevailed. Although she was among the top students in her senior class, she was not permitted to go along on a student trip to Washington, D.C. When the studious teenager pleaded to be allowed to attend a six-week summer honors course at the University of Missouri, her request was flatly refused.

But no infraction of the Isa clan's beliefs so inflamed them, so mocked, and so galvanized them as the forbidden friendship and young love that had begun without their knowledge between Tina and tall, handsome, black, twenty-year-old Cliff Walker, a quiet neighborhood youth who often shopped in the store.

It was in that store, while Tina worked as a cashier, that she came to know Walker and admire his easy laugh and calm maturity. Shyly at first, then in hours of tearful talks, she told Walker of her turbulent home life and her yearnings to enjoy the simple freedoms that seemed so ordinary to all of her classmates.

"I know my mom and dad love me and want what's best for me, but this isn't the West Bank. This is America. People shouldn't have to let other people tell them what they're going to do with their lives," Tina would tell Cliff.

They began dating in January 1989. When the Isa family learned what was going on, they were certain their most dire conjectures about Tina's corruption had been right. "There is your tennis and soccer. Lies! All lies!" Zein hurled into the face of Maria Isa. "All she wanted was to be with that nigger!" he spat.

Maria began to worry even more. Why would Tina choose to keep her schoolgirl infatuation from her own mother? Had Maria known, she might have been able to find some way to make the friendship more acceptable to the family. But going behind their backs brought shame on a God-fearing and respectable home.

In a fury fueled by what she believed was Tina's betrayal of her trust, Maria Isa stormed into a counselor's office at Roosevelt High School. One of her daughters accompanied her, watching and listening.

"Tina is to be removed from school today. She will not be coming back," Maria told a concerned Pamela Fournier, the girl's advisor.

"The problem was that Tina was seeing Cliff," the

counselor remembers. "They were absolutely against it. I knew this girl was in for a real stoning from her family."

Pamela Fournier argued that removing Tina from school would not bring about what they were demanding. Rather, it would only further damage the shaky relationship between Tina and her family. She convinced the pair that Tina should not be summoned from class to clean out her locker.

Although Tina was permitted to remain in school, Pamela Fournier was concerned the incident was far from over. Tina was a gifted and popular student. It would be a tragedy for her to not finish high school and go on to college. Fournier hoped her own diplomacy had calmed what she feared was a highly unstable situation.

Life for Tina and her contentious family did not get better. Almost daily, Maria came under new, sharp attacks from her opinionated daughters; they opined that Maria needed to take part firmly in reigning in her "baby" girl. Maria understood enough Arabic to know when the family was talking about her in their frequent gatherings. She needed no interpreter to understand the meaning of their smouldering side glances. They wanted her to know that she as well as Tina had become the shameful topic of wagging tongues.

Once, Tina let slip a secret that she and Maria shared. Maria had promised that, perhaps, if Tina could bend somewhat to please her father, there was a chance mother and daughter could take a trip to Paris the following summer. Tina, an eager student of French, had promised to try. Later, in a flickering moment of truce, she mentioned that possible dream trip to one of her sisters. Maria and Tina's innocent secret was revealed and strongly denounced by the family. The daughters hinted to Zein the secretly planned trip was most likely the beginning of a plot between the two to leave the clan and never return.

Zein's brooding deepened. Now he spoke more softly so Maria could not hear everything he said in his endless conversations on the telephone at work and home. Those snatches Maria did overhear worried her more every day.

Zein frequently spoke with an old friend from the West Bank, Abu Nafiz, now living in St. Louis, a man he reverently and affectionately called "my brother." He told Nafiz that his patience with Palestina was nearing an end. "She has no respect for her father," he complained once. "There is but one way for this child to learn and that is in another world," he added.

Even more ominously, Zein Isa bluntly told his daughter Fatima Abdeljabbar that he knew he would someday have to kill Tina. He would do it with a knife. "I'll put the knife in her hands after she falls down, of course," Maria Isa heard her husband tell Fatima.

The cheery greetings shoppers at the family store had become accustomed to were now subdued as weeks of turmoil continued to shake Maria Isa's home.

"Are you feeling okay, Maria?" concerned customers would ask.

She brushed away their friendly concerns with a weak smile. "It's nothing. Maybe a little flu," she would answer.

Maria Isa felt there was no one to whom she could speak or ask for advice about how to endure in a house so tragically divided. She had been guided by her husband's view of the world and by his decisions for nearly thirty years. In almost every situation, he had proven to be an honest, decent, caring husband and father. But was he right now about Tina? Surely the wild threats he had been making lately were only

7

hot-headed rhetoric, the kind of noisy but harmless bombast that spilled all over the pages of the PLO literature he read so religiously.

The climate in the Isa home heated to a flash point in early November 1989. Hard on the heels of Maria's threat to withdraw Tina from school unless she stopped seeing Cliff Walker, the girl told her family she wanted to take a night job at a nearby Wendy's Restaurant.

Zein shouted his firm veto of Tina's idea. It was another lying excuse, schemed up by Tina so she would have more free hours to spend with the black man. Maria did not find Tina's wish so unreasonable, but she would not face Zein's scalding ire to give her blessing. Tina adamantly insisted she would take the job. She was accustomed to her father's opposition to almost everything she wanted to do, anything that took her out of the stifling confines of his rigid world and into the freedom of life in America. She would risk his anger. She had ridden it out before.

Tina's first night on the job at Wendy's whisked by. The quick-to-learn honor student had no difficulty picking up the small food preparation tricks that distinguished that restaurant's fare from other fast-food operations. Her supervisor watched her cheerfully learn her tasks, pleased they'd been able to hire the friendly youngster, particularly for the hectic night shift.

Tina smiled and chatted animatedly that first night with the other young workers. They noticed, however, curious moments when Tina seemed caught up in moody, anxious pensiveness. She failed to hear and respond to some friendly remarks as they passed by her in the bustling work area. She often glanced at the small gold-banded watch she wore, then softly frowned, as though she had some secret quarrel with the advancing hands of the timepiece.

There had already been one ugly confrontation earlier that morning at the apartment on Delor Street as she prepared to leave for morning classes at Roosevelt High. The entire family was enraged that she had taken the night job rather than helping stock shelves and wait on customers at the small store on Shaw Boulevard.

As it neared time for her shift to end, Tina knew that another stormy clash awaited her when she returned home wearing the work smock and trousers symbolizing her disobedience.

Tina penciled in her time slip and told her shift supervisor she had enjoyed her first night of work and that she'd be in on time the next afternoon. She exited out onto the now nearly empty parking lot and glanced in several directions. She brightened as she saw Cliff Walker striding toward her with a broad smile, hands thrust in his jeans pockets against the late autumn chill.

"How'd it go?" he asked. "Did you eat all of Dave's burgers?"

Tina laughed. "After you wrap up a thousand of them, you're too tired to eat one," she said. Then her smile vanished, replaced by a tight-lipped shadow of worry. "There's going to be trouble at my house tonight. My dad and mom are really going to freak because of this job."

"You want me to talk to them?" Walker gently queried.

"I don't think so. That would only freak them worse," she quickly responded. "But I sure hope you're here to walk me home," she said regaining her perky grin.

"Why else?" Walker smiled back. He took her hand in his. They hunched shoulders into the late evening wind and set out on the walk through the city's tough south side.

At the doorstep of the apartment building, Walker asked again if Tina wanted him to go in with her. She told him it would be better if he did not but asked him to remain outside for a few minutes.

"If you hear me screaming, you'll know I need help," she said in farewell, adding an impish smile that Walker was uncertain exactly how to take. He knew how excitable and high pitched the Isas' family quarrels could become, but he did not think the girl he cared so much about was in danger of any real violence at the hands of her own mother and father.

Tina's parents had not retired for the night as she had hoped. They were wide awake and furious. The confrontation began immediately. It became loud, but unfortunately not loud enough for Cliff Walker, standing outside the building, to hear. He slowly walked the few blocks that would take him to his own home on Detony Street. He hoped everything was going all right for Tina.

Maria Isa was waiting at the door for Tina. She clawed at her daughter, tearing the girl's small handbag from her, pawing through its contents, searching for something she would not reveal when Tina challenged that violation of her privacy.

"Where were you, bitch?" Maria Isa snarled as Tina tried to protest her mother's harshness.

"I told you I was starting a new job tonight," Tina answered, her voice quavering with outrage and fear at her mother's rude assault.

Zein Isa appeared at his wife's side. He had just come from the apartment's small kitchen in time to hear Tina's reply to her mother. His right hand was held behind his back.

"We do not accept that you go to work," her father shouted. "Where is the black boy you disgrace us with? Were you with him again tonight?"

The argument grew more shrill. Zein and Maria

were resolved to address every wrong they believed their daughter had ever committed against them and their family honor. Tina stood transfixed in mingled dread and defiance. Her parents were now yelling at each other—as though Tina were not there—about whether they should throw their daughter out of the apartment right then with her soiled whore's clothes behind her.

Tina tried to interrupt their heated harangue.

"You want me to leave home . . . I'll leave," Tina said, choking back tears.

"She devil!" her father cursed. "Did you know that this is your last day? That you are going to die tonight?" From behind his back, Zein Isa suddenly thrust forward a black-handled, razor-sharp boning knife, the kind used behind the meat counter of small neighborhood grocery stores. From the startled girl's back, her mother pounced, seizing handfuls of her shining sable hair, pulling downward with a fierce force that slammed Tina prone, face upward on the carpeted floor. Maria Isa pushed all of her 200-pound girth down against the struggling girl. Zein Isa dropped to his knees and raised the slim-bladed knife above his head. Then he thrust it savagely again and again into the chest of his terrified daughter. He struck seven times deeply into her chest.

"Die! Die quickly! Die, my daughter, die!" Zein Isa breathlessly chanted as his maddened eyes watched the life flow from her. Once, the girl managed to wrest away from her mother's strong hands on her mouth and utter several tortured screams. Zein struggled up from his grisly work. He placed a stockinged foot over the girl's mouth to smother her last pathetic cries.

Tina Isa lay brutally slain on the floor of the apartment. Her mother slumped into a chair. Zein had collapsed onto a sofa, exhausted by the bloody attack. Still winded, his hands trembling, he reached for the living room telephone. He quickly dialed the numbers of each of his daughters. He told them that Tina was dead. She was with God now and God could do with her whatever he wished. It no longer was a concern of the proud Isa family. Honor was restored. Maria Isa was weeping hysterically. She moved as though to touch her dead child, to smooth back the beautiful hair that had been so cruelly strewn by her death throes.

Zein Isa snapped angrily: "Do not touch her, woman. It is time to call the police to tell them how this evil one tried to kill me with a knife tonight." He stared down impassively at the corpse of his daughter. Her eyes, opened wide in the starkness of death, stared accusingly back at him.

The call to the St. Louis police department central switchboard was handled patiently by a dispatcher who listened intently to make certain he understood what the caller was saying in halting and broken English.

"Your daughter tried to kill you?" the dispatcher queried. "You had to kill her to stop her? Are you sure she is dead? Do you need an ambulance there? Slow down now. Tell me your address."

Neighborhood patrol cars were ordered to the scene. Homicide detectives were told to roll also.

Zein and Maria Isa faced police detectives with icy calm. Odd, considering the horrendous trauma they had supposedly just gone through, defending their lives against a berserk, knife-wielding athletic young woman who had tried to kill them, whom they had needed to kill to protect their own lives.

Tina had come home in an angry fury. They told the cops she demanded money. Within moments she had rushed into the kitchen, returned with the menacing knife, and attempted to kill her father. Thank

God, during the struggle, Zein had managed to turn the knife toward his assailant while Maria heroically tried to pull the wild girl off her father by tugging on her hair. It was tragic, they sighed, but young people these days—especially that one! People were not safe in their own homes anymore, even from their own children!

But in the next forty-eight hours, cops began to hear a much different story as they interviewed people who were aware of the hostile camp the Isa home had become and what kind of girl Tina's short life proved her to have been.

The medical examiner's autopsy report had been rushed through the system. The stab wounds to the girl's chest all fell within a tight, circular pattern. They had been struck downward, their angle of entry showed conclusively the victim had been on her back when those fatal thrusts rained upon her. She had been virtually motionless, or those knife blows could not all have fallen in such a small radius. How could there have been the furious struggle that Zein had described, with the knife having been turned and plunged into Tina accidentally while she was on her feet, attacking her father? It could not have happened that way. The now-growing file on Tina's death added up to only one conclusion. Tina Isa had been murdered by her own mother and father.

Protesting outraged innocence, flanked by lawyers, family, and friends, the Isas angrily denied the first-degree murder charges brought against them. A sullen Zein railed that the tragedy that had struck his home was a page torn from scripture. He would be made a martyr for trying to raise his reckless daughter up into pure womanhood in the Sodom and Gomorrah of America, where such things were laughed at and reviled. Maria Isa remained mute. Her surviving

daughters echoed their father's denunciation of a
supposed system of laws that could make an innocent
man seem a murderer.

Tina Isa had been dead for only about a week when
investigators from the detective bureau and the prosecuting circuit attorney's staff were rocked by a bombshell discovery revealed to them through quiet,
unofficial channels. There had been a witness to the
brutal murder of Tina Isa, one that could not lie or be
misunderstood, one that took no sides. It had not
been a flesh and blood spectator, but a softly whirring,
secretly concealed electronic listening device placed a
year earlier in the Isa apartment by the Federal
Bureau of Investigation (FBI). The high-tech bug had
been approved under provisions of the Foreign Intelli-
gence Surveillance Act to permit the bureau to learn
more about Zein Isa's shadowy involvement in the
PLO. The tapes had been running during every quarrel that had reverberated through the Isa home. It had
captured each one of the incriminating phone calls
Zein had made to his daughters and others about his
growing anger and homicidal intent toward his teenage daughter. Most dramatic and telling of all, the
listening device had preserved indelibly on tape the
frightening, fatal, last few minutes of the slain girl's
life; every heart-wrenching second of her death agony
had been harvested and stored among hundreds of
feet of dark brown magnetic ribbon. Sadly, no FBI
agent was monitoring the equipment the night that
Tina met her death. Only the tape recorder had been
listening.

On the grounds of national security, federal officials
said they could not make all of the tapes that were
made of the activities and phone calls in the Isas'
apartment available to prosecutors. Only those that
were relevant to Tina's death would be released.

Lawyers for the defendants would strenuously challenge the admissibility of the selected tapes into evidence against their clients. That complex legal skirmish would wind its way through federal court hearings and appeals for several months. The court's final decision permitted the introduction of the tapes into evidence.

Few juries ever impaneled in American judicial history have faced a grimmer, more macabre task than that which would confront those chosen to hear the case against Maria and Zein Isa, for with it they would also hear the terrified, dying cries of a child begging her mother for mercy: "Mother, please help!" they would hear the eerie, electronic ghost of the helpless teenager plead.

"Shut up!" they would hear Maria Isa, her mother, coldly answer.

For seven unbearably long minutes, the slain teenager, like some Shakespearian spectre, would point an accusing finger from a cold grave at the two people who had sent her there. The jury that heard those haunting words reacted in unconcealable anguish. Several wept. Those who managed to keep their composure riveted their eyes on the Isas. Maria threw her hands up to her face, hiding it from view. Zein stared ahead as though he did not hear that horrifying reenactment of his heinous act.

Lead prosecutor Dee Joyce-Hayes felt a shudder pass through her, as it had when she first had heard the dreadful recordings. She turned to look away from the stunned jury. Later, she would explain why she had not been able to witness the jury's reaction: "It would almost be like going to a funeral and staring at the family to see who was crying," she told *St. Louis Post-Dispatch* reporters Tim Bryant and Fred Lindecke. The two newshands understood.

Joyce-Hayes and her coprosecution counsel, Robert Craddick, relentlessly battered the Isas' contention of innocence by reason of self-defense. They ripped into testimony that attempted to characterize Tina as some wayward, disrespectful, hellion teenager.

The tale the Isas had told to police was hammered mercilessly against the tapes that told another story. Zein struggled in Arabic, through a translator, to insist that the recorded chronicle of the slaying was being distorted by his legal tormentors. But had he not coldly told his daughter that she was going to die that night?

"When I said that, she already had the knife in her hand. I then directed the knife toward her to stab her until she fell down," Isa parried.

Did he want Tina to die because she would not yield to his demand that she break off her relationship with Cliff Walker?

Untrue. He had even offered Tina and Cliff $5,000 with which to start their own life if that was what they wanted. Walker had spurned the money, Zein said. He did not want to marry Tina. He only wanted pleasure from her.

In four hostile hours on the stand, Zein Isa defended his stern fatherhood and his belief that a firm hand was needed to turn Tina back onto the paths of righteousness followed by her sisters and by every well-brought-up daughter of Islam. He had not been implacable in his demands. He would have been content if his youngest child had been willing to meet him even halfway, he testified.

Maria Isa did not take the stand. The prosecution had real doubts about whether a jury would convict the mother of first-degree murder. Perhaps, viewed in tandem with her volatile husband, her participation in her daughter's death would not seem to have been entirely willing. But the dying girl's plea to her mother for help as she was being killed and the heartless reply Maria had given would weigh heavily against Mrs. Isa.

The jury heard a stinging denunciation of the Isas' crime from Joyce-Hayes and Craddick. Speaking an emotional eulogy for the murdered girl, Craddick defended her memory: "This vibrant young woman is in stark contrast to the way her family viewed her. She should have lived a beautiful life."

Joyce-Hayes called Tina's murder an assassination: "I can't think of any other way to describe this incident other than as a blood sacrifice," she said. Tina had died to "cleanse the family name through blood," she added. "You can't do that in America."

Craddick added another accusation about the way the parents had chosen to slay their child: "They wanted to make Tina suffer before she died," he charged angrily.

Despite an impassioned closing argument by Maria Isa's lawyer, the jury returned in four hours to find both of the parents guilty of murder in the first degree. The attorney had argued that Maria had, in fact, been the child's only protector, that she was guilty of nothing more than being married to Zein Isa. The jury decided otherwise.

When the clerk read the jury verdict, the Isas showed no emotion. They were led away by deputies as the jury reconvened to consider their recommendation to the judge. Should their punishment be life imprisonment or death by lethal injection?

Zein Isa sat almost indifferently in the witness chair to testify during the penalty hearing. Emotion overwhelmed him only once when he turned to the jury and asked them to spare Maria's life: "Punish me the way you want, but my wife has nothing to do with it. For me, it doesn't matter," he said.

Maria's lawyer told the jury that she had been trapped in a raging conflict between two cultures and had been unwillingly caught up in the killing because she was no more than "a puppy dog" in the hands of her fanatical husband. He pointed toward the gray-bearded, stony-faced Zein: "If it wasn't for this thing sitting right here, she wouldn't be here today," the lawyer thundered, holding his accusing finger fixedly at Zein. "But for Zein, she would not have been involved in this and she would not be here today. She obviously was the lesser element of that family," he argued as he tried to convince the jury that Maria's life should be spared.

The prosecution answered that the religious values of the Isa family were not on trial. Beyond that, Maria Isa had faced a clear and compelling moment before the lethal blows had mortally struck down Tina when she should have stopped and rescued her daughter. Tina had pleaded to her mother to save her. Maria had refused.

"We are not here to blame Islam or Islamic culture," prosecutor Dee Joyce-Hayes said. "We're here to blame these people," she added, gesturing toward the defense table where the Isas sat.

"Maria Isa held down her daughter while her husband killed her," Craddick said. "It's clear from the tapes that even while Tina is being stabbed . . . her mother's response is 'shut up,'" he added.

Now, tears had begun to fill and overflow Maria Isa's eyes. Craddick noted them and offered an explanation of them to the jury: "Maria is crying a lot, because she and her husband planned this murder and got caught," the prosecutor accused.

In four hours the jury had returned with their recommendation. They had determined that Zein should pay with his life, and so should Maria.

St. Louis Circuit Judge Charles A. Shaw felt the need to offer some of his own thoughts about the tragedy that had so vividly been detailed in his courtroom before he passed sentence on Zein and Maria Isa: "This is a country of laws, not men," he said looking directly at the impassive Zein. "The court does not believe culture can be used as an excuse for murder. The rule of law is the thread that binds this country together."

Shaw passed the sentence of death on the couple. He softly added that phrase that has become at once an accusation and a benediction American courts offer to those whom society determines must pay through their own deaths for lives they have taken: "And may God have mercy on your souls," Shaw said.

The Isa family reacted to the sentence as a solid phalanx that seemed unable to understand or accept the way in which their narrow and insular beliefs had been examined in harsh daylight by others and rejected as murderous zealotry. Those who had run the Isas to ground and now wished to kill them may have said that a religion, a culture, and labyrinthine Mideast politics were not at issue in the strange Western courtroom, but the family knew better.

"There is no justice," Fatima Abdeljabbar, their daughter, contended outside the courtroom. "The only reason this happened is my father is Palestinian," she charged, dark eyes flashing in contempt.

Another sister, Soraia Salem, added her view: Tina Isa's death could not be blamed on her mother and father. "The system killed her."

And what of Tina? Had she been the sinful, disobedient infidel her parents believed she was?

"She's gone now. She's not coming back. She don't need nobody to defend her," Saraia Salem shot back in reply.

2

Debra Jean Milke

SANTA CLAUS KNOWS THE NAME OF EVERY CHILD IN THE world. He knows where they live and what special things they want for Christmas. He loves them. With all of his tiny heart, four-year-old Christopher Milke knew that was true. There were few other hopes the sad, battered, unwanted little boy could cling to in his lonely life.

And now, though he could scarcely believe it, in an hour or so he would get to see Santa. Jim, his mom's new friend, had promised; and Mommy had said it was okay. Maybe there would even be a photo of Chris and Santa that he could proudly show.

Chris already knew what he would whisper into the fuzzy ear of the big, smiling man with the white beard when it was his turn to snuggle onto his ample lap. He would not ask for toys or games—well, not for many. He would see instead if Santa could somehow get his real daddy to come back home. And he would ask Santa if there wasn't something he could do to make Mommy like Chris better. Maybe the smiling old man who made wishes come true could tell Debra Jean Milke how much it hurt Chris when she was so angry at him all the time, when she slapped him and said she wished he had never been born, how she flew into wild, punishing rages when Chris made even little mistakes—the kind that didn't seem to bother other moms in the blue-collar Phoenix neighborhood when their kids did the same kinds of things.

If there really is a Santa Claus, Christopher Milke would never see him that afternoon of December 2, 1989. Instead, Jim Styers and a roustabout buddy named Roger Scott lured the excited child to a harsh patch of desert minutes north of the sprawling Arizona city. There, Styers roughly shoved the boy to the ground. He fired three bullets from a cheap handgun into the back of the youngster's head. He calmly walked back to the rattletrap car where Roger Scott nervously waited. "I think he's dead," Styers said, the gun still hot in his hand.

"You'd damn better be sure or you'll catch real shit from Debbie," Scott responded in a voice as gritty and dry as the sand beneath them.

Styers slowly walked back. He thought he saw the tiny corpse twitch. He poised the revolver to fire another shot. There hadn't really been a movement. It was just the whip of the desert wind tousling the thin cheap windbreaker the child had been wearing against the winter's chill. The kid was dead all right. Styers had seen plenty of dead children during his sixteen months in Vietnam. He told friends he still had nightmares about all the dead babies.

Styers did not try to cover the body that lay in the sand. He wanted the desert's ghoulish undertakers to come at dark and begin to pick the flesh from the child's bones.

Scott waited behind the wheel of the car. Silently, he wondered if now was a good time to ask about the $250 he had been promised for being the driver. He decided that had better wait until later. Jim Styers could be a crazy bastard, and even though they had been friends for twenty years, small things could set Styers off. Besides, Scott noted in panic as he glanced at his watch, they were starting to run behind the carefully planned time schedule that called for them to be at Metrocenter Mall at midday, while crowds of holiday shoppers were still thick. That's where Santa was. Scott stepped down hard on the accelerator. The car flew down Black Canyon Freeway. It was almost time to put on the show, the one in which the two murderers would tell mall officials that Chris Milke had wanted to go to the bathroom before he got into the long line of kids waiting to talk to Santa Claus and had then mysteriously vanished while they browsed nearby store windows.

At her house, the one that had no cheery Christmas decorations, Debra Jean Milke, twenty-six, worriedly glanced at a kitchen wall clock. She should have heard by now from Styers and Scott. Jesus! Couldn't they do anything right?

When the phone finally rang, Debra Milke knew who was on the other end of the line. She knew exactly what Jim Styers would be saying for the benefit of concerned mall employees hovering nearby. They had rehearsed the charade many times. There was a code word they had agreed upon to signal her the child was dead. Styers said it.

"Debbie, stay calm now, I have some bad news. Chris got lost here at the mall, but they're searching for him. Don't worry, he's probably just looking at toys somewhere . . ."

"Oh . . . no . . . oh, my God . . . You've got to find him, Jim . . . Oh . . . no . . . Do you think he could have been kidnapped by someone?" Debra Milke spoke her lines with mock fear and alarm.

Worried security staff at Metrocenter Mall had already fanned out in search of little Chris. Linked by handheld walkie-talkies, they scoured the huge complex inch by inch. Most of them were dads. Some of them were moms. They told Styers not to worry; kids wandered off all the time. They would find Chris Milke before long, they said. They didn't.

Debra Milke turned to the telephone again. Her first call rang in the home of her father in nearby Florence. Richard Sadaik could barely decipher her hysterical words. His daughter was alternately sobbing and screaming into the receiver.

When Sadaik finally managed to calm Debra down, he told his frantic daughter to get hold of herself, that Chris surely would be found. "It's Christmastime. Kids wander off at the mall all the time. Don't worry. They'll find him." Debra's dad reassured her.

"Chris knows his phone number, doesn't he? I bet he'll know enough to call you in a bit. Why don't you get some friends to come over to your place. You'll see. Chris will call."

For a moment, Debra's voice brightened, but then it fell again to a somber note: "Dad, I've got this terrible feeling that Chris has been kidnapped, probably by some woman who couldn't have a child or maybe child molesters have got him—"

"Stop talking like that!" Sadaik brusquely broke in. "I'm sure the boy is all right. Do what I told you now, and don't worry." After he hung up the phone, however, Sadaik had troubling thoughts. He knew his headstrong and self-willed daughter was not a very caring mother to little Chris. No, worse than that, she really wasn't a good parent at all. Sadaik sadly knew Debra didn't have a normal mother's heart. It seemed as though she had fiercely fought to keep the child after her divorce from the boy's dad, Mark Milke, mostly out of anger toward her ex-husband.

When Sadaik told his wife, Maureen, of the frantic call from Debra, Mrs. Sadaik's response was immediate. "I think I should go on up. Someone needs to be there." It did not matter to Maureen Sadaik that she was only a stepmother to Debra Milke and that they did not see eye to eye on the way Debra conducted her life. She felt her own mother's heart urging her to go. A little boy was lost. Someone who cared needed to be there.

Debra Milke had continued to work the phone, tearfully informing shocked neighbors and friends that Chris was missing. Before long, her carelessly kept house was filled with people who wanted to lend comfort and support to the anguished young mother and to pray together for the safe return of the vanished boy.

Some friends pressed her to eat. She said she was too upset to touch a bite. She did manage to drink two, perhaps more, rum and colas a friend mixed for her.

Throughout the long night of worried waiting, people who kept that vigil with Debra Milke recalled that all of their hopeful remarks that Chris had simply strayed off and become lost were firmly dismissed by the young mother. Silently they thought it strange she didn't cling to that fairly logical hope with them. But with growing certainty, Debra Milke brushed away those well-meant speculations from friends and relatives: "I have this gut instinct that tells me Chris is dead," she said. "I don't think I'll ever see him in this world again. I think he is with God."

When a uniformed Phoenix police officer arrived at the door of her home at about eleven P.M., a small murmur of amazement passed through the knot of guests who overheard the conversation between the policeman and Debra Milke. He said he had been sent to take her to the mall to join in the search for her son. The squad car was waiting outside. He knew she would want to come. He was a dad. He understood.

Debra Milke said she did not want to go to the mall. "I just can't handle that," she told the cop.

To those who had witnessed the cold vignette, she hastily explained her reasoning: "Chris knows our phone number. He might try to call. I have to be here," she said, miming a fresh shudder of grief by bringing her hands faceward.

The cop who had come to take Debra Milke to the mall had an odd thought trouble him as he resumed neighborhood patrol. Wouldn't Debra Milke have thought his visit was to bring some news of her missing child? But she never even asked a question. *Strange,* he thought, *That isn't the way my wife would have acted.*

When Maureen Sadaik reached Debra's home, a cluster of news reporters had begun to gather. They were ready to use their powerful voices to help Phoenix find the child missing at Christmas, to bring him back home where he belonged.

Maureen's arrival soothed Debra Milke. Her presence seemed to steady the obviously distraught mother. From her purse, Maureen produced a mild tranquilizer and watched Debra eagerly swallow it. Before long Debra asked that Maureen drive them both back to the family home in Florence.

"I have to be with Daddy," Debra Milke pleaded.

Mrs. Sadaik consented. On the ride to the suburban town, Debra leaned her head against her sympathetic stepmother's shoulder. "Something very bad has happened to Christopher," she wept as Maureen Sadaik piloted the car along the black desert highway. "Christopher is probably dead," Debra sighed.

Maureen Sadaik tried to speak words of calming dispute, but Debra had not finished her drowsy speech: "If they find Chris dead, I want him cremated and I want his ashes strewn in Daddy's yard."

"Hush, now. Try to sleep," a suddenly worried Maureen said. They drove in silence the rest of the way. Maureen's hands felt clammy against the steering wheel.

At Metrocenter Mall, the store-by-store search for Chris Milke had continued. Large air-conditioner duct covers were removed, and workmen crawled through them with flashlights. Behind the shops, big green dumpsters were carefully emptied. In the sprawling parking lot, security people peered into the interiors of countless cars; perhaps Chris had found one unlocked, crawled inside, and had fallen asleep. Other searchers fanned out for blocks. A missing child alert was broadcast. Hours dragged on.

At Phoenix police headquarters, night-shift detectives listened with concern as Scott and Styers told their story. They had no reason for disbelieving it. Attention was focused on finding Chris. Once they gleaned every possible detail from the pair of men, there was no need to detain them. Scott and Styers said they wanted to head back to the mall to take part in the search. Police would know where to find them.

By daybreak, with still no sign of the vanished child and no other reports of missing kids, kidnap attempts, or child molestation incidents that would validate speculation Chris had been abducted, weary police began to consider other likelihoods. Among them was the possibility that Scott and Styers might know more about the boy's whereabouts than they were telling.

Homicide detective Armando Saldate, Jr., had just wheeled his lawn mower out of the garage of his comfortable suburban home. This was a Sunday morning chore he liked. It freed his mind from routine and let him think intuitively about the deskful of cases he was working. After nearly twenty-one years as a Phoenix cop, Saldate had earned a reputation that landed the toughest cases on his desk. It wasn't just that he was a skilled investigator with a remarkably perceptive mind, it was the climate he always seemed able to create in an interrogation room across the table from the toughest con, the wiliest perpetrator, the most evil kinds of killers. Almost always, they chose Saldate as the man to whom they would finally decide to tell the truth.

Saldate invariably told rookie detectives the most important things he'd learned on the job. "It doesn't matter who the suspect is or how terrible the crime they've committed, they really want to tell someone about it. They want someone to understand why they did it. If you try to understand and tell them you won't accept anything less than the truth from them, the chances are you'll get it sooner or later.

"When they're lying, and you know they're lying, you tell them to cut the crap. You want the truth. There comes a moment, and you'll learn to know it, when that confrontation is what it takes. After that, they'll tell you everything you need to know."

Saldate's mower had just sputtered to life when his morning plans were interrupted by a phone call from downtown. He listened intently as a young sergeant briefed him on the details of the missing child case.

"Have you got these two guys down there now?" Saldate asked. "They've come back? Who the hell let them go? Keep them there. I'm on my way in. I want to talk to them."

Scott and Styers were told to stay at the station. When Saldate arrived, he sat down to put into his mind every detail then known to police. Record checks were ordered up on the two men. By midafternoon, Saldate was ready. "Get me Scott," he said.

Armando Saldate took a long measure of the man when Roger Scott sat down in a chair across from his. Scott nervously lit and fiercely inhaled a menthol cigarette. Saldate quietly sipped coffee from his bottomless cup. He idly flipped the pages of the missing child report patrol officers had filed after Scott and Styers had told them their story of how Chris had disappeared. He already knew it by heart.

He looked again at Scott: fortyish, unkempt, watery eyed, for the most part, nondescript, timidly perched on the edge of the chair, clearly uncomfortable under the steady eyes of the detective.

For a few minutes Saldate posed routine questions to Scott, referring occasionally to the report. Then he slowly removed his glasses, folded them, and placed them in his shirt pocket. He turned the report over and laid it face down on the desk between them. "I don't think we need this, do we, Roger?" he said calmly. "This isn't what really happened, is it? You know where this little boy is, don't you? Why don't we cut the bullshit?"

For a moment a look of shocked denial came across Scott's beard-stubbled face. Then, slowly and resignedly, his head lowered.

"The kid is dead. He's out in the desert, out by Happy Valley Road. I didn't do it, though; Styers did. I just drove the car. Hell, I didn't even think he was really going to do it . . ." The words poured out in a pleading jumble.

"It's okay, Roger. I think I understand. Can you take us to the boy? It's going to get dark soon. You know how dark it can get in the desert. I don't think we want to leave him out there alone, do we?

In the car, a heavy-hearted Saldate followed Scott's directions. The frightened man continued to spill out details of the crime. "This was all Debbie's idea," Scott said. "Jim Styers said he'd do it. He'd do anything for her. She has been planning it for months. She and Jim even brought the kid out here a couple of times before to do him then, but it made her too

28

nervous. There were some people around. I came out once before with Debbie and Jim and the boy, but she didn't want to do it that day. I think she just wanted to show us where to do it and get us used to the idea.

"Debbie's got an insurance policy on the kid. Five thousand bucks, I think. She said she'd give me and Jim $250 each for getting rid of the kid. I need the money. My lawyer won't do anything about getting my disability checks from Social Security until I pay him. And my mom needs money. She's an invalid. God, what is she gonna do now if I have to go to jail? Maybe we can work some kind of deal. I'm cooperating. I'm telling you everything I know," Scott said, his voice trailing off, lost in the sound of the car engine and the wind that whipped against the auto as they neared the twilight-bathed desert wash where Scott said the boy's body was.

Armando Saldate began to steel himself when the car reached its remote destination. He exited the vehicle with Scott. Other officers and a county coroner's wagon pulled up and parked nearby. Roger Scott said he wanted to remain near the car. "Over there," he pointed. "Twenty-five, maybe thirty, yards up that wash. He's over there."

Saldate stared down at the slain child. "He looks like he's just sleeping," he said to another detective who had turned away from the heart-wrenching sight.

Chris Milke was wearing a pair of Levi's, a cowboy shirt, a light jacket, and a pair of scuffed little cowboy boots. He seemed small for his age. Perhaps the innocent fetal position that death had curled him into made him seem smaller. He had a sweet face. He was a handsome little boy.

Saldate spoke again to the younger officer. "Right now, you're looking at evidence. That's what you need to remember. I know it's a little kid. A few days from now you'll want to cry your eyes out. Maybe you will.

But right now, he's evidence. Don't look away. You need to remember every possible detail you can."

On the drive back to the city, Saldate began a quiet rehearsal for his next encounter: the one that would pit him against James Styers. He hoped it would go as well as his confrontation with Scott.

Saldate ran through his mind the quick portrait that Scott had sketched for him of Jim Styers. The two had been friends for more than twenty years. They had known each other in high school. Styers had served for more than a year in Vietnam. He was taking some kind of medication to relieve depression and curb the vivid, frightening dreams he had about those months of war. He had a bad leg. It made him feel like less of a man. He worked sporadically as a construction laborer. He wasn't very good-looking.

A few years earlier, he had married an attractive young woman who divorced him after the birth of their first child. He had known Debra Milke for a year or so before he had moved in with her and Chris. Styers wanted to believe that Debra loved him, but he wasn't bold enough to make any real demands. He was twenty years older. He satisfied himself with the small scraps of affection she threw to him. They were few and far between. His devotion to Debra Milke was complete. He would do absolutely anything for her, Scott said. She was just using him as a baby-sitter and getting him to do other things for her, Scott told Saldate. Then he added another revealing insight: "Maybe I'm the same thing to Jim that he is to Debbie, somebody to order around who will do stuff even if someone doesn't appreciate what they're doing and is just using them maybe."

Saldate's interview with Styers did not go well. After more than an hour, the veteran detective knew Styers was not one of those persons ready to tell someone the truth. Saldate reported to his supervisor,

"He says he has no idea what we're talking about, can't imagine what made Scott say what he did. He says he loves the boy. Has always treated him like he was his own. He says there is no way in the world Debra Milke would want any harm to come to her son, says she's a good mother to him.

"He's trying to protect the woman," Saldate concluded. "She's got him in her pocket. I need to talk to her. Can you arrange a ride down to Florence for me? I'm told she's down there with her family. Now we know why she's eighty miles away while we're up here looking for her supposedly missing child. I'm looking forward to meeting her," Saldate said with a grim smile.

Ironically, the city to which Debra Milke had fled to be with her father and stepmother is the site of Arizona's primary state prison. Her father worked there as a prison guard. Because Florence was located in adjacent Pinal County, deputies from that county's sheriff's department were dispatched to the Sadaik home to inform Debra Milke that Phoenix police, investigating her son's disappearance, were enroute there and wanted to talk with her at the local sheriff's office. Once again, deputies carrying out that task could not help but note that Debra Milke asked them no questions about the progress of the search for her son. She merely said she needed a little time to freshen up before coming. She would be there shortly, she promised.

Armando Saldate wanted to be there, waiting. A police helicopter lifted off and whirled its way through the night. In less than a half hour, he had arrived at the Pinal County sheriff's compound and borrowed the only room available for his meeting with Debra Milke, a medical examining room for jail inmates. It would do, Saldate thought.

As Debra Milke entered the room where Saldate

waited, it took the canny detective only minutes to form his strategy. He would play a bold hunch. He would lay down an explosive, confrontational card on the table between them. "Debra Jean Milke, you are under arrest for the murder of Christopher Conan Milke. I'm going to read you your rights . . ." When he had finished, a stunned Debra Milke began to protest, then faltered.

"I know how you arranged your son's murder, and I know why," Saldate said soothingly.

"Do you? Do you really?" Milke answered. She told Saldate everything.

While the husky homicide cop listened to her rambling account, one part of his mind could not help musing about the way in which she was choosing to tell the story. It had an all too familiar ring.

We're alone here. She's trying to seduce me. She wants to charm me into being her friend. She knows that we know. She knows that I'm going to write a report, but she doesn't want me to tell on her. She thinks I understand all this, why she had to do it. She wants me to believe she really isn't a bad person, but there was no other way for her to have all the things she wants from life. They're the same things I want, that everyone wants. See, she's just like me, just like anyone else. She's thinking we could be friends, real friends. This cop is my pal. Look at him, he likes me. He believes me. He's going for it. I've got him. He'll tell everybody why I had to do this.

The little boy never meant a thing to her. He was just in the way of her ice-cold dreams. For all it mattered, he could have been some other neighborhood kid found dead, someone she barely knew. Too bad, how sad, but life goes on. My God, I'm glad she can't read my mind. I understand,

Debbie. Too damn well. Keep on talking. You want me to hear how it was, why nobody should blame a nice kid like you for something that just needed to be done.

"I feel better telling you about this. I was afraid no one would understand. You have nice eyes. Are you married? There's this guy at work—I'm with an insurance company—I really like him. I want to be with him. You know, you could tell them I'd never do anything like this again. They could fix me so I wouldn't have any more children. You could tell them that, can't you?"

Debra Milke tugged loose the bottom of her blouse. She dabbed at her eyes with it.

There aren't any tears there, Saldate noted to himself. *I wonder if she has ever shed a tear over someone else.*

It was time for handcuffs now and transport to jail. Debbie's eyes softened and reached out imploringly to Saldate. "Will you walk me out to the car. I'm afraid," she implored.

"Sure," Saldate obliged.

They passed a bank of pay phones as they walked down an empty corridor. Debbie paused. Escorting deputies looked to Saldate.

"My dad needs to know what's happening," she said to the detective. "He'd hang up on me if I told him. Would you call him now? He'd listen to you."

Saldate knew the woman was still at her manipulative game. He made the call all the same. He told Milke's father what he had learned from Debbie's confession.

"She'd like the family to come down. She hopes someone might go a bond," Saldate said.

"You can tell that little bitch the answer is no," Richard Sadaik responded. "Someone will bring her

33

stuff over to the jail, but that's the end of her and us."
He hung up the phone on Saldate.

"Families usually get over this kind of thing," the
detective said as Milke turned her face away.

She looked back. "Maybe you could come to see
me. Maybe we could talk some more. You have a good
heart," she said to Saldate.

"Maybe," he answered. "Take care of yourself."

He watched as the squad car pulled away. She
turned and smiled at him through the rear window.

Saldate never talked to Debra Milke again, but she
remained in his thoughts for some time. "She was
unique," he would later tell a colleague. "I don't know
what made her become what she was. I never knew
anyone who was born without a heart. Maybe Debbie
Milke was."

Debra Milke's family kept their promise. They took
the personal belongings she had brought with her
from Phoenix to the jail. After they had been logged
in, a death-knell discovery was made. In her purse was
a small box of .22-caliber bullets. Some were missing.
Ballistic tests showed they were of the same kind that
Styers had used to kill Chris.

As Phoenix detectives continued to methodically
develop the case against the trio, the shocking and
soul-numbing diary of misery that had been little
Christopher Milke's few years on earth was brought to
light. It seemed that dozens of persons had caught at
least a terrible glimpse of the abusive way in which
Debra Jean Milke had made life a terrifying hell for
her child.

Milke's sister, Denise Pickinpaugh, told stunned
investigators that Debra had often flung Chris across a
room when the child annoyed her. When the boy was
still a toddler, Milke was infuriated when the child let
his pacifier fall from his mouth. She firmly fixed it in
place with electrical tape and left it on for hours.

When Chris wet his pants, he was roughly stripped naked and placed out in the front yard. Milke locked the door. She ignored her child's frightened pleas for forgiveness. Pickinpaugh said that medication prescribed for Chris by a pediatrician was withheld from him by his mother as another form of punishment.

Kelly Hesse had been a co-worker of Debra Milke. Once she witnessed Milke administer a harsh spanking to Chris over a small incident. As she stepped away from the cruel scene, she heard the child shriek out an intense, piercing scream. Milke was beating the child again because he would not stop crying. Hesse told police she discontinued any friendship with Milke. She did not want to be around her again.

Susan Stinson had shared an apartment with Milke in 1988. She said she could not remember Milke ever showing love or tenderness toward her bright-eyed two-year-old. "She never should have had a child," Stinson added. Milke often dropped the youngster off at day-care centers but gave staffers there incorrect phone numbers so they could not locate her at the end of the day when she failed to arrive to pick the child up on time.

The cops' quest took them to Nevada where another former roommate of Milke's had since moved. Dorothy Markwell had shared an apartment with Debra and Chris for a few months about a year before the child's murder. "She told me she wished Chris was dead," Markwell related to police. "She also said she wanted her ex-husband, Mark Milke, dead."

Milke would often disappear during the time they lived together, Markwell said. She would leave Chris behind, alone. Markwell would care for the little boy. She would need to go to the store to buy food for him. Milke always forgot.

"Why in God's name hadn't someone done something about what was happening to this child?" angry cops asked each other. "Where in the hell was everyone?"

What sort of woman, what kind of mother could have so brutally tormented, then so ruthlessly conceived and stage-managed the lonely and terrifying desert slaying of her only child? Could a jury be expected to accept the almost unimaginable scenario of a young, pretty woman who looked for all the world like a typical suburban mom being the mastermind behind a heinous plot to murder an innocent little boy with Scott as her only accuser?

Investigators like Saldate and Deputy County Attorney Noel Levy needed to know who Debra Jean Milke really was at the labyrinthine center of her being.

Forensic psychologist Michael Bayless was brought in by the law enforcement team to review and analyze the puzzle pieces at hand. Bayless pored over what records had accumulated in the brief twenty-six years of Debra Milke's life. He watched and listened intently as detectives interrogated Milke. At night, he carried home a mounting pile of interview transcripts dogged cops had done with people from Milke's past, anyone who might shed some light on her true face, the one behind the cryptic, impenetrable mask she wore for the watching world.

Bayless was an old hand at mapping the mind of murderers. He had been part of the team in Atlanta that struggled to fathom the grisly trail of dead young black men who had fallen victim to the homosexual sex crimes of Wayne Williams. In Phoenix and across the Southwest, Bayless and a group of other professionals working under his direction were acknowledged as top specialists in their field. They were called on by both prosecution and defense attorneys when murder was at the bar and the judicial stakes were high. Prosecutor Levy and Detective Saldate had often worked with Bayless in the past. Sometimes they encountered him on the other side of the courtroom table. They liked it much better when the bright, wry, psychological expert was in their camp. Their respect for his shrewd insights and far-reaching knowledge of the human psyche was enormous. They also appreciated his way of explaining the complex workings of the mind in everyday terms cops could quickly grasp and use as an insightful tool in their investigations.

Saldate, Levy, and a half dozen others working the case crowded into a Mariacopa County Courthouse conference room that hushed as Bayless, his preliminary analysis completed, prepared to brief them about a tearless, stone-faced woman who had come to haunt their dreams.

"Let's go right to the heart of this," Bayless began. "You have Roger Scott copping out and telling you that Debra Milke and James Styers have been planning to kill this poor little tyke for months, that Debbie was doing the orchestrating, and that she was the one who wanted the child dead and out of the way.

"Styers says they occasionally took the boy out to the desert for an ordinary outing, but he's sticking to his story about the mall.

"Debra Milke confessed to Saldate but now denies it all. She says she loved her child, would never want him harmed, can't believe that Styers would hurt him.

"Was Debra Milke capable of manipulating two men into killing her son?" Bayless queried into the smoky haze that clouded the conference room. "There isn't any doubt in my mind that she was—and that she did!

"Debra Jean Milke is psychotic. She's a pathological liar. She has been for a good part of her life. She is incapable of forming genuine loving relationships of any kind. She's wrapped herself in a kind of emotional insulation that everyday healthy feelings and outlooks can't manage to filter through.

"Sometimes you'll hear someone like this called the 'victim' of a personality disorder. Debra Milke has a personality disorder, but she isn't the victim—almost everyone she's come in contact with have been the victims.

"There is only one person in this world that Debra Milke has ever looked out for and that person is Debra Milke and the hell with anyone else who stood in the way of whatever it was she wanted.

"She firmly believes that most people think and act in the way she does, and she finds it hard to believe that people are shocked and revolted by her actions.

"Is she sane? Yes. Is she normal? God, no! Debra Milke is almost a textbook example of a personality disorder.

"Her trouble hasn't been with the law. Her record is pretty clean. Her trouble has been with people. Once they come to know her and see through her, they don't want anything more to do with her. When she senses this, she sets up a situation in which she believes she is rejecting them, when it is really other people who are rejecting her. During one interview, talking about her ex-husband and her family, she says 'I divorced them all a long time ago.'

"People who exhibit her personality disorder make the mistake of thinking that God didn't give anyone else a brain and that they're too stupid to see through their manipulations and lies.

"Debra Milke has made her way through life up to this point trying to get what she wanted through cold, calculating, selfish lies. She's an attractive young woman, and sex is one of the ways she's employed to get men to do what she wants. Jim Styers was just one more perfect love-struck dope willing to do her bidding.

"She wasn't trying to get rid of the child just to build an uncluttered little love nest for her and Styers. She would have dumped Styers somewhere down the road sooner or later. I doubt if she ever had any feelings for him at all.

"She wanted the boy dead for several reasons. He meant absolutely nothing to her in the way we normally understand the mother–child bond. She could no more love him than she could love anyone else. Killing the child was also an act of revenge against her ex-husband. She saw a great deal of him in the child. Whenever the boy displayed the slightest trace of his father's personality, she punished him in humiliating and cruel ways or she beat him mercilessly. She saw the chance to make some money from her son's death from the insurance policy. In her mind, she was being paid for all the inconvenience the child has brought into her life and for having to give birth to a child she never wanted in the first place, fathered by a man she wanted to continue punishing.

"The bullets you guys found in her purse are about as macabre a personality indicator as I've run across in a lot of years of doing this," Bayless continued. "They're a souvenir of the child's execution. She was keeping them as a means of recalling, reliving, and relishing a moment of ultimate and total power, the power of life and death. That box of bullets was an object of pleasure to her. In my judgment, it shows that Debra Milke is beyond the emotional pangs of remorse. The only sadness she is feeling is about her own predicament now.

"Debra Milke is a depraved person. She is as cold as the bottom of the Arctic Ocean. She wanted that little boy dead. She got her way," Bayless concluded. "I hope you guys can make it the last time she gets her way," he added with a sigh.

While Debra Milke was held at the Durango Psychiatric Unit, she wrote sentimental and sometimes revealing letters to Jim Styers. She had a hard time understanding her unpopularity among other residents. "You wouldn't believe the remarks I hear from people when they see me. I'm so scared to be around people," she complained.

Staff at the mental facility noted that when Milke first arrived she had been jeered at and taunted with shouts of "baby killer" by other inmates. Milke was being held at the facility to keep her segregated from the general prison population. Authorities had real fears she might be attacked. Before long, center workers observed, any hazing of Milke had ceased. Police later learned why. Debra Milke had cornered one of her harassers and fixed her with an icy stare. "It didn't bother me about the kid, it wouldn't bother me about you either," Milke spat at the offender. After that, she was pretty much left alone.

Her letters to Styers also griped that food served at the unit was far too fattening. She was worried about keeping her trim figure. She said that her morning aerobic class was fun. She sweetly thanked him for sending her a hundred dollars. There were so many little things she needed.

In the eyes of some of the psychosocial experts who examined, observed, or interreacted with Debra Milke during her stay at Durango, the young mother was innocent. The director of psychiatric services for the facility, Dr. Leonardo Garcia-Manuel, said so flatly and added that many other members of the staff had reached the same conclusion. He could not say how many. "When she first came here, the predominant opinion of the staff was that she was guilty, but later that opinion changed."

A counselor at Durango, Rachel Roth, would testify she did not believe that Milke was guilty. Roth said that in her sessions with the accused woman, Debra Milke had shown genuine grief over her son's death and that she was suffering acute depression. "Debra Milke is not capable of having taken part in her son's death," Roth said.

Dr. Garcia-Manuel conceded that his role at the unit was an administrative one and that he had followed Milke's testing and evaluation at the hospital largely in that role. He also acknowledged that the psychiatrist who was in actual charge of the Milke case came to the opinion that she was guilty.

An inmate who shared a cell with Milke told cops the woman was winning over the staff with demure behavior and remarkable acting performances about her unhappy life. Some members of the staff had given her their home phone numbers so Debra could reach them at night in case she had just had one of those bad dreams. She called them often.

There had never been a doubt in the prosecution teams' mind that the death penalty should be sought against Debra Jean Milke, even though she had not been in that patch of desert wash near Happy Valley Road and 99th Avenue the night three bullets were pumped into the head of her son.

Under Arizona law, the death penalty can only be imposed in murders judged to have been committed in a "heinous and depraved manner." There seemed no legal doubt that her crime met that definition. Dr. Bayless and another respected Phoenix psychiatrist, Dr. Otto Bendheim, gave prosecutors another measurement by which to gauge whether Milke's soliciting of Scott and Styers to slay her son met that standard— the way in which her crime was perceived by a society woven together not just by laws, but by ordinary beliefs, values, and morality. "Debra Milke's crime is heinous, hateful, shocking, evil," Dr. Bendheim said. "In fifty years of practice I have never encountered an act that reached as low a level of depravity. I cannot find enough adjectives to fully describe how heinous her participation was. It is a total perversion of the mother–child relationship," the elderly expert added.

Dr. Michael Bayless also told Noel Levy and his staff that by any criteria—legal or moral—Debra Milke's complicity in the death of Chris would be viewed by the community as unequivocally compatible with the test demanded by the law. "A crime is heinous when it causes society to recoil," Bayless said. "To murder a child under the guise that you are taking him to see Santa Claus makes any normal human being recoil. It is the killing of innocence that was willfully planned and executed. It is indeed heinous.

"How can a four-year-old child harm you? There were so many options open to her. There was never a need to take this boy's life. Debra Milke is an extremely depraved woman," Bayless said. "She has shown absolutely no remorse over the death of her son. I don't believe society wants to have Debra Milke among them any more. I would not want the job of convincing a jury that she is innocent or that her life should be spared. It wouldn't be an easy task."

Debra Milke's four days in the witness chair were an unqualified disaster. She showed no emotion as the details of her son's death were spun out before a jury that glared at her in seeming disbelief and horror. Her second day of testimony came on what would have been Chris's fifth birthday. She seemed unmoved. She tried to refute the confession she had given to Armando Saldate. He had pretended to be her friend. Now she knew he wasn't. He had twisted her words, she complained. Yes, Saldate had read her her rights, but she was in shock at the news of her son's death and the wild charge that she was involved. How could she have understood what was going on or call a lawyer, even though she was told she could?

Why had Saldate reported that she had said she wanted the child dead rather than in the custody of her ex-husband? That isn't what she had told him. "I said to him that I didn't want Christopher to grow up to be like Mark, that I would rather die first than have Mark take care of Christopher . . ."

She had never wanted children, she had told Saldate. It would be better for Christopher to die. She wanted God to take care of him. Saldate had turned those words on her, Milke told the jury. "God, I just wanted to take care of him." That was what she had told the cop she had foolishly trusted.

Defense Attorney C. Kenneth Ray finally asked of Debra Milke the question that had become a topic of thousands of daily conversations in Phoenix. "Were you involved in the death of Christopher Milke," Ray asked.

"No, I was not," she replied in a steady voice.

The jury did not believe Debra Milke. They found her guilty and recommended to Judge Hendrix that she be put to death in the gas chamber.

The judge heard two particularly shocking witnesses before sentence was passed. Denise Pickinpaugh, Debra's sister, who had just begun a family of her own, said she believed Debra should be executed for her crime.

Milke's father, Richard Sadaik, said this of his daughter: "She was never meant to be a mother and if given the opportunity to have more children would probably continue to murder again."

Her ex-husband, Mark Milke, angrily called her "baby killer." "Give her the same sentence she gave my son," he asked the judge. It was the sentence the court imposed.

Judge Hendrix told Milke her cruel act had made

her the most reviled woman in Arizona. "That a mother could plan the death of her own child is shocking and repugnant. Had it not been for your wishes and desires, this crime would not have been committed," the judge said.

"I don't deserve to be punished for something I didn't do," Debra Milke said.

Within months, both Styers and Scott also received the death penalty for their roles in the murder of Chris Milke.

All of the cases are on appeal.

Scott repeated his confession. Styers claimed it was Scott who did the killing.

Now retired from the police department and serving as a constable in West Phoenix, Armando Saldate, Jr., has sharply fresh recollections of the woman he was instrumental in bringing to justice. "She could never cry for that little boy. It was like he never mattered, never mattered at all. She has something to cry about now," he added.

(The state of Arizona adopted the gas chamber as a method of execution through a state constitutional amendment passed in 1933. A public outcry had arisen two years earlier to substitute the deadly gas for hanging after the horrifying botched execution of housekeeper Eva Dugan, sentenced to the gallows by a Tucson jury for the murder of her employer. When the trap door fell and the bulky Dugan plunged downward, the violent impact at the noose's end was so powerful that it snapped off her head. It rolled grotesquely toward the witnesses gathered for the spectacle. They fled in shock. Eva Dugan was the last Arizonan to be hung, as well as the only woman ever to be put to death for a crime in Arizona.)

3

Lafonda Foster
and Tina Powell

A FULL MOON, A STEALTHY HUNTER'S MOON, STAGE-LIT A weedy patch of nowhere in Lexington, Kentucky's gritty, workhorse east end that cool late April night in 1986.

The theater of death illuminated by its cherub face was the third such horror show Lexington lawmen had rushed to in as many hours. This one shrieked even more of lunacy than the others. Two people were horribly slain, a third was dying of wounds too cruel to believe. Two others had been killed at the earlier sites. All were victims of a furious, maniacal savagery beyond anything the veteran cops had ever seen. Raging, demented, unfathomable violence had visited their city under the full moon's guiding lamp. Quietly, reluctantly, the investigators had begun to say among themselves the word *lunatics*. They desperately calculated how many fleeting minutes they yet had to run to ground whatever tortured minds might have made the moon their accomplice for that eve of insane mayhem. It was a night that made ancient fears plausible.

Dr. John Hunsacker, associate Fayette County med-

ical examiner, looked up wearily from the grim work
he had just completed. He slowly peeled from his
hands a crimson-spotted pair of disposable forensic
gloves and paused briefly to notice as a CNN news
team shifted their camera away from the tragedy they
had just recorded and aimed it skyward—toward the
full moon.

"They must be thinking what everyone else has
been thinking," Hunsacker heard the voice of metro-
squad detective Frank Root speak beside him in a low
tone.

Hunsacker shrugged. He didn't believe in myths.
"Murders this crazy bring all kinds of theories out of
the woodwork. People want to believe there's some
way to explain them rationally . . . even cops."

"Then what do you make of all this, John? What the
hell is going on here?" asked Root. "We find the first
body in front of Godfather's Pizza. The victim looks
like she's been part of some horror movie. Godfather's Pizza? Is that some kind of sick joke . . . or a
clue?" Root demanded.

"The second one we find is shot, stabbed, run over
with a car, and now . . . here . . . it looks like they
tried to burn the old man alive after they've ripped up
the other two victims enough to kill half the east end.

"This is too damn weird. Do we have crazies
running loose? Are they done? Have they just gotten
started? Why would they kill people like the ones
we're finding? They don't seem to be anyone in
particular."

County Coroner Chester Hagen had walked over to
join them. Together he and Hunsacker gave the nod
that permitted morgue attendants from the University
of Kentucky Medical Center to tuck into garish green
rubber body bags the corpses of the latest victims.
They transported them to an autopsy room. There a

long and painstaking night awaited Dr. Hunsacker and the other pathologists. They would attempt to make the victims' wounds yield some useful clues.

Hager shook his head in bewilderment and spoke with a sadness the others shared. "I've been doing this job for twenty-nine years now and I've never, ever seen anything like this. We've never had anything like this happen in Lexington. Who are we living among these days? I heard on one of the radio stations a few minutes ago that they're saying some moonlight maniac is on the loose."

"Just dandy. Just what we need right now: Panic at eleven . . . Police paralyzed . . . Stay tuned, folks." Root groaned.

Hunsacker interjected a calming presence: "Let me tell you what I can tell you, Frank, from a preliminary look. The trauma inflicted on these victims is the most violent I've seen in ten years. This is almost a text-book case of ways to kill people. Gunshot wounds, stab wounds, throats cut, burns inflicted, and massive injury from driving over a body with a vehicle. The amount of overkill here is incredible. I couldn't even count the number of stab wounds on some of these bodies," the doctor told the detective.

"I'm no psychiatrist. I can't tell you who did this or why, but I can tell you that the only cases I've been involved in where there has been this crazy kind of violence has had a psychotic perpetrator. They some-times apparently have to go on killing their victims over and over. These aren't ordinary circumstances, Fran. These are scary," Hunsacker concluded.

The wail of yet another approaching police siren caught Root's ear. The vehicle that sharply braked moments later brought Root's boss, Lieutenant John Bizzack. He had sped there from a family quarrel that had mushroomed into a hostage taking. He was drained. It was far past his shift hours as midnight now approached. Bizzack had ordered Root to take on the bloody events; his first major homicide investigation. Bizzack clapped a reassuring hand on his subordinate's shoulder and asked for a briefing.

"There's a lot more we don't know than we do know, John," Root began. Four persons had already been pronounced dead by Dr. Hunsacker. A fifth was dying at nearby Humana Hospital. He would not make it through the night.

Shortly before nine P.M., employees at a pizza parlor on Mount Tabor Road heard the sound of screeching rubber out in the parking area. Then they heard what sounded like a heavy thump. Tina Modelli stepped out to look. She cried out in shock and fear at what she found. The tattered and bloodied body of Trudy Harrell, fifty-nine, lay in a rag-doll heap on the patched asphalt lot. Trudy Harrell had suffered a hideous death. She had been shot in the back of the head. Her throat had been cut. She was repeatedly stabbed. Then she was dragged for some distance beneath a car and finally run over by that vehicle. She may have lived through all that brutal horror until the car crushed her.

Within minutes another body had been discovered near a paint store loading dock at Codell and Palumbo Drives. Another woman. She was identified as forty-five-year-old Virginia Kearns. She, too, had been inhumanly killed. She was shot in the head, and her throat was slit. There were other ugly knife wounds. She also had been crushed beneath the wheels of a car. Her body had been found less than a mile away from that of Trudy Harrell's.

Again a call. Firemen extinguishing a blaze consuming a 1983 Chevy on a nearby east-end parking lot found a frightening scene. Roger Keene, forty-seven, was beneath the burned-out hulk. He had been shot twice and stabbed five times in the chest and twelve times in the back. Parts of his body were roasted by the blaze. Tire marks criss-crossed his chest.

Theodore Sweet, fifty-two, also lay near the wreckage. He had been shot twice, once through each ear. He too had been stabbed with wild ferocity in the face, neck, and chest.

The final and ultimate act of barbarism was not seen until the red-hot shell of the car cooled. In the back seat authorities found the near lifeless body of an elderly man.

Carlos Kearns, seventy-three, husband of the earlier-discovered victim, had also been run over by a car, stabbed mercilessly, and shot three times in the head. Amazingly, he was still alive when his killer roughly threw him in the back seat of the auto, sloshed gasoline through an open window, and then ignited it.

"My God," Bizzack sighed when his subordinate had finished the briefing. "What are we up against here?"

Within sight of where Bizzack and Root then stood, Carlos Kearns clung feebly to his life in a hospital on Eagle Creek Road. It was at that hospital, even as the worried detectives planned their counterattack, that the bizarre facts behind Lexington's most explosively murderous night began to emerge.

Police officers and trauma staff turned sharply as the doors of the emergency room at Humana Hospital were flung open. Through them walked two blood-drenched women quarreling loudly. They appeared intoxicated.

Lafonda Fay Foster, twenty-two, and Tina Marie Hickey Powell, twenty-seven, said they needed attention for wounds they had inflicted on each other

49

during a fight. Foster belligerently demanded that a taxi be called to take them back home after their injuries had been treated.

Police Captain John Potts and Officer John Jacobs moved toward the women to put an end to their disturbing behavior in the already clamorous emergency room.

When Foster responded with a stream of curses, the officers arrested both for public intoxication. They would be transported to Central Fayette Detention Center, downtown, for booking and videotaping. But first Potts conducted a frisk. In the jacket pocket of Lafonda Foster he found a blood-smeared buck knife. She said it was the one that had injured them both during their fight. Doctors, however, found no wounds on either woman. Potts observed that it was a most unusual knife. From a single body, two six-inch blades swung out in the same direction. Anyone cut by such a weapon would have received a telltale wound. He assigned Jacobs and Officer Gerald Ross to make special note of the knife when Foster's belongings were logged in to the property officer on duty.

During their booking on the drunk charge, the video camera recorded a not uncommon arrest scene. Both Tina and Lafonda were somewhat unsteady on their feet, their voices slurred by alcohol. Lafonda hurled insolent "fuck you's" at bored cops, many of whom recognized both her and Tina from previous arrests and previous performances. Lafonda was able to respond to the usual questions. She accurately gave her phone number and her Social Security number. A struggling Lafonda and a meekly obedient Tina were taken to their cells.

Lola Slowin found herself a reluctant cellmate to the still angry Lafonda. When Foster finally fell asleep, Slowin attracted a center matron and asked to be put in another area of the jail. She trembled as she pointed to the blood-stained pants she was now wearing.

"That crazy broad made me change clothes with her," she said, pointing to the bunk where Lafonda lay.

"She flushed her damn bloody socks down the toilet . . . and her shoestrings too," Slowin added.

Lieutenant John Bizzack had still not made his way home. While Detective Root began assembling facts that were now known and examining evidence taken from the crime scenes and the victims, Bizzack began juggling the schedules of peacefully sleeping cops who would now be awakened and summoned downtown. Bizzack and Root wanted Lexington's best counterattacking whatever it was that had happened. Sleep didn't matter now.

The victims had all been tentatively identified. Wallets and purses gathered by investigators now lay on a table before which Root stood, sifting and sorting their contents. Some of the names sounded vaguely familiar to Root. He called them out to Bizzack and the half dozen other plainclothesmen who had by now arrived to lend their skills.

"My God, John," Root suddenly said. "I think the victims all lived in the same place—Green Hills Apartments—out on Jennifer Road!"

"Get somebody down to records and run all of them," Bizzack ordered. He had hardly given the command when Officer John Jacobs entered the busy squad room. He carried with him the bloody knife taken from Lafonda Foster. Root stared at it intently. He remembered the oddly configured wounds on Carlos Kearns.

"Where did this come from?" Root asked.

"A coke-head hooker and her girlfriend we collared for intox a little while ago. Here's their book and their priors," Jacobs answered, handing Root the manila jackets that miraculously ended the authorities' earlier fears. It hadn't been the moon. More likely moonshine.

Root quickly scanned the files. The woman who had surrendered the bloody knife had been interrogated by patrol officers less than twelve hours earlier. There had been a complaint that she was creating a disturbance at an apartment in Green Hills, the apartment of Carlos and Virginia Kearns! The beat cops responding to the complaint noted that they had calmed down the quarreling parties. No further action was required, their report concluded.

It was early morning now. People at Green Hills Apartments were not going to be happy when the detectives Root quickly dispatched began knocking at their doors, but that was the way it was. Root felt the tremendous tide of relief that washed over him.

Root picked up the cold cup of coffee on John Bizzack's littered desk and poured it down a sink.

"Why don't you go home and get some shut-eye, John? I think we can take care of the rest of this now. I think it's going to be pretty much case management from here on in . . . pretty much by the book."

Once Bizzack had left, the younger detective began poring over in more depth the files that the uniform officer had brought in. He stopped short when he saw Tina Hickey Powell's name on the second rap sheet file. He remembered her well from his days in narcotics division. Timid, petty felon, street chick, everyday loser on the way to being totally chewed up and thrown up on the seedy, hopeless streets of Lexington's down and out core. How in God's name could she have gotten herself mixed up in anything as crazy as the blood orgy of that night? Root thought the answer had to lie in the other file, Lafonda Foster's. He turned to it next.

Lafonda Fay Foster called herself Fay. Her mother

was sixteen when she gave birth to Fay in a small Indiana town. Her father, Bill, had a long criminal record and deserted his wife when Fay was twelve. At thirteen, she was busted for shoplifting. Taken by the court from her mother, she was sexually abused in a foster home provided by an uncle. A frequent truant at Crawford Junior High School in Lexington, she tried for a while to attend a dropout school, but teachers would note she sat in classrooms in hostile silence and refused to do any work. In a five-year span in her teen years, Lafonda was remanded to five different youth homes. At eighteen she was booked on a robbery charge. She and two accomplices entered a woman's home, where she held a gun on the victim, helped tie her to a bed, and made off with jewelry, food stamps, some small change, and a shotgun. She told arresting officers she needed the money to pay off drug debts. She was using heavy amounts of quaaludes, Valium, and LSD. She had started getting high years earlier, inhaling glue and household solvents. She had tried three different times to kill herself, the records showed. There was a haunting but unsubstantiated note that she had met up briefly with her absent father in a downtown bar and that he had turned her on coke—and turned her out as a hooker to pay for both of their habits. The robbery bust had caught her ten years at the Pee Wee Valley women's prison, but she was out in six months when an elderly local businessman said he would give her a job as a convenience store clerk and see that she had a place to live. Not long after, the sixty-five-year-old man who befriended her died a suicide. Root did not bother to count the numerous arrests for public intoxication, driving under the influence, and disorderly conduct. Root sighed. Lafonda Fay Foster was only twenty-two years old.

Another detective reporting in stopped briefly to get

his orders from Root. He glanced at the file and saw Foster's name.

"Has Fay made the big time?" he queried, half in jest.

"I don't know yet," Root answered. "You know her? Could she do something nuts . . . like whack a bunch of people . . . I mean really whack them?"

"If Fay was way into the shit, she could do anything," the other cop answered. "She is meaner than hell and smart in a sick, crazy way."

Root opened the squad room's window blinds. The sun was coming up. The moon had vanished. Hyped-up cops began streaming back in to report what they had learned in the neighborhood around Green Hills. They gave Root the highlights before sitting down to type their reports. Root was almost certain he need not look further for Lexington's full-moon murderers. They were already locked up in the county drunk tank.

Root and the ten investigators working the case then began to fit all the pieces together. Within hours, dozens of persons had been interviewed. Each had lines to speak in the gruesome drama, some tinged with sad irony.

Candace Christison, a neighbor of the Kearn's in Green Hills, told police she had been approached by Lafonda and Tina on the morning of the murders. Lafonda said she needed to scrape together a little money to buy another half-pint of Jim Beam. The bottle from which she was drinking was nearly empty. She offered to sell something to Christison—a buck knife with two long blades, each of which swung out in the same direction. Two dollars would be plenty. Christison said, "No, thanks."

Scotty Hicks told investigators he was on his way back to his job at a printing plant, driving his pickup truck down New Circle Road when he saw Lafonda and Tina hitchhiking. He stopped to give them a ride. He reckoned it was about two-thirty, maybe three in the afternoon. They wanted to go to a liquor store on Eastland Parkway. Hicks obliged. Then Lafonda asked if Hicks would take them to Green Hills Apartments. When they arrived, Lafonda fixed Hicks with a seductive smile. She offered him sex.

"She said it would be cheap," Hicks told police. "I told her I had better things to do with my money, and besides, I had to get back to work."

Hicks told police he watched as the two women entered a building in the Green Hills complex.

At four P.M., Lexington police dispatchers answered a call from Virginia Kearns. She told them two drunken women were creating a disturbance in her home and refused to leave.

Officers Mark Boggs and Gerald Belcher responded. When they arrived, it was their judgment that Mrs. Kearns was herself badly intoxicated. The women she demanded be ordered to leave were questioned by the patrolmen. Lafonda Foster and Tina Powell did not seem to be creating a problem. They told police that they had been trying to give a soothing bath to the elderly Mr. Kearns, an invalid whom they feared Mrs. Kearns and Trudy Harrell, the Kearnses' friend, were not caring for properly. Lafonda said Mrs. Kearns and Harrell were recent patients at a regional mental hospital and had let the old man's health deteriorate badly. They said they were good friends of Carlos Kearns and had attended to his needs before.

Officer Boggs and Belcher had ordered the loudly shouting Mrs. Kearns to go back inside her apartment. Lafonda and Tina obligingly agreed to leave the complex—just to keep peace—even though they had meant no harm. Boggs' later testimony would add yet one more sad note to the case. "We considered Ms. Powell and Ms. Foster to be sincere in their concern for Mr. Kearns," he would say under oath.

Witnesses who helped police put together what next happened observed that Lafonda and Tina did not keep their promise to leave. They remained at the complex, leaning unsteadily against parked cars, talking to out-of-work residents who knew them or who had nothing better to do that afternoon. Both women laughingly said they were in the middle of a hell of a trip. They had been on drugs and booze for the past three days, perhaps longer, they weren't sure.

When Virginia Kearns once again appeared outside her apartment door, Lafonda turned angry and ugly. Candace Christison recalled that scene for investigators. "She hollered and told Virginia she was going to kill her," the young neighbor said.

"They were mad. They said they had it planned for one of them to give Carlos a bath while the other went through his pants pockets for some money. I guess I just didn't take it seriously when they told Virginia they were going to kill her," Candace Christison softly remembered.

Other binding links between the two troubled women and their victims also came to light as police scoured the apartment complex. The pair had been frequent visitors in the Kearnses' small apartment. They had drunk together often. The victims themselves lived broken lives. Elderly Carlos Kearns was an alcoholic with an old man's liking for young women to whom he could play the role of benefactor with the slim proceeds of his Social Security check and an Air Force pension. Lafonda had more than once taken advantage of the elderly invalid.

Margie Barbee had known Kearns for years. He had confided in her that he feared Foster. "He said that once when she was giving him a bath she deliberately put shampoo in his eyes, then stole $450 from him. He told me he was scared of her and didn't want her coming around. She scared his wife, too."

Virginia Kearns was almost thirty years younger than her husband. She, too, was an alcoholic. She would often wander the complex in nightclothes attempting to sell new apparel that her husband had bought her. She told friends that she heard voices that guided her. Without tranquilizers, she constantly paced, drummed her fingers, and chain-smoked. Seventy-three-year-old Kearns admiringly told their friends he had fallen desperately in love with her raven black hair when he had first hired her as a house cleaner six years earlier. He called her Ginny. She couldn't cook or really keep house. That was why Trudy Harrell, who also drank far too much, was allowed to move in. She was neat as a pin.

Roger Keene had once worked as a Kentucky coal miner. Now he lived across the hall. When Kearns wished to visit, the rugged Keene lifted him gently up and brought him over. Keene, too, had a bad drinking history but a big and generous heart. Theodore Sweet, down on his luck and driven by failure to three-month drinking bouts, was always welcome in Keene's small place. They all became fast friends. They laughed together, drank together, not knowing they were fated to die together.

Police could not determine how Lafonda and Tina had been able to patch up their earlier quarrel with Ginny Kearns, but by about five P.M., all were seen piling into Kearns's white 1983 Chevrolet, with Lafonda behind the wheel, careening erratically from the parking area out onto Richmond Road.

The lightning-fast investigation conducted by the metro cops had produced an astonishingly accurate chronology of the movements that night of the victims and their killers.

By seven P.M., the Chevy roared into a small bait shop on Seventh Street. Lafonda wanted manager Charles Cowan to lend them fifty dollars on Carlos Kearns's credit worthiness. Cowan said he would cash a check for twenty-five dollars but no more. He did not like what he saw. Lafonda hurled an insult at Cowan, calling him a cheapskate as she screeched the car away from his shop.

At the home of a male acquaintance, Foster apparently borrowed a .22-caliber handgun. At eight-thirty she pulled into the Sportsman's Liquor Store on Walton Avenue and demanded of manager John Haggard that he lend her some bullets. He asked her why she wanted them. "I need to shoot some rats," she told him. Haggard gave her four shells. Within half an hour, the Chevy pulled up again. Foster told Haggard she needed more bullets. He told her he had no more. He noticed blood on the passenger side of the car. She should wash it off, he told her.

At about nine P.M., the body of Trudy Harrell was discovered.

The newspaper headlines screamed bloody murder the next morning. Television coverage of the grisly crimes added to the shock waves of horror and disbelief that swept Lexington. Metro detectives confronted Lafonda and Tina with the volumes of evidence they had already gathered. The women stuck to their emergency room story. Tina, however, seemed nervous and frightened.

Bizzack and Root took what they could prove to Fayette Commonwealth prosecutor Ray Larson who reviewed their night's feverish work. Larson had the complaint drawn that would charge Foster and Powell with the first-degree murder of Carlos Kearns. Charges in the other four crimes could wait until every follow-up lead could be pursued and tied down.

Larson knew how Lexington was reeling under the blow of these crimes. He had earlier and often stated his position on the crime and punishment of murder. He had vowed to seek the death penalty in every case. He did not plan to make an exception now because the apparent killers were women. He would demand their death in Kentucky's electric chair.

Shackled hand and ankle, drably clad in blue county jail coveralls, Foster and Powell faced Fayette District Court Judge Lewis Paisley in a jammed hearing room for arraignment. They entered pleas of not guilty in the two-minute proceeding and were held on $100,000 bond. Bizzack and Root told scurrying reporters the motive for the slaying of Carlos Kearns had been robbery. He said other charges involving the remaining victims would be filed soon. The women were also being held on the drunk charges. Counts seeking they be held as persistent felons were also filed. Public defenders were named to help them. Psychiatric tests were ordered. The results of one such session would return during the trial to badly harm the case Lafonda's dedicated lawyers would build on her behalf.

Interviewed on videotape by Lane Veltkamp, professor of psychiatry at the University of Kentucky, Foster answered self-damningly to the probative questions asked. Veltkamp asked if the murder victims had reminded Lafonda of herself in any way.

"Oh, yeah," she replied. "They were all alcoholics and they were just pitiful. They were useless. They had no desire. No ambition to better themselves in any way. Yeah. It scared me."

While they were held awaiting final grand jury action, the part of Foster's persona that cops and social workers had labeled manipulative and cunning did not work to her advantage. Wardens at the detention center were monitoring letters she sent to Tina in which she clumsily warned her friend not to vary their story. In another letter to a friend whom she hoped would testify on her behalf, Foster urged the woman to emphasize the large amounts of drugs Foster had been using. Lafonda wrote her friend that her strategy was to convince the jury she "was mentally deranged from large amounts and excessive use of cocaine."

Yet another heavy blow would be struck against Lafonda Foster. It would point the finger of guilt largely at her for the chilling crime spree. Tina wanted to tell all. Not long after all five charges of murder had been filed, counsel for Tina Powell notified the court his client wished to enter a guilty plea in all five slayings but only if a jury, rather than a judge, would pass sentence for the crimes. In a hearing on the motion, Tina told such a confused story of her involvement that the court rejected her plea and finally ordered that she and Foster stand trial together.

Tina Powell had already been described in the media as a not-too-streetwise twenty-seven-year-old misfit whose troubles with drugs and booze frequently landed her in trouble with the law. It was mostly two-bit loser raps: altering prescriptions to obtain larger amounts of drugs, public intoxication, failing to show up for court appearances. Her parole officer, Rod Planck, once arrested Tina on the spot when she came for a required meeting high on drugs. In Planck's opinion, Tina lived only to get stoned on booze and drugs. She frequented cheap bars where elderly and lonely men came. She used her youthful good looks to wheedle gifts of money from them. "Even if you don't have a sex act, the old men come up with money," Planck said in describing Tina's wiles.

Another part of Tina's life came to notice. She had been Lafonda's lover for at least a year prior to the murders. Fighting to keep herself from the electric

chair, Tina would say she was Foster's battered
spouse, taking part in the murders only because she
feared Lafonda would turn her murderous rage on her
if she refused. In the letters Tina wrote to Lafonda
during their early detention, she unfailingly closed
with "Love ya and miss ya."

Eight women and four men were selected to hear
the case against Lafonda and Tina in the small
courtroom presided over by Judge James Keller. It
would hold only seventy persons in the ten uncomfortable hardwood pews reserved for spectators and
the media.

Commonwealth prosecutor Larson and his chief
assistant, Mike Malone, were confident the jury would
find the women guilty. In fact, the battery of public
defenders representing Foster and Powell saw their
primary task as persuading a jury to stop short of
imposing the death sentence once that verdict had
been reached.

The continuing investigation had produced additional evidence that added even more weight to the
prosecution's case. Shocked jurors heard that after
Foster and Powell had killed the two female victims,
they laughingly pulled into the Parkette Drive-In and
ordered food for themselves and the three trembling
men awaiting their deaths in the rear of the car. Those
same jurors gasped in revulsion when they viewed the
crime scene and morgue photos of the victims and
heard testimony from cellmates who alleged Foster
had bragged that she had carried off the killings with
skills rivaling Charles Manson.

It took the jury only two and one-half hours to find
Foster and Powell guilty of the murders they had
taken about an equal time to commit. Neither prosecution or defense expressed surprise. The real battle
had only begun. The same jury would now determine
whether the women should live or die.

Tina Powell's attorney, Gene Lewter, argued that his client's life should be spared because Lafonda Fay Foster had forced her to take part. "Tina knew that Fay had a gun in her hand. Tina knew you don't mess with Fay now," he explained.

Larson demanded to know why Tina had not told the police who arrested them that Foster had just committed five murders. She could then have their protection had she truly been so afraid.

Lewter asked that Tina be sentenced to twenty years each for her part in the slayings. He seemed certain what the jury was thinking when he added, "I'm not standing here telling you that you should let Tina Powell go free."

In his closing argument on Lafonda's behalf, attorney Kevin McNally asked the jury if enough lives had not already been taken. "Good people don't kill unless it's necessary . . . Juries don't impose the death penalty unless it's necessary . . . The American jury is not a sword of vengeance," he argued, asking that Foster's sentence be life in prison without possibility of parole for twenty-five years.

Powell's attorney, Lewter, bitterly attacked prosecutor Larson in the final moments of the penalty hearing, charging him with misstating facts "because he wants you to kill these people," as he pointed to Tina and Lafonda.

Larson angrily struck back. "I'm not killing them. You're not killing them," he thundered to the jury. "They wrote and signed their own death warrant on April 23, 1986. By their own conduct, they forfeited their right to live under our law."

Tears filled Tina Powell's eyes as she pleaded with the jury to spare her life. "Sometimes when I'm in my cell at night, I think about these people and I try to come up with a reason or some way that what happened that night could have been prevented, but so far I've come up with no reason . . . There's no words to say how sorry I am because there's no reason for what happened. That's really all I can say."

This time the jury that had found the women so swiftly guilty struggled much longer before determining their recommendation to Judge Keller. After more than twenty hours of deliberation, in over three days, they reached a decision. Lafonda Foster should die by electrocution. The life of Tina Powell should be spared, but she never again should be a free woman.

Now the fate of Lafonda Foster was in the hands of yet another man. Judge Keller would consider the jury's verdict. He could uphold or modify it. Lafonda asked to be allowed to read to the judge a four-page statement she had penned in her cell.

The courtroom was only half filled. Dressed in a black jumper and crisp white blouse, Lafonda Foster at last appeared softly feminine and vulnerable. She sobbed through the ten minutes it took to address her remarks to Keller. She fought to control the tremor in her voice: ". . . even though I've been through a lot of suffering in my life, I'm not much different than other people," she began. "I am a woman of twenty-three years who appreciates beauty, who cries at sad movies, who loves children and once had a dream of having a husband and children and a decent life."

She pleaded for mercy. "I know that if you let me live that somehow or someway I can turn the pain I felt around and help other kids who are right now going through what I went through. That's all I have to say. I'm sorry for what happened, but I can't bring them back," she concluded with a final rush of tears. "I wish I could." Head bowed, still weeping, she waited to hear her fate.

"You took the lives of five innocent people, brutally and for no reason whatsoever," Keller intoned. "There's no justification for what you did."

The judge imposed five death sentences on the trembling young woman standing before him. He ordered that her electrocution be carried out on April 22, 1988. She had committed her crimes on April 23, 1986.

Because all death sentences imposed in Kentucky are automatically appealed, there was no finality behind the judge's sentence. In December 1991, the Kentucky Supreme Court ruled that Foster was entitled to a new sentencing hearing because the jury had been prejudiced by hearing Tina Powell's testimony at the same time. It was, in effect, as though Foster had faced two separate prosecutions, the court said. New motions and cross-petitions continue to complicate the case.

4

Deidre Hunt

CAROL HUNT SEEMED TO BE SEARCHING SOME FORBIDding, iron-fenced, dead-of-night graveyard in her own
soul as she struggled to give an account of her daughter, Deidre.

The forty-eight-year-old mother could not do so
without releasing from the dark and shuttered closet
of her own life a slithering parade of ugly, misshapen
gargoyles and griffins. They might now accuse her of
being the cruel hand that had shaped the doomed-tohell life of her twenty-year-old child. Perhaps Carol
Hunt was the original sinner behind the sins for which
her daughter now faced death in the electric chair.

Carol Hunt described the day on which she had
taken tiny Deidre Michelle home from the maternity
ward to a bleak flat in South Weymouth, Massachusetts. "She wouldn't stop crying, so I slammed her
down in the crib," she remembered. Through therapy,
the unwed mother sought to control her continuing
violent abuse of the pretty child. She could not stop.

At age eleven, Deidre was raped by a thirty-year-old
man in the sorry neighborhood. Her mother did not
report the terrifying assault to police. "I couldn't deal
with it," Carol Hunt would recall.

Life for the troubled mother and her two children
—Deidre and a younger brother—seemed to Carol
Hunt a depressing and futile trial, so cold a sea of
despair that she made plans to kill the children and
then herself. The dreamy refuge of alcohol and the
sweet rush of cocaine would calm her and spare her
children from that death, at least.

Her daughter often asked the whereabouts of her
father. Carol Hunt's answers were vague, her frown
menacing. Deidre took the loom of a little girl's
imagination and wove together a hopelessly wonderful chain of romantic yarns about who her father was
and how he really wanted to be with his daughter and
would be, were it not for some mysterious, urgent
matter that kept him away. When, in answer to a
thousand prayers, she would meet that man, Dennis
Driscoll, his chilly indifference turned love and yearning into their bitter shadows—hatred and a desire to
hurt others.

When only twelve, Deidre ran seriously afoul of the
law. She and a band of toughs from the projects were
nabbed burglarizing neighborhood homes. The boys
she was with were far too old to be a twelve-year-old's
playmates. They used Deidre for other things. She
would help them tug the jeans from her slim, coltish
frame and eagerly do whatever they asked. High on
cheap drugs, they would treat her roughly. She seemed
to be asking for it. Deidre had been slapped around
before. She stood the hurt. Sometimes the boys could
be awkwardly tender, too.

Deidre learned to turn twenty-dollar tricks with
stubble-bearded dock workers and old men who had
just cashed their pension checks in wood-floored
seafront bars. Sometimes, a man who sensed and
stroked the most secret levels of her desires could get
change back from his twenty or a week or a month or
longer of a Deidre who followed him home to whatev-

er shabby place he lived. She searched for something she could not name herself, then abruptly left when she did not find it.

Deidre Michelle Hunt liked people to call her Dee. You could also call her Cheri. Cops in several worn-out textile towns in New England called her trouble. They had been following her determined progression from one predictable broken-home-kid kind of scrape to another for years. The file that bore her name as a juvenile offender had grown to more than 200 pages, filled with arrest reports, psychological evaluations, and observations by social workers and cops who weren't ready to stop hoping that the cute, bouncy teenager would finally catch on that she was heading for big trouble. When the family moved to near Manchester, New Hampshire, Deidre enrolled at Goffstown High but didn't stay long. She missed more than fifty straight days of class as a ninth grader and then left altogether. She told a frustrated guidance counselor she already had learned all she needed to know.

At eighteen, Dee did pass through a graduation of a kind. She was involved in an armed robbery. The victim was shot. Deidre and a friend, Bridgette Romano, were charged by police with attempted murder.

Cops said a young woman had been sitting in her car on a street that fronted Derryfield Park, waiting for a friend to get off work at a nearby nursing home. The woman said she looked up to see Deidre and Bridgette weaving toward her vehicle. It was nearly nine-thirty P.M., and it was dark. Deidre approached the car, an unlit cigarette dangling from her mouth.

"Got a light?" she asked the waiting driver.

Before the woman could answer, police said Bridgette Romano thrust a .25-caliber automatic into her face.

"We want money," Dee Hunt demanded. When the

victim said she had none, Bridgette allegedly opened fire erratically into the car. The woman was struck four times but fortunately survived her wounds. Her assailants fled without any money.

Three days later, Manchester police detectives received a crimestopper phone tip. The caller said Deidre and Bridgette were the pair they were looking for. The tipster claimed Deidre had laughed about the incident and said she'd taken part in the clumsy heist because she and her friend desperately needed money for drugs. Cops found Deidre at home, on Remmen Street, chatting breezily on the phone in her bedroom. They handcuffed the teenager. She was an adult now. On the drive from the rundown neighborhood to police headquarters, one cop scolded her the way a father might have done: "What's the matter with you, kid? This isn't nickel and dime stuff. You're going to do some hard time here if you don't cut the crap."

"This is a goddamn roust," Dee spat back. "I want a lawyer." Her pixie face was hard with defiance. She refused to talk to investigators.

"She was tough as toenails," a veteran Manchester police detective would later recall when Deidre made headlines across the nation. "She got lucky on the charges we had her on. It had been dark. The victim had some trouble with identification. The charges got reduced. She didn't do much time, maybe six months. I guess she decided to head south after that. Nobody up here missed her. Not us anyway," the cop said.

South for Deidre Hunt turned out to be Daytona Beach, Florida.

The lights were kept low at the Top Shots Pool Hall on the frayed ocean boardwalk in Daytona Beach. Konstantions "Kosta" Fotopoulos imagined that gave the seedy gathering place for tattooed bikers, drug-hungry runaways, aimless beach riffraff, low-budget whores, and felons-in-waiting a sinister, dangerous ambiance. He postured as a man born to be the still-water, mysterious overlord of just such a cauldron of intrigue. At first blush, Kosta Fotopoulos might seem to the uninitiated no more than a bragging buffoon, the laughable, small-time, and small-potatoes proprietor of a sleazy little hole in the wall. But to those in the know, those whom Fotopoulos let in on what was really going on, Top Shots was only a cunning facade, a mob-connected front for a web of deadly, desperate criminal adventures. He hinted that those enterprises included international drug trafficking, money laundering, counterfeiting schemes, and assassinations for hire—all being directed by the thirty-year-old pudgy-faced, vainly groomed man who only a few years previous had paid his small bills by waiting on tables at a nearby hotel.

The electrifying glimpses that Fotopoulos pretended to let slip about his danger-cloaked life had their intended effect on the court of losers who camped and caroused at Top Shots. Kosta Fotopoulos was a big-time operator, a valuable man to know. Freckle-faced runaway teenage girls from heartland towns too small to confine their growing up were especially impressed by the stories Fotopoulos told. He would elaborate on them in much greater detail after he'd helped find them a cheap little room in the faded tourist cottages south of the boardwalk. He spent more than a few evenings with various girls there.

Things were not nearly as glamorous when Kosta Fotopoulos went home at night. He was no longer quite the dashing figure he once had been in the eyes of his twenty-seven-year-old wife, Lisa. Four years earlier, while still a waiter, Kosta had met Lisa Paspalakis, daughter of a wealthy and influential Greek family. Kosta set out to capture Lisa and he did. Their wedding was held at St. Demetrious Greek Orthodox Church, an important bedrock of Greek community life in Daytona Beach. There was no doubt the elaborate affair had cost the bride's family a very pretty penny.

After their wedding, the family agreed to Kosta's wish to run Top Shots. Lisa ran a nearby amusement arcade called Joyland for her family with sound business sense. From her office in the arcade, it was a short walk to Top Shots. What she began to see and hear there worried Lisa Fotopoulos. The people with whom Kosta was making friends were not the kind that she would ever welcome into her comfortable and respectable home. Grimy motorcycle thugs, crazy-eyed teenage girls, ten-time losers carrying on whisper-voiced transactions in which small packages and crumpled currency changed hands. Lisa told Kosta she did not like what was going on at the pool hall. Kosta would eye his wife narrowly and make no reply. In Greece, where his parents lived, women were not so bold as to venture an opinion about the business dealings of their husbands. He would storm from their house, his dinner uneaten, and return to the smoky provinces of Top Shots where his affairs were his own, and women more respectful.

Deidre Hunt lazed on the sparkling beaches at Daytona for a few sunny days to recover from yet another cruel wrench. A few months before, she had found another man. They had taken a small but comfortable place to live. She got pregnant. He was not ready. The beating he gave Deidre was worse than any other he had given her. Deidre miscarried, but she forgave him. She wanted them to remain together, but he would not stay.

Feeling lost, Deidre reconnoitered the pastel, palmlaned city she planned to call home for a while. The magnet of the boardwalk brought her inevitably to the door of Top Shots. She could tell from the people loitering nearby that it was a place worth checking out.

Kosta Fotopoulos had a finely honed instinct about what lay behind some of the carnival of faces that came through his doors. He could be a sympathetic and understanding man when a girl told him she was a little down and out and needed a job, maybe a few dollars until payday if that wasn't asking too much.

"It just so happens I need a waitress right now," Fotopoulos told Deidre Hunt. She eagerly pulled her chair closer to the small table where they were seated.

"I think I'd make a good one," she smiled.

"Don't kid yourself. It's hard work waiting on people, and you have to be smart," Kosta answered, sounding very much like a man who knew. "You're a fine-looking lady, and I think maybe you are smart, too," Kosta added. His voice then dropped to a cautious hush. "There may be some other ways a smart girl could make some money here with me. There are things I can't tell you about right now, but . . . maybe, maybe later. We'll see . . . We'll see."

The pay phone rang on a wall nearby. Kosta let it shrill six times as he moved slowly toward it. Without answering, he picked up the receiver and put it back down. He returned to the table where Deidre sat. Before she could speak, Kosta put a finger to his lips to indicate silence. "That was a secret code," he said. "It will ring again in my office in an hour. The people from Washington must have a little job for me to do."

Wow, Deidre Hunt thought. *Who is this guy anyway?*

The apartment Kosta Fotopoulos found for Deidre Hunt was on Lenox Avenue, a slight cut above the accommodations he usually provided, paying the first and last months' rent for the ladies in his life who needed a little help until payday.

Deidre was a quick study. From other Top Shots waitresses and customers she soon learned more about her employer's covert, daring ventures. She and Fotopoulos had already made love. In those misty minutes after, he somberly hinted that there was more, much more to him and his life than he could reveal to her . . . unless she was made of the same fire-hardened steel that he was, unless she was prepared to enter with him into a world where she had to prove just how cold and ruthless and tough she was, where she had to meet certain tests.

Kosta's cigarette hovered close to Deidre's naked breast. He brought it yet nearer. She cupped his hand and drew it forward. She did not cry out at the pain.

"I think perhaps there are things I can tell you about," Kosta said approvingly.

"I want to know them all," she replied.

Day by day, Kosta revealed more of his shrouded life to a breathlessly enthralled Deidre.

"You see this check?" he told her, slipping only a part of it out of the envelope in which it had arrived at Top Shots.

"It's from the CIA, their payment for killing a man they were afraid knew too much."

"My God," Deidre exhaled. "How much do you get paid for that?"

"It all depends," Kosta said cryptically. "If it is easy, it can be only $2,000. If it is difficult, it can be $100,000."

"Is this something you do all the time," Deidre wanted to know.

"I have killed eight people . . . so far," Kosta answered darkly.

Somewhere—perhaps someday he would tell her—

Kosta had buried $100,000 in mint-perfect counterfeit currency. He was only waiting for the signal from his underworld contacts to put it into circulation. He bragged that a secret-numbered Swiss bank account held a huge amount of money he had arranged to launder for some very big people making illicit fortunes in the drug trade.

One night, Fotopoulos brought with him a videotape. He played it for Deidre. It appeared that several people were being horribly tortured on the tape. A shadowy figure, back turned to the camera, was their apparent tormentor. Deidre had no trouble recognizing it as Kosta Fotopoulos.

"Video cameras are a useful tool," Kosta told Deidre as she intently studied his eyes. "They can be used to teach people very valuable lessons."

Deidre had been told by Kosta that things were not well between him and his disapproving wife. He also complained of his treatment at the hands of the powerful Paspalakis family. Lisa's father had recently become the target of an IRS probe. Kosta smiled knowingly when he spoke about that, cautiously implying, but careful not to assert as fact, that he had a hand in arranging that headache for her father through highly placed connections in Washington.

As the summer of 1989 passed, Kosta's conversations with Deidre seemed more and more to turn to Lisa. "She has money, that one. There is a big insurance policy on her, too. It would be nice to have a lot of money—all at once. Then I wouldn't have to do so much to keep you in style," Kosta said in a teasing, testing voice.

"What are you thinking about, Kosta?" she asked.

"I think it is time for Lisa to go so we can be happy," he answered.

"Yes, yes!" Deidre said, clapping her long, thin hands.

73

There was a serious problem about how to snuff out the life of Lisa Fotopoulos, Kosta explained to Deidre.

He could not, of course, kill his own wife. He would be the first person suspected. And even though he had a roster of professional assassins whom he used for such things, it would be unwise to hire one of them for this job. It was too dangerous to mix business with personal matters. It just was not done.

"We need someone that we know, someone that we can trust," Kosta said. "Can you think of someone like that and then see if they might be interested in helping us?"

In her months at the pool hall, Dee had made some friends of her own. There was Yvonne Lori Henderson, just turned a troubled twenty years old. She was a daughter of a well-respected Volusia County lawyer who served on the district's public defender staff. To her parent's dismay, she was a frequent Top Shots visitor, choosing her companions from the ragged ranks of pool hall patrons. Deidre thought of Henderson as her closest friend. She confided in her many of the things Fotopoulos had related. Some of the boardwalk wise guys snickered about Deidre and Yvonne's close relationship. They believed Deidre lusted after her curvy friend.

A twenty-two-year-old street-hardened dodger named Mzimmia James had also become a friend of Deidre's. The lithe, good-looking, resourceful black youth was a well-known character along the boardwalk where he occasionally pimped and worked other hustles.

Deidre liked to tease another friend, Mark Ramsey. She often caught him watching her, admiring her body as she made her way around the pool hall in tight-fitting cutoff jean shorts and sexy tank tops. She would brush against him, then laugh when he stammered some embarrassed exclamation in his cute North

Carolina drawl. Deidre thought the good-looking
nineteen-year-old had possibilities. She invited him to
share a few cold beers with her at the apartment on
Lenox Avenue.

"If I needed help with something, would you help
me?" she asked Ramsey, joining him on a sofa, sitting
close, making him uncomfortable but pleased. "You'd
have to do something first, something like an initiation to prove you aren't chickenshit," she added,
peeling off the tank top that clung to her with nervous
sweat. She reached to extinguish the lamp that was the
room's only light. Mark Ramsey reached for Deidre's
fullness. He said he would not mind some silly
initiation if that was what she and her boss wanted.
He knew what *he* wanted.

Lisa Fotopoulos watched silently as her husband
rummaged through a bedroom closet. He found what
he was looking for. From a shelf, he took down an
expensive video camera. Without a word, he left.

Kosta Fotopoulos had already considered the can-
didacy of Ramsey as his wife's potential killer. He did
not share Deidre's faith that the nineteen-year-old
could handle the tricky assignment. But, Fotopoulos
mused, maybe the kid could serve another useful
purpose, perhaps more than one.

Fotopoulos, Deidre, and Mark Ramsey drove
through the humid, almost-autumn Florida night.
From Daytona Beach, they headed west, down Clyde
Morris Boulevard, until they arrived at a stand of
remote pine scrub near the Strickland Shooting
Range. Kosta, a gun buff who loved exotic weapons,
knew the area around the shooting range well.

On the way, Deidre kept up a stream of banter with
Ramsey. As they pulled off the road and came to a
stop, that cheerful chatter faded. Ramsey had asked
unconcernedly just what kind of hazing he was ex-

pected to go through that night. Fotopoulos gravely told the youth he was to be prepared for acceptance into an assassin's club. That is, if he proved his courage.

Ramsey nearly laughed, then thought better of it. What the hell, Dee had already told him that the Greek got off on this kind of stuff, that he would fire a couple of rounds from a gun at Ramsey's feet, and then they would go somewhere and get snot-flying stoned.

Ramsey made no protest as he was tied to a tree. He grinned at Deidre. Nor did he feel any alarm when Kosta Fotopoulos unsheathed from an expensive leather case a long-barreled rifle. Inside her waistband, Deidre carried a small silencer-equipped .22-caliber handgun her boss had given her. Fotopoulos retrieved from the car another item he had brought: a video camera.

Fotopoulos stood behind Deidre and raised the camera, focusing it on a smiling Ramsey. He had told her that she, too, would face a test that night. He ordered Deidre to shoot. She looked at him for a long, questioning moment, then raised the gun.

The slight cough of the small weapon was lost in the pine woods, but it was captured by Kosta's whirring video camera. Through the viewfinder he saw the handsome blond teenager's leg jerk in pain. He heard him groan, then cry out to God. The small weapon in Deidre's slim hand sputtered yellow-blue flame twice more. Ramsey slumped against his bonds, his chin on his bloodied chest. The camera saw Deidre stride forward toward the boy. Without a tremor of hand, she filled her fingers with his hair, pulled his head upward, and fired a fourth shot into his brain. Deidre was breathing hard. Her eyes blazed in wild, almost carnal triumph. Fotopoulos lowered the camera.

Deidre and Kosta returned to Lenox Avenue. They

clawed away each other's clothing and made white-hot, hurting love. Mark Ramsey was alone in the woods that night, dead.

Kosta's farewell to Deidre broke the spell of dangerous excitement and torrid passion. "Don't forget, I have the tape. Don't ever try to cross me, Dee," he said as he stood by the door.

"Don't forget everything you've told me," she answered softly to herself after he had gone. "Maybe I've told other people. Maybe I've written it all down."

A dozen blood-red roses were delivered to Deidre's the next morning. Kosta called not long after. "I love you, sweetheart," he whispered. "You're a soldier. You're my lieutenant. We need to talk right away, but not on this line. It could be tapped. Go to a pay phone and call me. We need to get going on the other thing."

That other thing was Lisa's death. Kosta had become almost frantic as he talked about it now. He had to have the money that would come to him as her widower. Who had Deidre found that could be talked into the job? Trust was no longer a concern; anyone could be used to commit the murder of his wife. And he had a surprise for whoever would do it—they, too, would die when they finished their work. No one would ever know what had happened. No one but Deidre and Kosta, and they weren't about to talk, were they?

Deidre Hunt agreed to comb her list of friends to find someone else who could be induced into accepting the contract on Lisa Fotopoulos's life. She could offer big money and whatever else it took. The trigger man would never live to collect the bounty, Deidre knew. She asked her friend Yvonne to help. Among the swaggerers and connivers who frequented the pool hall, Deidre managed to find five different men who said they were willing to murder for money and for her. Two would later turn tail. Another schemed to kill

Lisa at a Halloween costume ball, then lost his nerve when he saw the size of the crowd of revelers. Mzimmia James was the next to try. He cornered Lisa in the small office of the amusement arcade, armed with a gun Kosta had provided. It was to appear as though a robbery attempt had led to her murder. The noisy electronic blipping of the quarter games would drown out the commotion of her slaying. Lisa reacted swiftly when confronted by James. She dove between his legs and darted to the safety of the boardwalk. She recognized the grinning young black man as someone who hung out at Top Shots. She confronted her husband with her suspicions and demanded to know what he knew about the frightening incident.

"I have no idea what you're talking about," Kosta answered coldly.

Following that suspicious bungled attempt on her life, Lisa Fotopoulos was warily mistrustful of her husband. She told her family of her concerns but continued to live in her own home. An agitated Kosta determined that the scheme needed much more intense direction to keep from making a boner of the kind that had permitted Lisa to escape death in Mzimmia's earlier foiled plot.

This time a more foolproof scenario would be employed. A burglar would break into the Fotopouloses' riverfront home in the early morning hours. There had been other recent burglaries in the neighborhood. The phony thief would create a scene that would make it appear that Lisa had been awakened by his prowling. He would shoot her with the .22-caliber pistol Kosta provided: freshly cleaned, neatly oiled, but not exactly an ordinary .22 handgun. It had been rigged so that only the first round in the clip could be fired. The designated burglar would not know about that. Deidre and Kosta would.

Brian Chase was only a little more than eighteen

years old. Beneath the bluff, wanna-be tough guy was a kid who could be manipulated. Deidre knew how. He went with her to the apartment on Lenox. The bargain was sealed in her bedroom.

Deidre kissed Brian Chase passionately, lingeringly, as she curbed her car a half block from the home that Lisa and Kosta Fotopoulos uneasily shared. It was a Judas kiss. He would never taste another. His last warm breath of desire stayed in Deidre's throat as she pulled away, her deadly errand completed.

The night of November 4, 1989, was cloudy, starless. It looked like rain. Kosta Fotopoulos listened intently to the light breathing of his wife, attentive to her smallest, dreamy toss and turn. A foggy iridescence from a streetlight provided a thin slice of light in the master bedroom. Kosta heard Brian make his planned forced entry into the house. He tensed, his hand crept quietly toward a drawer in the lamp table near his bed. He felt the cool metallic thrill of his .9-millimeter automatic. The nubby grips on the sides had been crafted to fit his hand. Chase paid him no mind. The script called for Fotopoulos to be sound asleep. The burglar stood for a moment above the slumbering form of Lisa, her lithe, tanned legs splayed in innocent seduction. He fired a round into her head. He saw her spasmodic thrash. Her head flew up from the pillow, her handsome Aegean face a mirror of confused pain, her sleep-tousled raven hair a sudden compress for the sharp spurt of blood obscenely streaming from her wound, painting the spotless bedsheets scarlet with murder.

Kosta had framed the intruder in the sights of his heavy sidearm. He listened as Brian pulled the trigger on the second round, knowing the only sound would be an empty click. Whatever surprise passed through the mind of Brian Chase was never uttered. Kosta

Fotopoulos fired the full cargo of the gun's clip into the betrayed assassin's body. The sledge blows of the powerful bullets gyrated the youth like a top. He fell, gushing his own blood onto the plushly carpeted floor.

Lisa Fotopoulos lay seemingly lifeless as Kosta made his rehearsed, shaken call to summon police. He did not look at the face of his dead wife. Had he done so, he would have observed her faint, barely audible breathing. Lisa Fotopoulos was alive!

An astonished and fuming Fotopoulos struggled to keep his story straight when cops and an ambulance arrived. While emergency medics rushed a comatose Lisa to nearby Halifax Medical Center, Kosta hurried to brush off the police intent on gathering all the information they could about the incident. He nervously paced outside the operating suite where Lisa hovered near death. The bullet was too close to critical areas of the brain to be immediately removed, but Lisa at last was stabilized. Kosta could now make his frantic exit, still posing as the shocked and grieved husband tragically forced to kill a man to defend his wife and home.

"Get hold of James! I want to bomb that fucking woman's hospital room," Kosta shrieked when he slammed the door behind him at the Lenox Avenue apartment. Deidre had spent a sleepless night. She had seen the TV news reports of the blundered burglary.

"He can act like he's delivering flowers, then he can stick a can of charcoal lighter under her bed and light it," Fotopoulos sputtered. Neither James nor anyone else could be found to make the insane delivery. They had seen the news, too. They knew Brian Chase was dead.

Fotopoulos managed to calm himself. He told Deidre about the bloody charade that had taken place in his bedroom only hours before. "The punk looked like meatloaf," he laughed. "He pissed himself, too. All over my carpet. Not a class act."

When Lisa Fotopoulos regained consciousness, she told police of her suspicions. Only three days passed before homicide detectives had followed the clumsy trails of elephant tracks the blowhard Greek waiter/ phony soldier of fortune and his troubled lover had left behind. Some of the layabouts Deidre had tried to hire to kill Lisa told cops about the offers. Fotopoulos and Deidre were placed under arrest. Yvonne Henderson and Mzimmia James were charged with conspiracy counts.

"Keep your mouth shut!" Kosta threatened Deidre. "Remember the tapes."

She didn't oblige. "I want a lawyer and I want to talk to the DA," Deidre said. She was willing to cut a deal. Deidre Hunt offered to cooperate in hopes she could pay with only prison time. It proved to be the mistake of her life. Her choice to plead guilty to the charges and assist the state in its prosecution of Kosta Fotopoulos meant that a jury would never hear her case, only a stern, no-nonsense S. James Foxman, a veteran circuit court judge. He became the sole weigher of the facts of her troubled life. Early on in the preliminary proceedings, he seemed unmoved by the argument that Deidre was the product of her hurtful childhood and the frightened, threatened tool of a sinister, manipulative Kosta. When Deidre wanted to withdraw her guilty pleas, Foxman ruled she could not. Her deal with the prosecution never materialized.

Deidre had already led cops to the awful place where Mark Ramsey's corpse waited to be discovered. Woodland insects had already found him and had begun their ghoulish scavenger work.

She admitted to police that it was she who had enticed and hired Brian Chase to be the executioner of Lisa Fotopoulos.

"You knew you were sending that boy to his death, didn't you?" her interrogators asked.

"Yes," Deidre Hunt replied.

This lurid tale of murder for thrills and murder for hire unfolded with new revelations every day. Spellbound residents of Daytona Beach and surrounding counties gleaned each startling tidbit from a cascade of ink flowing across the pages of the *Daytona Beach News-Journal.* Much of the dramatic coverage was pounded out in rushed takes by a thirty-year newsroom veteran who covered the police beat with a quiet, low-key style, a solid reputation for fairness, and a deft knack for finding and reporting the stories other area news hands wished they had filed first. Kathy Kelly was a familiar and respected front-page byliner at the *News-Journal.* The community liked the way the enterprising, wry cop-shop lady took them behind the scenes. Kelly was getting phone calls from friends she'd made during her many years at the paper. They didn't want to wait until the next edition came out to find out what Kathy had turned up and would be reporting when the big presses rolled again on their latest cycle.

"I'd never seen so much interest in a story. People would stop me on the street and say, 'Tell me what's happening. I need my Fotopoulos fix for the day.' It was a real-life soap opera," Kathy Kelly remembers.

At the Volusia County jail, someone else was anxiously reading each new story that flew from Kelly's green-glowing video display terminal to the endless wide ribbons of newsprint down in the pressroom. That someone called the newsroom's city desk and asked to speak with Kathy Kelly. It was important, urgent, a matter of life and death. It would sell a lot of newspapers, Deidre Hunt's husky voice on the line said. Kathy Kelly had finished her tour for the day and had gone home. The call was quickly patched through to her.

"You're not getting all the facts. You're not being told everything," Deidre Hunt told Kelly as the newswoman rummaged through her handbag for a narrow brown reporter's notebook. "I can tell you the true facts. And when you write about me, please call me Dee, not Deidre. Can I call you Kath? I know all your friends do."

What Deidre Hunt wanted Kathy Kelly to know had certainly not been revealed at the daily police and prosecution briefings held for reporters. The cops didn't believe any of it.

"Fotopoulos held a gun on me the night I shot Mark Ramsey," Deidre confided to Kelly. "I had two choices. I could do what he told me or I could die. Oh, God. I was so scared."

After she fired that unbelievably ruthless fourth bullet into Ramsey's skull and the video camera had stopped recording, one more shot was fired, Deidre claimed. It had been fired by Fotopoulos because the teenage victim was not yet dead.

"Kosta walked over and touched Kevin. I could hear him moaning like he wanted to say something," she alleged to the reporter. Fotopoulos was angered. " 'Damn it, I knew this would happen,' " Deidre now asserted her lover said, then shot a fatal coup de grâce into Ramsey's head with the rifle he had brought along.

Deidre's voice faltered as though she had been overcome by remembering the events of that night. The most haunting memory of all, she said, was Mark Ramsey's strange inability to understand he was about to be slain. "That was the worst part. He had a smile on his face like he thought it was a joke," Hunt informed Kelly in the telephone chat.

There was something else, something terribly important her readers needed to know, Hunt continued in a conspiratorial voice. "I tried to warn Lisa Fotopoulos that Kosta was planning to have her killed," she said.

For a week before the final murder attempt, Hunt claimed she had dialed a phone number she knew rang only in the Fotopoulos bedroom. She hoped to catch Lisa there alone and give her an anonymous warning. The times she had called, however, it was Kosta who had answered and she had hurriedly hung up.

"I figured if I told her, she would take him out of her will and he would leave her alone," Deidre said.

"Why didn't you call the police and tell them?" Kelly quietly interjected.

"I didn't tell anyone because I didn't want to involve anyone else," Deidre answered haltingly.

Deidre said her own life was now in danger. Fotopoulos would find some way to reach through her cell bars and silence her with death. Another inmate had already told her as much. "I don't think I'll make it to court," she said in a trembling tone.

Deidre said it was terror, not love, that had enmeshed her in Kosta's deadly plots. "We had something going, but it wasn't love," she said.

When she discovered that Fotopoulos was married, early in their relationship, she told him she couldn't see him anymore. She had a firm rule about not dating married men. Once, she had packed her bags and told him she was moving out of the Lenox Avenue love nest. He grabbed her violently, manacled her hands behind her back with a coat hanger, and burned her breast with a cigarette. She wanted desperately to flee but didn't. She remained his helpless sex slave. He continued to torture and abuse her. She did not try to leave again.

Money had never been important to her, Deidre told Kelly. Those rumors that she stood somehow to gain from the reported seven hundred thousand dollars in life insurance carried on Lisa were mean and untrue. Even though she knew Fotopoulos was "filthy rich," she asked him for nothing and got very little while she had been his mistress. A few dresses, some occasional flowers, that had been all. She was indifferent to that, having come from a family background where there was never enough. She was philosophical about money. "It's better not to have any rather than have it and lose it," Hunt told Kelly.

Kelly carefully crafted the story she would write from that interview. She had formed an opinion about the teary twenty-year-old. This sad spectre had come uninvited into her peaceful home late at night to seduce her with a self-serving story clearly at odds with what a thorough police investigation was uncovering. *This is a very tough cookie,* Kelly thought. *Why do they always want you to like them? Why do they think you will?*

Deidre read Kelly's story eagerly and apparently approved. She began writing letters to the reporter, asking her to write back and to come visit her. The letters from Deidre were again almost diametrically at odds with other information Kelly had gleaned as she worked the ongoing story.

"I had a good childhood and my schooling was not bad," Deidre wrote. "We never had much money, but my mom did try her best."

The scared little girl who desperately wanted a friend again reached out to Kelly after she had replied to one of Deidre's letters. "Thank you for writing," she began. "If we ever meet, don't be so formal. Call me Dee. Even in the next letter if you don't mind. Please don't write anything till we meet so you can have a better story . . ."

Deidre repeated her belief that Fotopoulos would have her killed before she could testify against him. "I'm convinced that he will make several attempts on my life before I go to court. I really hope I make it, but if I don't, there will be a sealed letter addressed to you containing a lot of details. If I die, I don't want anything covered up. I want the public to know of the things he did to me.

"Also I don't want everyone going on what was written already. OK? Thanks," Deidre wrote.

Deidre also related to Kathy Kelly a much different version of her armed robbery arrest in New Hampshire than had been proven as fact during her hearing there. "I physically stopped the girl from killing the lady," Hunt asserted. "They had to give me something because I didn't go to the police and tell them what was going on. Instead I tried to stop the robbery myself."

That was not the train of events New Hampshire court records showed. The "something" she had been given was a six-month sentence for the armed robbery and shooting of the woman near the park.

Kathy Kelly remembered something similar Deidre had told her during their first talk on the telephone. It had to do with the night Hunt had raised a pistol and coldly shot Mark Ramsey to death. "I'm not totally innocent because I didn't call the police, but this man held a gun to me and ordered me to shoot someone to death," Deidre Hunt had said.

The case of Deidre Hunt had begun to attract attention far beyond Daytona Beach. When prosecutors let it be known that the gruesome fifty-seven-second videotape of Mark Ramsey's slaying would be shown at Deidre's sentencing hearing, dozens of reporters found themselves packing travel bags, bound for the arms-open tourist town to cover the year's most sensational murders.

Deidre Hunt was available for some limited interviews. The details she was now willing to provide became steadily more revealing. She told the story of her brutal rape at eleven, then added that only a year later she had been the victim of yet another attempted rape, this time being stabbed in the assault. She had not told her mother of that incident. She no longer believed Carol Hunt would care or do anything about it.

A few years later, while she continued to dream that one day her father would come home and she could be part of a normal family, she made a heart-breaking discovery. The mother of one of her schoolmates had begun dating a very handsome man, that friend told Deidre. When she caught a glimpse of him, it proved to be Dennis Driscoll, her father, who didn't care about Dee at all.

At sixteen she was a hooker on the streets of Boston, cocaine crazy most of the time, in and painfully out of brief relationships in which the men she chose seemed always to turn violent in anger and in love. She found a job muling coke for a mob-backed operation, but she had to run for her life when quantities of the product showed up missing on inventory.

The miscarriage—the lost baby she wept for—had brought her to Daytona Beach to pull her shattered life back together, Deidre told reporters. It was there that the most wretched chapter of her life would begin on the day that she met Kosta Fotopoulos.

It was hard to describe the numbing terror he had subjected her to, Deidre recounted. Much of it was sexual torture, but he used other frightening threats and tools to keep her in bondage and make her a helpless accomplice to murder. "He told me one day that he had gotten the addresses of all of my relatives. He would hire people to kill them if I didn't do what he told me. He told me he would kill me and have my body stuffed and keep it around and do terrible things to it," she wept.

He had a small weapon that used a cartridge to fire a knife with pinpoint accuracy. He would push a terrified Deidre up against a wall and sadistically torment her by firing the blades dangerously close to her while she trembled in fright and pleaded with him to stop. After he had viciously burned her with a cigarette for her attempt to escape, she became too fearful for further resistance. "From then on I was really in bad shock," she said.

Deidre's mother spoke to the media as well, making humiliating admissions about her life and the unloving way in which she had reared her daughter. She recounted that first day on which she had brought the child home and angrily threw Deidre down in her crib, then added; "After that, I started making bargains with God, promising it wouldn't happen again," she told the *Boston Globe*. "But it did. I hit Deidre a lot."

Carol Hunt also confessed frequently considering suicide as her children were growing up. Her addictions to alcohol and cocaine and her own loneliness had cast an ever-present pall of depression over their home. "I was drinking a lot. I wasn't looking at Deidre and the problems she was having," the mother said.

Carol Hunt said her sorrow was now enormous. What had happened to her daughter was a heavy pain that could never be lifted. "All she's ever looked for was someone to love her," Carol Hunt wept. "And look what she's found."

Judge Foxman heard six days of presentencing testimony before determining what punishment should be meted out to Deidre Michelle Hunt. During that hearing, Foxman watched as the brutal murder of Mark Ramsey came to life again in stark, macabre, cinema verité on a television screen. The judge could barely conceal his shock.

Deidre's attorney, Peter Niles, said he had opted for a verdict by judge rather than risk the impact of that taped horror on any jury that might have been empaneled. Niles could see that even a hardened criminal court judge could not avoid giving heavy weight to that horrifying tableau.

Niles argued that Deidre's tragic background, her virtual slavery to Fotopoulos, and her willingness to help police bring the real mad killer to justice should result—in simple fairness to his client—to a sentence of life in prison without possibility of parole for twenty-five years. "This person should be pitied," Niles said, pointing to a ghostly white, drawn, and diminutive Deidre, quietly crying at the defense table. "When you take someone like that who is a cripple, do you kill them? A mental, physical, and emotional cripple? Do you kill them? I say no."

The prosecution would not let that impression stand. Assistant state attorney David Damore also pointed to the weeping twenty-year-old defendant. "Deidre Hunt has a newfound remorse, your honor," he sharply accused. "She now knows she faces the ultimate penalty for her actions." Damore charged the facts were clear and unforgivable. "Deidre Hunt wanted money. She set out on a wave of murder and intended to kill anyone who stood in her way to get that money. She chose, in essence, to be the messenger of death on one occasion, in the case of Brian Chase, and she chose to be the bearer of death in the case of Mark Ramsey," Damore added.

Deidre Hunt then rose to speak what she hoped might be the right words to keep her from a rendezvous with Florida's electric chair. She wore the unflat-

tering, outsized jail-issue jumpsuit over which a matron had draped a fading navy blue sweater against the
chill of the courtroom, against the chill of that day in
her life.

Deidre told Judge Foxman she wanted to apologize
to the families of the two dead young men and to Lisa
Fotopoulos, but she maintained she had no choice
about her participation. "It was my decision of living
by shooting Mark Kevin Ramsey or dying with Mark
Kevin Ramsey," she said in a voice trembling and
breaking. "I take responsibility for my action, but I
feel my action was not first-degree murder."

Of the man whose servile pawn she claimed she had
become, Deidre said, "This is someone who has
mastered the secret of manipulating the human mind.
He makes Ted Bundy look like a teddy bear. This
person was sick, evil."

Judge Foxman remained unswayed. His sentence
was death. He cited the damning power of those
fifty-seven seconds of video. It was as though he had
somehow been transported from his quiet chambers
and forced to come face-to-face with the awful realities of violent death that few judges have ever witnessed. "Never before has this court seen a victim's
suffering so graphically or visually established," he
intoned.

That monstrous scene would play again, within
months, when a stunned jury watched it in the murder
trial of Kosta Fotopoulos. The nine men and three
women who would determine the bogus soldier of
fortune's fate were then required to view the spine-
chilling incident again and yet again, the second time
in surrealistic slow motion. The dying cries of Mark
Ramsey strung out like some eerie banshee's shriek as
the television set's speakers slowed the sound as well.

Kosta Fotopoulos was also found guilty. He, too,
was sentenced to die. Both cases were appealed to

Florida's high court. The justices turned down all sixteen points upon which Fotopoulos's appeal were based. But Deidre was granted a new sentencing hearing. A date for that new chance to live is pending.

Carol Hunt was stopped by reporters as she left the Volusia County Courthouse following the guilty verdict. She was embittered by the outcome. "There is an evil that lives in this city and Deidre was caught up by it," she said. "Deidre may be twenty-one now," Carol Hunt added before briskly walking away, "but after all she's been through, she is still only a child."

Lisa Fotopoulos divorced her husband and took back her maiden name. Her father died. Kosta passed a jailhouse rumor that he had arranged the death. The body was exhumed. Lisa's father had died of natural causes.

Deidre Hunt was sent to Florida's death row for women, housed in the Broward Correctional Institution at the edge of the remote Everglades. From a small window in her eight-by-ten-foot cell, she can catch the wild and free cries of loons and see the tall bayonet grass bending in the wind.

Deidre occupies her time writing black, haunting poetry about death and pain. She sketches pictures depicting different methods of suicide. She does not leave her cell except for three weekly showers and brief exercise periods. She says that her former lover has hired assassins to kill her and that she is not safe from him—even on death row.

Her poetry is as bleak as her future. In one verse she wrote, "There is evil lurking all around. The screaming voice in your head does pound."

"I write mostly about torture and blood and being beaten down to nothing," she says. "I wish myself dead all the time."

Deidre has made a new friend. Judy Buenoano, on death row for the poisoning of her husband, has become almost like a mother to the haunted hooker whose own mother still grieves her failure. Deidre and Buenoano, forty-eight, are allowed to chat on the intercom that links the six pastel pink-painted cells. They swap small luxuries like new shades of nail polish. Deidre favors red.

Kathy Kelly shared the memory of Deidre Hunt that will stay with her, after all the yellowing words had gone their way to the *News-Journal's* clipping morgue. "When I watched that tape, when I saw that boy dying right in front of my eyes and knew that it was Deidre Hunt on the other end of his death, it made me believe that all of those tears she shed later were very convenient tears. My first impression of her was the one that stayed with me. Deidre Hunt is a very tough cookie."

5

Yvette Gay

EVEN BY THE HARDSCRABBLE YARDSTICK AGAINST WHICH
life is measured in the poverty-cordoned black section
of small farm town Washington, North Carolina,
Yvette Gay and her twin sister, Doris, dwelled in
wretched want and scant hope. Home for the pair of
twenty-seven-year-old twins was an old school bus,
towed from a junkyard and crudely converted into a
house. There they made do, raising Yvette's two
illegitimate children without such ordinary comforts
as heat, water, or indoor sanitation.

But there was now hope. In the past few weeks, as a
sweet new April came warm and green to recompense
winter's cold, gray, mountain drear, the comely,
winsome-faced black woman found reason to rejoice.
Renwick Gibbs, the man she had loved so desperately,
so singly, for the past five years, had again left the wife
with whom it seemed he could not peacefully live. He
had come back once more to a patient Yvette. "And
he's promised to be better with our kids this time and
not to beat up on me anymore when he gets mad,"
Yvette gushed to Doris. "This time Ren is going to
stay . . . really stay," Yvette smilingly asserted to her
sister with love's blind certainty.

Doris looked away as her sister said those words. It was a script of plaintive hope she had heard before. The final scene inevitably ended the same way. Renwick Gibbs had stormed out of his firecracker marriage to Ann Farris Gibbs at least a dozen times before. He would take Yvette's comfort and love and then leave her without a backward glance when he managed to persuade his wife to give him just one more chance.

When Yvette gave birth to Ren's first child, he had promised marriage. It was the same when a second daughter was born. They would wed soon, Gibbs would pledge. Then he would buy them a real home. Yvette, the kids, and her sister would not have to endure the squalor of the rickety old school bus he had found for them so long ago as a "temporary" place to live.

Now he was back with the same kind of sweet hopes, but beneath his mood was a vein of darkest anthracite. Brooding, brawny, twenty-seven-year-old Renwick Gibbs had returned to borrow another full cup of Yvette's love in a state of mind more frightening than her concerned twin had ever before seen.

Doris could not help but overhear the anger and hatred that loudly spilled out of Renwick Gibbs while he again drew Yvette Gay into his explosive orbit. "I'm gonna clean house this time, by God. I'm gonna kill that bitch and I'm gonna blow away her smart-ass daddy and her meddlin' momma and that's gonna be the end of it, Yvette. Then it's just gonna be you and me and the babies. We can make it look like somebody busted in and robbed them. Hell, they got all kinds of goodies in that new house of theirs. Everybody gonna think they was showin' off a little too much for their own good," he added.

Doris watched the faces of Renwick Gibbs and Yvette as those reckless conversations took place.

Could her sister seriously be considering any of Ren's craziness? Yvette's placid features seemed to take on an eerie cast when Ren spoke about killing his wife.

Doris had been drawing her own conclusions about the murderous plot that Ren daily elaborated upon and enlarged. She could place real belief in the possibility that Gibbs might want to take some kind of sullen, sneaky revenge against his wife's parents. Over the five fractured years of marriage to their daughter, the Farris family had always given Ann a haven in their rock-solid, respectable home when the couple's latest spat boiled over. Their standing in the community and their righteous willingness to defend their daughter from the abusive husband had been a galling and demeaning roadblock to Gibbs. It had made it difficult, sometimes impossible, for him to hector his wife into forgiveness with his insincere promises to mend his marital ways.

William "Pop" Farris, Sr., was a tough, hard-working, church-going, responsible citizen, who brooked very little of Gibbs's nonsense. His cheerful and sturdy wife, Louise, was a well-loved, devoted mother who could turn a sharply honed tongue on a cowed Gibbs when events demanded. She also proved a wise advisor to Ann. She was a formidable wall between her daughter and the sly-mouthed Gibbs.

William Farris had worked hard to make his home for his family. He took enormous pride in the growing accomplishments and Christian goodness he saw bearing fruit in their two youngest children still at home. Sixteen-year-old Shamika was a blossoming beauty. Her father could not look at her without a quiet rush of wonder and satisfaction. It was no accident that thirteen-year-old Bill had earned the nickname Pop, Jr. He was growing up to be a fine young person. He would be a real man like his dad, friends would say.

As Renwick Gibbs had arrived yet once more on their ramshackle doorstep that shimmering spring of 1990, Doris made quiet conjectures of her own about his true intent. Maybe Ren would try to scare or even rough up his wife's parents, but she was certain that Renwick Gibbs would never commit a fatal violence on Ann. Doris knew that Ren was still passionately in love with his wife and wanted to have her back. He demanded it with an insane determination that at its roots could not pass for love. It was jealousy or anger that something he wanted had been taken from him. How could a man hold his head up in the face of that?

Yvette Gay did not want to confront that unhappy truth, her sister believed. Instead, Yvette remained a willing stand-in for Ann when conflict wrested Gibbs and his wife apart. The facts were plain enough to Doris. Yvette was being badly used and treated like a whore by a man who didn't really give a damn about her except when he wanted to cheat her out of sympathy and love for a selfish while.

The look that came over Yvette's face when Ren had drunk enough poorhouse wine to bluster about his intent to kill Ann was scaring Doris. Surely her sister wasn't being taken in by all this dangerous nonsense! She would certainly not help to take part in this wild scheme to kill Ren's wife and her parents.

When Doris was able to speak alone to Yvette, she found her sister's reaction to Ren's escalating persuasions disturbing. "If Ann wasn't around, things would be a lot different," Yvette said. "Ren is smart about these kinds of things. He knows how to take care of stuff like this."

"The only people he wants to get rid of is her daddy and momma," Doris interjected. "Then he wants Ann back. Just like always."

Doris had some hope that Yvette was taking her warnings seriously. But her twin was a seesaw of odd

personality contradictions. When they had been children, their mother's mind had progressively begun to
deteriorate. She was haunted by bad dreams and
irrationally provoked by paranoid suspicions of
everyone around her. Her Bible-believing husband,
Randy Gay, had faith that God would restore his
wife's tortured mind if only enough anguished prayers
were said, but morning- and night-murmured petitions did not bring about that divine intervention.
When their mother required treatment at an institution, it was Yvette who took on the duties of caring for
the rest of the wounded family. After they had grown,
Yvette remained the caregiver. Her twin would always
be welcome to live with her in whatever circumstance
she could offer. She shared without reservation or
complaint. As penniless as they frequently were,
Yvette always managed somehow to care for her two
little girls and her sister and always to have waiting,
like some biblical bride, the trimmed lamp and soft
cushions she was willing to provide for Ren Gibbs.

But her sister knew there was yet another side to
Yvette Gay. She seemed foolishly to ignore harsh
realities or to bury them somewhere inside because of
a cavernous yearning to be loved. Renwick Gibbs had
often beaten Yvette. When she shyly appeared at a
small county clinic for treatment of her injuries, it was
always with some made-up story of how she had been
hurt. There was never any mention that she had been
the victim of Renwick Gibbs's volcanic temper. And
when Ren returned to his wife and openly chased
other women, too, Yvette meekly submitted to
Gibbs's harsh command that she not see any other
man during his philandering absence. It was an order
she obeyed in patient loneliness until there were only
a few remaining friends with whom she had any
contact. One of them once told her, "Girl, Abe
Lincoln freed the slaves. You oughta tell Ren about

that." Yvette Gay turned away that remark. "You don't know what love is all about," she sharply rebutted.

Finally, those days and nights of Ren's tense presence at the squatter home reached a deadly crescendo. A first draft for death was presented by Ren. Ann and the rest of the Farris family would be killed at the parents' home. The murders would be made to appear as though robbery had been intended. The sketchy order of battle called for the victims' death to come early in the morning, while most of the neighborhood still slept. If the two teenagers had already left to catch their school bus, that small providence would spare their lives. If they were in the house, they, too, would die. There could be no witnesses.

The crucial linchpin to Renwick Gibbs's bloody strategy had been talked around for days now. Renwick's bold attack plan was ambitious. It would require help. He could not do it alone. There were too many people who might make a sudden move. What if someone unexpectedly arrived? The plan would not be foolproof unless another person was there to help Ren carry it out. "Will you do this with me?" Renwick Gibbs asked of Yvette Gay.

"Yes," she answered. "Then we can be together, can't we?"

"Yes," Gibbs replied. He reached across a littered table and took her hand in his. He saw the sudden cloud of worry come over her face.

"The babies . . . Someone is going to have to watch them if I go with you," she said with concern.

"Doris can be a little late for work. She can baby-sit the girls. She'll do it if you ask her," Gibbs said, waving away her disquiet.

Doris Gay would never have imagined she could have been ensnared in so awful a misadventure. She had always been the more practical one. Later, haltingly, convulsed with grief, she would testify against the sister she loved, making the admission that she had, indeed, succumbed to the delirium that had first enticed Yvette. She had yielded to a powerful emotional demand, clinging to a reasoned hope. How could she deny a plea made of her by the twin with whom she shared so much and loved so deeply? And she thought Renwick Gibbs might skulk and bellow, but he wasn't really tough enough to risk a murderer's punishment, was he? The answer was no. Renwick Gibbs valued his own tricky hide too much for that.

"All right," Doris Gay told Yvette and a smiling, confident Gibbs. Her eyes burned with the contempt she felt for Gibbs; she could no longer conceal it.

They woke early that May 1990 morning, somewhere around five A.M. Renwick Gibbs stepped outside and returned with two rifles. One was a heavy and powerful Winchester 30/30 caliber, the other, a small game piece. He reached into his pocket and pulled out a fistful of large, copper-jacketed cartridges and began loading the large gun. He explained to Yvette how that weapon and the smaller one worked. He demanded that she repeat and mimic his careful instructions. Gibbs left then, saying he needed to scout out the area just east of Washington along Highway 264, down behind Gurley's Flower Shop, where the Farris family lived in their secluded new home.

As Gibbs slowly cruised toward Glen Haven Road, he saw what he knew was a bathroom light blink on in the Farris house. He noted that his wife's car was not there. She was staying with other friends. He already knew that. It was part of the plan he had failed to reveal to Yvette. There would be one surviving member of the Farris family after the "robbery" had removed the rest from his path: Ann Farris Gibbs, the woman he loved, the woman he was certain would desperately run to him for solace before the bloody day was out.

Gibbs returned to the old school bus where Yvette anxiously awaited. Doris was up, too, but there was no cheerful chatter over coffee cups that morning. One of the girls was fussing. Yvette picked up the child and rocked her back to drowsy serenity. She heard the crunch of the tires of her aged Buick Regal on the scattered patch of loose gravel outside. It was Gibbs returning. Yvette placed her daughter back on the rumpled bed and stepped wordlessly out to join Ren Gibbs. He was impatiently racing the engine of the tired car. He smiled broadly as she slid onto the cool, morning-damp seat beside him. In the back seat, the barrels of two rifles leaned drunkenly against each other. Gibbs sensed her fear. He gave her a peck on the cheek.

"Don't worry, sugar girl," he said. "This isn't going to take long." He stomped the engine into reluctant, clattering motion, pointing it toward the house where the ordinary, sleepy morning rituals of his intended victims had begun for the last time.

A soft, hazy dawn had already started its journey above the zephyr-tossed pines and fragrant magnolia that shaded the Farris yard. Gibbs and Yvette slowly approached in the car. Gibbs suddenly cursed. He had glimpsed his father-in-law's car pull away from the house. Pop Farris had apparently been called early to work that morning. Gibbs gunned the old Buick.

"I ain't lettin' that old motherfucker get away from me," he shouted. Then, inexplicably, Gibbs thought better of the chase. He slowed, then turned, heading the auto once again toward the house. He parked the vehicle at a distance, out of sight. Soundlessly exiting the car, he reached into the back, handing the smaller rifle to Yvette, hefting the 30/30 hunter style, grasped at midpoint in the palm of his large right hand. When they reached the house, Gibbs motioned quiet to his accomplice. He pulled a pair of cutter pliers from his back pocket and expertly snipped the telephone wires that serviced the Farris home. Then he moved rapidly to the front door and signaled Yvette to cover him with her weapon.

"Are you ready, baby?" Gibbs whispered. Yvette nodded she was.

In a whirlwind assault, Gibbs threw open the screen door, snatched the knob of the interior kitchen door, and attempted to hurl it open. It was locked. Gibbs began a rain of kicking and cursing that alerted Louise Gibbs and her children. Mrs. Farris and the two children screamed in alarm. The door yielded. Gibbs burst through it with Yvette hard at his heels. He swung the Winchester level with his hip and pointed it at the terrified mother and the two teenagers.

"What are you doing here, Ren?" Louise Farris challenged as much in anger as fear.

"You're all done getting between me and Ann," he shouted. "You're all done doing that today."

Prodding the frantic family with the barrel of the gun, Gibbs forced the children to tie their mother's hands behind her back with knee-length socks he scooped up from a neatly folded stack of clean laundry. Then he forced another stocking into the frightened woman's mouth to end her stream of pleading for her children. He pushed her, face down to the floor, warning her not to move if she didn't want her children harmed. Gibbs grabbed other articles of clothing from the pile and handed them to Yvette. He ordered her to bind and gag a trembling Shamika and a defiant Pop, Jr.

Yvette balked. "Where's Ann?" she demanded.

"That bitch must have got away, but I'll get her later," Ren lied.

Hesitantly, Yvette tied up the youngsters. Gibbs pushed them roughly to the floor. Yvette dashed back and forth from the heart-wrenching scene. Part of her role was to watch through the front window of the home for any surprise visitors. Her stomach churned as she saw Renwick Gibbs gloating over his paralyzed captives. She saw his eyes roam over Shamika, who had not yet finished dressing for school. Then Gibbs barked a sudden, wildly shrill command, "Shoot, woman . . . Goddammit, shoot!"

Yvette recoiled in shock. She could not form the words that roared through her mind. Did he mean that? How could he ask that? She had never agreed to killing someone herself. He had never asked it. Was he afraid to do it? Finally, she stammered out her refusal.

For a long moment, Renwick Gibbs hesitated, stood stock still as if in some freeze-framed shard of eternity. Doris must have been right. Ren Gibbs could talk murder but couldn't pull a trigger. Her questioning eyes met his. They seemed lost in terror. Then in a pounding heart beat, Gibbs thrust the Winchester 30/30 to the back of Louise Farris's neck. The heavy cartridge that screamed from the barrel blew away much of her head. It sent fragments of her skull skittering across the floor, spattering her children with gore. Shamika had desperately tried to rise. Gibbs arced the gun to within inches of her pretty face. The projectile exploded that innocent visage into dozens of bloody bits, dashing them obscenely against the wall. A third blue blast dispatched the thirteen-year-old boy just as grotesquely. The hot, spinning bullet made Pop, Jr., unrecognizable as it tore through his head and wreaked its crimson mutilation.

The echoes of the gun's thunder seemed to reverberate in the house like some voice of judgment. The morning was cool, but Yvette Gay was drenched in sweat. Framed by sunlight pouring through a kitchen window, Renwick Gibbs seemed to Yvette a man who had just glimpsed hell. He was wild eyed, shaking, breathing in torn gasps. He seemed on the verge of panic, unable to take into himself the bloody work he had done. Without looking at Yvette, he began a dazed rush toward the door. Outside, he ran, with Yvette in hysterical tow. Several hundred yards from the house, he flung both of the weapons into a small stand of woods. He fled to the car, dropped the keys several times before he was able to start it. They sped back to the old school bus. Neither spoke.

Safely back at home, an uneasy sort of calm seemed to return to Gibbs, but none of the earlier bravado. Yvette watched him as though they had never met before. Gibbs abruptly announced he had another idea, one that would further divert suspicion from them. Near noon he left.

Deborah Blount was not surprised to see her brother, Ren, pull up to her home in Yvette's car. It most likely meant he and Ann were quarreling again. In the past she had helped Ren pursue peace with Ann. Now he would ask for her help again, accompanying her to the Farris home where he said his wife would be waiting for them.

When they arrived, Gibbs entered first, asking his sister to wait until he had announced their arrival. Moments later, a stunned Deborah Blount watched in shock as Ren reeled out through the door, shouting and weeping that the house was filled with dead people. He fell to the ground sobbing. He tore at his hair, screaming and vomiting. Deborah ventured, shaking, into the house. The horror that screamed up at her sent her fleeing to a nearby flower shop where she called the police. She returned to comfort her anguished brother.

"My God," he shrieked, "who could have done this?"

Washington Police Department Sergeant Mary Ann Buck was in the first squad car on the scene. Buck had just won her detective's badge. She had never imagined this bloody baptism. As she approached, Gibbs was still acting out his charade of frantic disbelief and trauma. Buck restrained the hysterical man who continued to beat his head against the ground in affected grief. As he spilled out a description of the terrifying sights inside the Farris home, Mary Ann Buck gently guided him to a seat in the back of her vehicle. As soon as more help arrived, she would see that he was taken to a hospital for treatment of the injuries he had done to himself.

Within minutes, however, other officers had located Pop Farris at his job and brought him home. When told that his family had been slain, a shocked William Farris had no doubt who was involved. Crime scene investigators had already noted that rooms in the Farris home had been ransacked, drawers pulled out, and their contents wildly strewn about. Did Mr. Farris keep large amounts of cash in his house? Were there other unusual valuable there?

"There was no robbery," Pop Farris said through a voice that shook both in horror and rage. "It was him," he shouted, pointing at Renwick Gibbs.

Sergeant Buck took Gibbs to the hospital as she had promised but not only as a patient. He had become a prime suspect in the senseless murders. He had torn the life just as surely from the heart of a fourth victim: a broken, never-to-be-mended Pop Farris.

Buck questioned Gibbs on the drive to the hospital and as he was being attended to by emergency room staff. Gibbs said he could not believe anyone would imagine he could harm the Farris family. But his answers weren't adding up. Why had he gone to the Farris home at a time of the day when it was unlikely anyone would be home? His wife's car was not there.

Why had he told his sister that Ann was waiting for them there? How did he know if she was or wasn't? Had he been there earlier in the day? Why would he have walked inside a house where he knew he was unwelcome? Mary Ann Buck stepped out to a pay phone in the hospital corridor. She called Lieutenant John Taylor and told him she believed the assassin of the Farris family was in the next room.

Taylor had Gibbs's records pulled. Detectives fanned out to interview anyone who knew him or knew of him. From Raleigh, polygraph expert Bill Thompson was asked to come down and bring his lie box with him. Gibbs, his minor cuts attended to, was brought to police headquarters.

When special agent Thompson and Renwick Gibbs met, one on either end of the truth-detecting apparatus, the suspect said he was confident the test would show his innocence. He asked how long it would take. "Ann, my wife, is going to need me." he said.

As the needle jumped sharply again and again at his responses, Thompson quietly asked, "How long do you want this to go on, Ren. You aren't telling me the truth and you know it."

Renwick Gibbs asked if he could have a cigarette. He lit it, didn't really want it, and snuffed it out slowly, head down, watching its fire die. "I did it," he said softly.

"Who else was involved?" Thompson quietly pressed on.

"No one," Gibbs responded. "There was just me. I did it alone."

Despite his confession that he had acted alone, the investigation by police continued. There remained puzzling, unanswered questions despite Gibbs's admissions. The police inevitably found themselves at the door of the old school bus.

Yvette and Doris were brought to police headquarters. Doris heard that Gibbs had confessed. She agreed to tell what she knew but insisted her sister had acted under coercion. Her own involvement in the crime, she said, had been only the sin of silence. Hours passed. It was Yvette's turn to be questioned. At first she was evasive, but police sensed something deeply troubling in the words of their second suspect.

"I don't want to feel like this anymore," Yvette finally told Detective Taylor and State Bureau of Investigation Agent Eric Tellefsen. "I want to get this off my chest."

"I held a gun and watched the doors, but I didn't kill anybody, sir. I never could kill anyone."

"Then who did all that shooting?" they asked.

"Ren did," she murmured. "Renwick Gibbs did all of that."

Within hours, the downcast woman was arraigned on three counts of first-degree felony murder. Doris agreed to testify. She was held on the lesser count of conspiracy.

Defense lawyers Maynard Harrell and Teresa Smallwood were appointed by the court to defend Yvette. District Attorney Mitchell Norton told an outraged community he would demand the death penalty for Gibbs and Yvette, even though the evidence showed she had not fired any of the fatal shots.

"Asking that she pay with her life is not some desire of this office, it is our duty," Assistant District Attorney Robert Johnson added.

Harrell was clearly moved by the plight of the young, unsophisticated, and marginally educated young black woman he represented. He and Smallwood came to know their client with unusual intimacy in the months preceding her trial. They came to resolutely believe that on the day that she was led timidly into North Carolina's gas chamber or drowsed into forever-sleep by lethal injection, yet one more helpless victim would be added to the lives Renwick Gibbs had already stolen or broken.

Harrell shared with a reporter for the *Washington Daily News* his compassion for his client. "I have a lot of feelings for her. I care about her. She's just a little girl that's going to be killed because of one night." The night she said yes to Ren's demand that she prove her love to him once again.

"I just want to get it off my chest." Those were the words with which Yvette Gay had begun the confession to cops that would seem to seal her fate before a jury. Yet her lawyers believed that penitent preamble spoke relevant volumes about the real Yvette Gay, a pliant child-woman who was at her core a person who cared for her family. She would not have broken so deeply rooted a commandment had there not been a hellish temptation put in front of her beyond her ordinary ability to resist.

Harrell and Smallwood turned to experts in the art of understanding why humans often do the unfathomable. Psychiatrist Bob Rollins of nearby Raleigh was asked to probe the avenues of Yvette Gay's mind, to study the files about their client's life. Who was Yvette Gay? What was she?

In a small cubicle at the Beaufort County jail where Gay was held without bail, Rollins patiently talked with the prisoner. Together they visited shadowed, walled-off corridors of her being he was certain she herself had never visited before.

Rollins then reported to the defense team the strong conclusions he had reached after his sifting of the life and crimes of Yvette Gay. "You have to understand that I am coming to this case a few months after these murders were committed. That makes it somewhat more difficult to pinpoint the exact state of mind of Yvette at the time they took place," Dr. Rollins began. "But this much is certain. Yvette Gay was essentially a slave to Renwick Gibbs. She had been totally brainwashed by this man. There was no way she could have refused any demand that Gibbs made of her.

"You could compare Yvette to a prisoner of war in Korea or Vietnam, the ones who finally did or said whatever their captors told them to do. Gibbs totally dominated her. She responded to his directions in an automatic way."

Dr. Rollins said the defendant had lost the ability to think independently. Her own will was not strong enough to resist Gibbs. Yvette's progression toward a mental state that Rollins characterized as a post-traumatic stress disorder had begun in childhood, according to his diagnosis.

Yvette's pressurized home life—growing up in the confusing aura of a mentally ill, frequently absent mother—had weighed heavy responsibilities upon her long before she was emotionally ready to understand and assume them. Then she had been dominated by the strong, religious personality of her father. It had made her a perfect, wet-clay candidate for her total subjection for another authoritarian male, a man like Renwick Gibbs.

Something else had been explored under Rollins's lengthy examination. Yvette now told the understanding psychiatrist about those trips to the hospital emergency room where she had always insisted that her injuries were the result of some clumsy accident. Her hurts had always come at the hands of an angry, sometimes lusting Renwick Gibbs. He had often abused her physically and sexually, making her perform acts she did not believe were proper, even between passionate lovers.

She also told Rollins a new version of what had happened on that awful morning inside the Farris home. Yes, she had broken into the house willingly, had helped tie the victims, dumped out drawers, and rifled closets to create the phony burglary illusion, but as she saw those intimate, everyday possessions being strewn violently across the floor, the enormity of the rape of the Farrises' home began to overwhelm her. Pictures of a smiling Ann and Ren at their wedding, Shamika laughingly hugging her mom, Pop, Jr., handing his dad a platter of buns for the burgers ready to come off the backyard grill. These images whirled crazily as Ren ripped them from walls and dashed their glass frames to bits on the floor.

The monstrous fear that had risen up and claimed victims and killers alike had a scent that had filled the house. Yvette still remembered it. She had been shaken like a willow limb when her boyfriend demanded that she fire the shots into the helplessly bound and gagged victims. She knew the Farris family. She had no personal dislike for them, save one. Seeing them desperately pleading for their lives with their eyes had struck her with a numb and nameless horror. When Gibbs saw her ashen reluctance, he struck her five times with the butt of the rifle he was wielding.

"Then he pointed the gun at me. He said, 'Don't you try nothin' funny, bitch.' He looked like he was wild enough to kill me, too."

Why hadn't she told police that Gibbs held her virtual captive at the actual moments of murder?

"I still loved Ren then. I thought he loved me, too," she tried to explain. That love had lasted through months of imprisonment. Six months after the murders, Yvette revealed her continued, unwavering devotion in a letter to the sister of Renwick Gibbs. "I still love Renwick. He's just a fine young man," she wrote to Deborah Blount. "When nobody loves him, I will, no matter what happens."

In still another letter, she offered a prayer for her lover: "May the Lord be with him and take care of him," she wrote.

The two defense attorneys hoped that the insightful evaluation that Dr. Rollins could offer to a jury would convince them that it would not be just to make Yvette Gay pay with her life for her role in the death of the Farris family, that she had made one desperate attempt to escape and would have died even if she had been able to break Gibbs's hypnotic spell. That testimony would be offered to show that Gay had a diminished capacity to refuse, that she was the victim of a serious mental/emotional disturbance and, hence, could not be found guilty of first-degree murder under North Carolina law.

Yvette Gay met the standard that mental health experts have described—but not in total agreement— as the battered spouse syndrome. That would be the defense Harrell and Smallwood would strenuously put forward in her behalf.

Prosecutor Mitchell Norton and investigators who had worked the case were not willing to accept Dr. Rollins's assessment of Yvette Gay.

When Dr. Rollins took the witness stand to testify for the defense, Assistant DA Robert Johnson attacked those conclusions and wondered if Dr. Rollins had ever pondered the topic of Yvette Gay's basic truthfulness.

The defendant had no trouble in telling police that Renwick Gibbs, not she, had committed the murders. Why would she not have said at the same time that she feared Gibbs might have killed her, too, had she protested in any way?

And if she was such an honest person, why had she written the letter Johnson now held in his hand. It was to her family and written while she was in jail. At the top of the first of the jailhouse-issued sheets, Yvette had written the words "Very important truth."

But what followed was not the truth at all by her own admission. In the letter she said she had not even been with Renwick Gibbs on the morning of the murders. She said she had confessed her involvement to police only so she would be placed in custody "to get away from Ren and protect my two daughters."

Why would Dr. Rollins now expect the court to accept as truth the other come-lately claims Yvette Gay was making? Did it not appear, even to someone without Dr. Rollins's years of learning and experience, that Yvette Gay was much more cunning than she wanted people to believe, that the prospect of her own death had made her more than willing to tell any self-serving lie she might persuade or flimflam others into believing?

Yvette Gay sat through her trial without visible emotion. Each day she carried a small Bible into the courtroom with her. The jury's face was unreadable.

District Attorney Norton said the state had no need of experts to help explain why Yvette Gay had freely planned and just as willingly taken a deadly part in the murder of the Farris family. "The fact is that she wanted Ann Farris out of the way and she thought Renwick Gibbs was willing to do that. What Yvette Gay wanted was Renwick Gibbs all to herself," Norton said. It was a motive as old as the North Carolina hills.

Yvette Gay took the witness chair in her own behalf to deny that allegation, but cross-examination was piercing. Here were the letters she had written from jail, confessing her unshaken love for a man who might lead her to execution. What were her judges to make of them?

"I don't love him no more," Yvette Gay said, her

words barely audible. "He made sure I never saw my family again. He made sure I never see another man or talk to another man."

But she had told everyone she desperately wanted to marry Ren. "Isn't it true that Ann and her family had to be out of the picture?" Norton demanded sharply.

"Yes, I wanted to marry him, but I never wanted the people out of the way," she tearfully answered.

Under the harsh glare of accusation, Yvette Gay lost all composure. She fell limply from the witness chair to the courtroom floor, her collapse placing her directly in front of startled jurors now looking down at the sobbing black woman. The small Bible had careened in front of her. "Why did he have to do this to me?" she cried out loudly.

With quiet gentleness, her attorney retrieved the Bible and placed it back into her trembling hands. He shepherded her back to the defense table and asked the court to recess. When the gavel fell again, it would be up to the jury to decide which of the two Yvette Gays who had been presented to them should be believed.

As that jury retired for its deliberations, they took with them vivid images of violent murder and its cruel wake. While Superior Court Judge Gregory Weeks had kept a firmly impartial reign on some of the grim evidence the prosecution wanted the jury to see, he allowed the viewing of carefully selected photographs of the bloody crime scene. They had a visible impact. The savagery of the deaths of a gentle mother and two innocent teenagers, captured by police and autopsy cameras, was a shriek in the night. Then there had been the heartbreaking testimony of Pop Farris, describing in a weary, now old, and quavering voice how devastating had been the brutal madness that had visited his once happy home. When asked to view and identify a picture of his young son, he broke down completely. He had not been able to return to the job in which he had taken such competent pride. He was not certain that he ever would.

The jury had been out for only about ninety minutes when it notified the bailiff it had reached its verdict. As they quietly trailed back to the jury box, Yvette Gay paid scant notice. She sat, head down, reading again from the small Bible on her lap. Someone had thoughtfully lent a simple pink dress for her to wear that day. It did not fit well. She seemed imprisoned and uncomfortable in it. She did not betray any emotion when the verdict of guilty on all three counts of murder was read.

That same jury returned a few days later to take up the most arduous part of their civic duty. They would deliberate on what recommendation they would make to the judge regarding whether the sentence imposed on Yvette Gay should be life in prison or the somber death of her choice—the gas chamber or lethal injection.

The jury returned in ten hours. They agreed with the prosecution that Yvette Gay had aided and abetted in the murders. She had acted in concert and with a common purpose with Renwick Gibbs. That purpose was the "heinous, atrocious, and cruel killings of the three victims."

"She was as responsible as Gibbs," DA Norman Mitchell had argued before the jury was sent to consider her fate. "It was as if she had pulled the trigger herself. She was with him every step of the way." So said the jury.

Judge Weeks pronounced the sentence. Death, three times, death for the murder of each of the victims.

"You can only kill a person once," defense attorney Teresa Smallwood grimly reflected as she heard the harsh sentence fall.

Yvette Gay asked to address some final words to the court. "I'm real sorry this happened to the Farris family," she said. "To this day, I still love those people. I forgive the jury and I forgive all of those who are against me," she added. She did not say if she had forgiven Renwick Gibbs.

Her lead attorney, Maynard Harrell, a twenty-year veteran of the courtroom's life and death struggles, was crestfallen at the verdict. Yet he managed to retain some of the stoicism every criminal defense lawyer needs to wear as daily armor. "I don't always agree, but I always respect a jury's verdict," he told reporters. He mused another thought to them: If Yvette Gay deserved three death sentences for her part in the crimes, what possible punishment was left for the community to impose on Gibbs?

As deputies prepared to transport a shackled Yvette to a death-row cell at a state prison in Raleigh, she seemed to those who watched the personification of the meek, abused, forlorn woman some deeply believed she was. As she was led off in her ill-fitting pink frock, head bowed, her father, Randy Gay, felt the hurt of that scene and shouted after her, "Hold your head higher, and be happy." For a moment, it seemed that she tried.

Yvette's father angrily denounced the sentence. He told reporters the trial had been unfair; the verdict, racist. He said evidence about the cruel treatment Yvette had received at the hands of Renwick Gibbs had been kept from the jury. He accused the prosecution of having deliberately suppressed them. "They don't know one-tenth of the things Renwick Gibbs had done," he protested.

In the same courtroom, not long after, attorney Harrell had his question answered. Gibbs was quickly and decisively found guilty. Three sentences of death were also imposed upon him. Harrell had already begun preparing the appeal motions to be filed on Yvette's behalf. It would be a long journey, he knew.

Because of her willingness to cooperate and in exchange for her testimony against her sister and Gibbs, Doris Gay received only a prison term but something else she may have rued as much. She blanched when defense attorneys implied she had carried on a secret relationship of her own with Gibbs. Had the wily conspirator made love slaves of both of the twins? Did the one know about the other? The question remained unanswered.

6

Faye Copeland

EDITH CHILEN FRETTED. SOMETHING WAS AMISS. MAY 27 had come and gone and the telephone in her small home in Dardanelle, Arkansas, had not rung. She'd been certain he'd call. But there had been no cheery "Hi, Mom, happy birthday," no bubbling-over good wishes from her twenty-year-old son, Paul Cowart, up in Chillacothe. That wasn't like the boy. He didn't seem to stay in any one place that much, but he wasn't ever one to forget his mother's birthday.

In Normal, Illinois, silver-haired Grace Beck clucked the same sort of worry to herself. How many weeks had it been now since the concerned seventy-five-year-old grandmother had heard from her wanderlust grandson, Dennis Murphy? He said he'd call her with an address when he arrived in Missouri to take his new job as a cattle buyer. He hadn't yet.

John Freeman had left Tulsa, Oklahoma, in early December 1988. He planned to hitchhike his way from there to Booneville, Indiana, to surprise his ten-year-old son with a Christmas visit at the home of his ex-wife. It had been months since his brother,

Don, had dropped him off on the shoulder of Interstate Highway 44 to thumb his way. It seemed as though I-44 had just swallowed him up somewhere along its gritty-gray breadth as it quickly crossed the Sooner State and wound its way up through Missouri. Finally, Don Freeman, not certain what else to do, filed a missing persons report with police.

In Bloomington, Illinois, Laurie Ann Prather wistfully reread the only two letters she'd received from her boyfriend Wayne Warner. He had gone away on the promise of a job in northwestern Missouri and said "so long" with a pledge to send for her once he'd settled. She'd stayed in touch with the staff of the Home Sweet Home Mission where they had lived when times were tough. No one there had heard a word from Wayne either.

The mother of Jimmy Dale Harvey was becoming frantic at the lengthy, unexplained absence of her son. He suffered from epilepsy. Jobs weren't easy for him to find. He needed to take medicine. There had been some word of his whereabouts from a friend, Stan Sanders. He said that before Jimmy had left Springfield he'd told him his luck had changed; he'd just been hired for $20,000 a year to buy cattle for this rich farmer up near Chillacothe, Missouri. He'd be calling before long now, Sanders opined. The cattle buying business was a tricky trade to learn.

The tiny market-road village of Mooresville, Missouri, was no more than a quick pickup truck ride from Chillacothe. It was a frayed-edged photo of what rural life was sadly becoming: a gaggle of sagging, thinly whitewashed old barns and weathered, turn-of-the-century, dour-faced houses hunkered down on mostly small hand-to-mouth acreages. Ragged rows of nubby field corn were scoured behind their ears by a sharp, dusty, dry central plains wind. Sad-faced cattle kept a sharecropper's vigil over the rows, barely barred from hungry felony by rusting, sway-backed fences.

Only about 130 souls called Mooresville home. Among them were Faye and Ray Copeland, an elderly and taciturn couple who'd bought a tired forty-acre place in the early 1980s, settled down on their grange without many, except their nearest neighbors, taking much notice. They kept to themselves. Their curt acceptance of welcomes implied rebuff, making it clear they weren't the Methodist-church-pancake-breakfast or barn-dance kind.

Some things were apparent to their neighbors. Even though a slightly stooped, seventy-five-year-old Ray had reached and passed the age at which most area farmers had turned the plow over to their sons or sold out and moved into a small house in town, he was a man who woke up the rooster and was still busying himself at some chore or other long after the cows had languidly come home. He listened to local gossip on his quick errands and used it to guide him to odd jobs on several more prospering Livingston County farms. No one who hired him ever got to know Ray Copeland well, but his energy and skills told most everything they really needed to know. The gray, hatchet-nosed old man could put hired hands half his age to shame when it came to the backbreaking tasks needing to be done every day. Haying, fence mending, barn shingling, and equipment fixing were all in Ray Copeland's agile tinkerer's bag. He was a mutely shrewd old rascal, too, concluded those who thought they had come to know him somewhat. With the money his handyman industry brought in, Ray Copeland and his wife bought and sold small trailerloads of cattle at the bustling auction barns that were the heartbeat of the county's economy. Faye and Ray Copeland had become familiar figures on the bidding floors of sawdust-covered sale rings. They would whisper among themselves as a small lot of angular feeder calves were poked out in front of prospective buyers, but it was always Ray's brusque nod that signaled a bid to the chanting, hawk-eyed auctioneer. Faye kept a dutiful, old-fashioned farmwife's silence.

Plump, graying, sixty-nine-year-old Faye Copeland would never have the harsh rural indictment of slugabed passed on her either. She was always up before her husband, chapped, callused hands aiding her struggle into mud- and manure-spattered jeans and crusted rubber feedlot boots. She would brew an acid, eye-opening pot of coffee while the fields outside were still draped in night, carefully poach one prudent egg each—laid by her own hens—for their spare breakfast, then set out briskly to shovel heavy scoops of corn to bawling knots of cows impatiently awaiting her arrival.

Not far down the road, at the Holiday Motel, Neela Patel, the owner, could set her watch by the prompt arrival of Faye Copeland, reporting for another day of work at her part-time job as housekeeper. The money she earned helped finance their cattle-buying ventures.

There hardly seemed enough hours in the day for Faye to finish all the tasks Ray expected her to perform. And it was not as though her gruff mate showed any appreciation for the long, almost joyless train of years she had been his forbearing wife, the mother of his sturdy sons and proper daughters. Ray seemed to think that was no more than what Faye should have expected as her lot when she'd married him so many years before.

Their children were gone now, making homes of

their own. None had stayed on the farm past their teens. They fled to freedom from the harsh, gloomy reign of Ray Copeland and their mother's meek unwillingness to take their side when their father handed down even the most unfair edict about how their lives were to be run. The children had memorized their mother's standard response when they appealed to her for fairness: "You father is right. Do what he says."

Betty Gibson, one of their daughters, had determined she would not fall hostage to a marriage like that between her mother and father. "I never heard my father ever tell my mother that he loved her. Not ever!" she sadly remembered.

Christmas might have been a happy time in most of the snow-roofed farmhouses that hug northwestern Missouri's winter landscape, but it was a bleak affair for the Copeland kids. There were small presents under the tree from their mother and one each that bore a tag saying it was from their dad. But the kids knew their mother had bought and wrapped all of the gifts. Not once had the children seen a present waiting for their mother from their father.

When the topic of their parents came up as the children gathered at each other's homes for pleasant barbecues and beer, their conversations often turned to their mom's grinding leaden years on the small farm in Mooresville. "It'll always be the way it's always been," Betty Gibson would sigh. "Mom idolizes him. She goes to him for the littlest thing like she was going to ask the Lord."

It was already a hot summer morning as Faye knelt down carefully to pick an apron full of pole beans from her thriving garden out behind the clapboard house. She'd make a mess of them for lunch, with bits of country ham tossed in and a pungent palmful of wild dill on top, just the way Ray liked. Soon, it would be time to pick them by the bushel, put them up in dozens of mason jars, and store them in the root cellar. She'd serve them, sparingly, over the winter to the ever-hungry drifters that Ray found up at the Victory Mission in Chillacothe and inveigled to come to work for him as truck drivers and cattle buyers. He would offer the lure that they'd quickly be making more money than they'd ever seen before, the kind of money that would soon let them find a small place for themselves to set up on and start living a real life, not the vagabond existence that had borne them, broke and forlorn, to the doors of a soup kitchen and flop house.

Faye looked up from her garden work as she heard the sound of Ray's black pickup truck pulling in the lane. She saw that someone was sitting on the seat beside him, chatting away into her husband's reluctant ear. She quit her task and walked toward the truck. The passenger exited lithely, walking in front of the vehicle to stand before Faye, at his new employer's side.

"This here is Paul," Ray Copeland said by way of tepid introduction.

"Paul Cowart, ma'am. Pleased to meet you. You've got a nice farm here." The dark-haired boy smiled.

"Yes . . . well . . . I'll let you menfolks get on to your work," Faye Copeland said. She had instantly liked the husky, sunny-faced boy, but it wouldn't do to start thinking on him too much or mothering him some. He would not be with them that long, she knew. It made it awfully hard when it came time for them to leave. It would keep her from sleeping on the night when Ray would fire two bullets into their heads with an old Marlin .22 rifle as they lay tiredly slumbering in the back bedroom. He would angrily scold her if she dropped the end of their bodies she was carrying out to the pickup for midnight transport to the lonely, shallow grave Ray had selected for them.

Later, sometimes, she would go to the jumble-stacked closet in the basement and stare at some of the mournful objects that had accumulated there over the past few years. The tattered tan suitcase had belonged to Wayne Warner if she recollected right. The new-looking pair of Levis had been John Freeman's, she thought. Had the faded plaid lumberjack shirt been left behind by Dennis Murphy or had that been an old garment Ray had cast off? Did it really matter? *Why are we keeping them?* Faye Copeland would wonder to herself.

Ray and Faye Copeland were not easy people to work for. They sharply upbraided idleness and ran as grudging and somber a place to live for their employees as they had for their children.

"I don't wanta see you smoking no tobacco, drinkin' no happy water, or foolin' with no women around here," Ray would sternly warn the roamers whose pockets he'd promised to soon line with profits. "You ain't allowed to use the telephone, and if you want to mail a letter, give it to the missus. She'll see to it for you."

Being a cattle buyer for Ray and Faye Copeland was a tricky business indeed. Unknown to the hapless men persuaded to join in the enterprise, it was a criminal business as well. The truth was, the Copelands were 1980s cattle rustlers, driving off herds of beef paid for with worthless checks. Not as glamorous as spooking away longhorns off a tumbleweed range beneath a lightning-torn sky, but rustling just the same.

Pawns in their schemes, like Paul Cowart, who knew almost nothing about the business, were driven to trusting small banks that dealt with usually honest patrons and didn't ask a lot of big-city questions when someone who seemed all right opened a new checking account with a respectable enough initial deposit. Next thing they knew, they were standing next to Ray and Faye on the mysterious, exciting, highly charged bidding floor of an early morning cattle auction, where they felt a sharp thrill of pride to be raising their buyer number. They liked rubbing elbows with Stetson-crowned, freshly barbered, bay-windowed, big-time beef barons who drove to the sales in gleaming new Lincolns and whose pert-bosomed, pool-tanned daughters smiled out from the front page of local weekly newspapers when they were named high-school homecoming queens.

The checks they wrote to the sale barns for their first few small purchases were good. Then it was time for their curtain call. With Ray and Faye in the shadows, their excited employee would be directed to make a bigger buy of animals. The cattle would be hurriedly trucked off down the mazes of gravel byways Copeland knew well, delivered to unsuspecting waiting buyers. The check that would be written then, bearing the name of the unwitting dupe the Copelands had puppeteered, would bounce higher than a silo when it had wended its way back to the bank. Should they ever be asked about the person who might have appeared to be their protégé, the Copelands planned to disavow any connection between them. The bad-check artist would just be someone they had met and thought to be a respectable farmer and legitimate buyer like themselves. And, of course, who would ever say otherwise? The homeless wanderers they had used as cat's paws would never talk. They had been buried. Ray and Faye chose remote, unlikely-to-be-discovered cemetery sites on some of the farms where the old man had done such diligent hired-hand work.

Paul Cowart had completed his final, fatal transaction for the Copelands. So had Dennis Murphy, John

Freeman, Wayne Warner, and Jimmy Harvey. From the scuffed carrying case for an old Polaroid camera, Faye Copeland extracted a small folded piece of paper on which she had written a list of names. She had placed an X by some of them. She added another next to the name of Paul Cowart. Then she carried down to the basement some of the clothes the boy had left behind when he went away.

While Ray and Faye Copeland were fairly confident their "business" wasn't being minded by any of their neighbors, they might have thought better of that, knowing their whole lifetimes that country folks can be every bit as curious about other peoples' doings as Robin Leach is about the rich and famous. The comings and goings of such a parade of hired men to the Copeland place over a few short years had begun to raise more than one village eyebrow. So intrigued was neighbor Bonnie Thompson that she began to secretly spy on the Copelands with a pair of binoculars she focused on their farm at different times.

She saw the men Ray Copeland brought to the farm unload a suitcase or backpack when they arrived and over a few weeks got to recognize their faces. Then, unaccountably, they no longer appeared in her high-powered scans. She had not seen them leaving, loading up whatever rude carryalls they had arrived with. Mrs. Thompson puzzled about that. On another day, she swung her binoculars quickly to the neighboring farm after she heard several sharp cracks of a weapon being fired. She saw Faye Copeland, slowly lowering a handgun that had apparently been the cause of the reports she had heard. A few days later, she bumped into Faye at the grocery store.

"I thought I heard some gunshots over at your place the other day," she queried Mrs. Copeland.

"Oh . . . I just took a shot at some starlings that were getting after my garden," Faye answered, hurriedly pushing her cart down the aisle, ending the conversation. Through her binoculars it had looked to Bonnie Thompson as though Faye was target shooting at an old tin can.

At the Livingston County sheriff's office, the Copelands had also lately come to some minor notice. Checks to a sale barn on their own accounts appeared to have been written in confusion and bore the name of one of the many bunko artists who had of late given bad paper in payment for cattle. Investigators wondered what the link might be between the Copelands and a growing number of similar rubber checks that had victimized other area auction houses. Sheriff Leland O'Dell ordered deputies to have a closer look at the Copelands' operations.

It had come time again for Ray Copeland to take one of his recruiting drives up to the mission in Chillacothe. It looked like an upward trend in beef prices was in the offing. It might be a good time for some brisk buying and selling.

The drifter that Ray Copeland chose to be their next pigeon was a different kind of bird. Jack McCormick was pushing sixty but was tough as mule harness. He'd bummed around the country for years, in and out of scrapes with the law that had included credit card fraud, embezzlement, and countless beefs that arose from his self-confessed slavery to vodka. He could tick off the merits and the menus of dozens of county jails and homeless shelters from one coast of the country to the other. He had stopped trying to be respectable about his drinking after his wife had died of cancer some years back. He'd blustered his way into all kinds of jobs on his foggy pilgrimage. Up in Idaho, he'd even been a cowboy. When Ray Copeland parked in front of the Victory Mission where McCormick had alighted a month earlier, a newly sober Jack McCormick seemed to remember meeting the beefy, bib-overalled farmer somewhere before. When Copeland approached the muscular-looking McCormick with a job offer, the former Idaho cowhand's memory clicked.

"Didn't you hire a friend of mine to work for you a few weeks ago . . . a black fella named R. C.? He still with you?" Jack McCormick wanted to know.

"Didn't work out. You know how they are," Copeland replied. "He moved on. You look like a man who could do some work for me, though, if you're of a mind to."

"What kind of work we talking about?" McCormick asked.

"Cattle buying, mostly," Copeland responded, then leaned in closer. "I'm losing my hearing some. I can't stay up with the auctioneer anymore. I need a man who can go with me to the sales and do some buying. Might even be able to do some buying on your own and make some good dollars."

McCormick accepted. Chaplain Don Pease logged out Jack McCormick with reluctance. He'd come to like the bluff, noisy wanderer and thought a few more weeks in the mission's Christian Life Program would do him a world of good. It was July 25, 1989, when Jack packed his bag. He stepped energetically up into Copeland's black pickup and waved a smiling farewell to Pease as the vehicle turned out onto the road that went down to Mooresville.

There was something about McCormick that made Faye jittery. He wasn't like the others Ray had brought home. Not cowed or beaten down by life, McCormick seemed to telegraph a strong sense of self-confidence about himself. He was older and had been a lot of places. He seemed to be only half listening as the pair laid out the rules of the house in their practiced stern fashion. He seemed to be slyly laughing at them, especially when they came to the parts about not drinking or seeing local women. They didn't need to explain to McCormick how cattle sales worked or what a cattle buyer did. He stopped them in midsentence, telling them this wasn't his first rodeo, jibing them a little about the smallness of their spread. There were bigger hen houses up in Idaho, he chuckled.

He did listen intently when the Copelands invited him to sit down at the kitchen table shortly after his arrival to tell him they were willing to open an account for him at a bank in Brookfield. He'd be able to start cattle buying. When the personalized checks arrived in the mail not long after, Ray and Faye sat down with their new hireling once more. They needed him to sign one blank check and leave it in the care of Faye. It would never be cashed of course, unless Jack got hurt some way and couldn't write his name.

These two old farts are in the right business, McCormick smilingly thought to himself. *There's more bullshit flying around here than in a Chicago stockyard.*

Jack McCormick hadn't taken too long to piece together a fairly accurate picture of what the elderly couple's game was. The Copelands were eyeing him warily. They speeded up the timetable. They made only one quick buy in Sedalia with a good check issued in McCormick's name. Then they told him they'd like him to make a carload buy in Green City. The Idaho cowboy insisted on going to the auction alone. Estimating that there weren't many dollars left in his account, McCormick bought only three head of cattle instead of the forty or fifty the Copelands were expecting. They were furious when he returned. He told them to go to hell, he was leaving and was closing the account in Brookfield. Faye and Ray stormed from the house. She was almost late for her job at the motel. After a hurried conversation with Ray, she left.

Ray rushed back into the house shouting for Jack. "Come help me," he said. "There's a damn raccoon got into the barn. Get a stick to poke him with, I'll shoot him."

Brazenly, McCormick sauntered down to the barn with Copeland, keeping the old man ahead of him. There was no coon in the barn, as Jack McCormick knew. What he did see in the back of Copeland's truck was a large folded square of heavy clear plastic sheeting. Next to it, a round-headed shovel. Turning back to Copeland after that grim distraction, McCormick saw that Ray was pointing the rifle, a .22 Marlin, at him.

"You'd better put that up, old man, before someone gets hurt. There are people who know I'm here. You're going to drive me into town now. Did you give old R. C. one of them plastic suits?"

Shakily, Ray Copeland put the gun down. After McCormick was dropped off in town, the nervy nomad did some shaking of his own. Some vodka helped calm his nerves. He went to a small used car lot and asked to test-drive a likely-looking junker. He took it and drove straight through the night to Nebraska. When he got there, he was sober. He dropped a quarter in a pay phone, dialed information, and asked if he could have a number for the crimestopper line. Jack McCormick rubbed the back of his hand against his stubbled jaw. Unless he was mistaken, there was a nice reward for people who offered tips that led to the arrest of criminals. He had the names of two people in mind that fit that bill nicely.

Sheriff Leland O'Dell's men had been probing into the Copelands' business affairs for a considerable time. They had begun listening carefully to the small-town gossip that the tight-lipped couple's odd way of doing things had generated. Seemed awful funny, one neighbor told deputies. He knew the Copelands were bringing in men to work for them, so he sent his own jobless son over to hire on. The Copelands rudely turned the boy down. Some curious missing person flyers had started to trickle their way across investigators' desks from nearby states. Quite a few of them said the missing men had mentioned something about heading to Missouri to work for a flush cattle-buying operation. When Nebraska authorities alerted O'Dell's office to the strange call they had gotten from a drifter by the name of McCormick, a lot of pieces suddenly fell into place. An arrest warrant was prepared against the Copelands in connection with the bad check. A search warrant was obtained to allow a careful going over of the farm.

Faye Copeland answered the sheriff's knock. She was placed under arrest. Had she ever known any of these men, O'Dell asked, reading off a list that contained several of her former employees.

"Never did hear of any of them," she replied. "The mister will be home soon. You might ask him."

O'Dell realized his department now faced an investigation beyond the resources of a small county in rural Missouri. He appealed to the state highway patrol for the kinds of experts he was certain he would soon need. A nine-county network of area sheriff departments sent specially trained deputies to help O'Dell under a plan designed to meet just such criminal emergencies. The state attorney general's office flew down several of its best and brightest to stage-manage a thin-iced legal pond that might have to be crossed. Heavy earth-moving equipment rumbled down gravel roads that led to the Copeland farm. Sheriff department squad cars followed. Shovel handles protruded out of opened rear windows. Excavations began, moving each day to different spots. O'Dell declined to tell reporters what it was the men under his command were expecting to find. He didn't need to. Rumors flew. Police crews were digging up other places not far from Mooresville, too. "My God! What have these old people done?" Bonnie Thompson wondered. Her peering binoculars offered no clue.

The first three bodies were discovered on a farm near Ludlow owned by Neil Bryan. Copeland had done many odd jobs for him. An old house on the farm was being rented by John Hovey. A huge barn, used for storage, sat idle on the property. It was there the badly decomposed corpses were found, covered only by a light shroud of earth. Hovey said he'd noticed a bad odor coming from the ramshackle structure and mentioned it once to Copeland who told him some small animal had probably crawled in there to die. He'd take a look.

Forensic specialists in Columbia sent for medical records of men who had been reported missing as they pored over the slim remains of the three bodies taken from the barn. Dental X rays finally confirmed the names of the victims: Paul Cowart, John Freeman, and Jimmy Harvey.

Held in lieu of $500,000 bond at Livingston County jail on murder charges, the Copelands were apparently following the search for more victims each day as it was being reported in the *Constitution-Tribune* newspaper. After a story about one fruitless scouring, Faye wrote a letter to Ray and penned an observation about that failed effort. "Nothing found, nothing gained," it said. She added the paper had reported the search warrant was good only for ten days. Maybe things would cool down after that, she went on.

Within days a fourth body had been discovered, also buried in a shallow grave on another nearby farm.

Hundreds of huge hay bales had been stacked on top of it. The partially mummified remains of Wayne Warner were taken to Columbia by hearse. Now Laurie Ann Prather knew why the man she loved had not sent for her.

Joe Adams remembered an old abandoned well on a farm he owned. Ray Copeland had once hauled a load of trash out there for him and said he dumped it down the crumbling shaft. Deputy Ray Reith cautiously crawled through earth that had been tunneled away to permit a check of the well. He gasped when he came face-to-face with the mold-speckled body of Dennis Murphy, slumped in about four feet of rubble-strewn muck. A chain was wrapped around his waist anchoring him to a cement block. As Reith tried to dislodge the man's corpse from the cold prison, its head ghoulishly rolled off into his hands.

The ghastly finds in the sleepy farm community drew hordes of print and broadcast news reporters eager to cover the upcoming trials of the accused pair. The intense media attention created a hostile climate in which the Copelands would never get a fair trial, their attorneys, public defenders David Miller and Barbara Scheckenberg, argued before the court in pretrial motions. Photos of the crestfallen elderly couple, handcuffed and wearing bright orange jail jumpsuits, hurled every day onto doorsteps and beamed into homes had already left any prospective jury with a damaging certainty of guilt, they argued. The state attorney general's office was blasted for attempting to convict Faye and Ray before a jury could hear any evidence.

The jury would not be made up of citizens of Livingston County, the court ruled. A panel would instead be drawn from nearby Vernon County. They would be brought by bus to a Chillacothe courtroom each day to hear the trial. A wing in the Grand River

Inn was booked. All television sets, VCRs, and radios were to be removed while the jury was sequestered there. Books could remain, including the ubiquitous Gideon Bible.

Psychiatric testing and counseling were ordered for the defendants. Faye's attorney said the old woman was depressed. The couple would no longer be required to wear the damning scarlet letter implied by the glowing jail jumpsuits. They would still, however, be handcuffed while being transported to and from the courtroom because of the serious nature of the charges. Once in the court, the accusing manacles were to be removed.

An inch-by-inch search of the Copelands' cluttered house had produced hundreds of items police exhaustively examined to determine what blank in the puzzle they might fit. Almost by accident, the list Faye had kept hidden in the Polaroid camera case came to light. It contained almost twenty names. Stunned authorities nervously mulled the meaning of that list and the crude letter X that had been placed by some of the names. They began attempting to locate the whereabouts of each of the men. Their investigation was stumbled onto by the press. Headlines screamed that the digging machinery would soon be at work again, perhaps even in other nearby states. How many homeless drifters had the Copelands buried in lonely, half-dug graves?

The police task force knew for certain now that at least two other men had rented post office boxes, opened bank accounts, and unknowingly bought cattle with bad checks. They almost certainly had been ensnared by the Copelands. A nationwide alert to locate them had turned up nothing.

Sheriff O'Dell was unwilling to claim those men were also likely victims of the Copelands' schemes.

"We can't say these guys are buried out there someplace. All we can say is that we have not been able to locate them," the veteran county lawman said.

Cops had turned up yet more logs for the fire of growing suspicion that many more wandering men lay hidden beneath the clotted farm earth. The clothes, toiletry items, and other personal effects jammed into the basement closet were shown to people who had some acquaintance with the Copelands and their agents. Lothar Borner had been hired by Ray from a homeless mission in Joplin. He had been riding one day in the black pickup with the old man when they stopped to give a ride to a hitchhiker. Borner knew the man as another one-time resident of the rescue shelter although he could not remember his name. Borner went his own way, luckily, when they reached Joplin, but the hitchhiker stayed in the vehicle with Copeland. Among the items taken from the basement, Borner recognized the clothing the unknown drifter had been wearing.

Lawyers for Ray had won the court's permission for exhaustive examinations of their seventy-five-year-old defendant to determine his competency to stand trial. Faye had been examined and found fit to assist in her defense. She was to be put on trial before her husband would face a judge and jury. The defense pleaded for a combined trial, arguing a sound rural reason that masked a deeper concern. "Separate trials for these two defendants is just throwing taxpayers' money down the toilet," defense lawyer Barbara Scheckenberg argued. Beyond that, she quietly feared a trial for Faye. The old woman, who at worst was an obedient accomplice, would be put squarely in the path of the white-heated anger and a desire to punish someone quickly.

Judge E. Richard Webber's courtroom was packed

when the state of Missouri placed Faye Copeland on trial for her life in the first-degree murders of five unfortunate itinerants.

David Miller and Barbara Scheckenberg flanked their bent, softly weeping client, then guided her toward the defense table. Miller rose to tell the jury that their good conscience could not permit them to find Faye Copeland guilty as the state had charged. "The first and most important thing I hope you will keep in mind is the first words the judge said," Miller pled. "This is the case of the state of Missouri versus Faye Copeland and not Ray Copeland."

Miller added that he would conduct them on a dark journey into the sad, empty, half-a-life that had been Faye Copeland's. Her hard, thankless, numb existence had cruelly pressed her down under the dictatorial thumb of her cold, money-obsessed husband. It had snuffed out the smallest flicker of independent reason or the most ordinary exercise of her own broken will.

"This is a picture of a lady who was trapped, in the worst sense of the word, in an old-fashioned marriage. She was literally incapable of questioning the action of her husband. Her whole life experience told her that Ray's business was Ray's business. Our evidence will show a woman dominated and isolated, as much a victim as anyone else. She took no active part in the crime. She didn't even know what was going on," Miller argued.

The jury heard a Kansas City psychologist bear out the image of Faye Copeland the defense hoped it would come to understand and accept. "Faye Copeland is the victim of what has been termed the battered spouse syndrome," Dr. Marilyn Hutchinson testified.

Dr. Hutchinson said she had met with Faye Copeland nearly thirty times as the elderly woman awaited trial. Faye suffered from the aftermath of a long, abusive relationship with her husband, she concluded. The emotional scars inflicted on Faye were a catalog of what professionals expected to find in such a dominant–submissive marriage pairing. Faye was chronically depressed, confused about sexuality, was cut off from normal, healthy relationships, exhibited a bottomed-out level of self-esteem, suffered guilt pangs about her faulty motherhood. She had become the tragic victim of learned helplessness.

Faye's children took the stand to help shed some redemptive light on the senselessly cruel and avaricious offenses of which their mother stood accused of being a knowing and willing co-conspirator. Their years with their mother had convinced them that if she had taken part in the heartless slayings, she was guided, without the power to resist, by the iron hand of their father.

Al Copeland, their son, said his father constantly browbeat their mother into doing things his way, with robotish compliance. "I think he treated her a lot worse than trash," an emotional Al Copeland said.

Even after he had left and started a family of his own, his despotic father tried to go on managing the young man's life. "My father tried to domineer me in my way of lifestyle and what my family did. You did it his way or no way."

Betty Gibson, a daughter, repeated for the jury the memories of her gaunt childhood. "My dad ran our home. He told us exactly what to do, when to do it, and how to do it. His word was final," she testified.

Another son, Wayne Copeland, offered his recollections of a mother who seemed sympathetic to her children's plight in a home presided over by a flint-edged dictator but who, in the end, did not dare to challenge his arbitrary rules. "Mom was there. You could talk to her," he said. "But she didn't say anything to Dad. That's just the way things were."

The nation focused its attention on what bore the earmarks of sensational serial killings. Five were known dead, but the search for other missing transients might yet lay even more deaths at the doorstep of the Copeland farm. A circus of attention swirled around the case.

Livingston County prosecutor Doug Roberts was joined in the court by whetstone-sharp, rising stars from the state attorney general's office who helped shape trial strategy. Ken Hulsof, one of those assistants, would take part in the hammer-blow courtroom clashes methodically prepared to project another vision of Faye Copeland to the jury, one calculated to prove she was her husband's more-than-willing helpmate in homicide.

Yet another off-stage consideration was making its presence felt in the drama. Confinement had begun to take some toll on Ray Copeland. A Yale University neuropsychiatrist had been brought in to examine him. What was learned signaled repercussion for both sides of the courtroom.

The diagnosis was disturbing. Dr. James Merikangas filed his report. Magnetic resonance imagery tests—MRIs—had shown a portion of the elderly man's brain had abnormally shrunken in size over the years, but another area, related to the retention of memory, had grossly swollen. Those conditions made him suffer both short-term and long-term memory loss. Copeland had a significant heart murmur. There were indications of strokes and rampant high blood pressure. Other testing showed him to be functionally illiterate, having great difficulty deciphering documents. Without the aid of his wife helping him read and write, Copeland could not be viewed as a totally independent agent in his actions, the medical psychiatric evaluation had concluded, then added the most volatile wild card of all: Ray Copeland was not in his right mind. "He cannot rationally assist in his defense because he is irrational," Dr. Merikangas was prepared to state under oath following his extensive examination.

Of course the state of Missouri would bring him to trial, but what might be the outcome? Perhaps, pondered both prosecution and defense, Faye Copeland might be the only person ever called before the bar to face responsibility for the shocking murders.

Hulsof and Roberts began tearing at the Grant Wood portrait of Faye Copeland that Miller and Scheckenberg had expertly painted. The physical evidence was more than convincing. The bullets taken from the shattered skulls of the victims perfectly matched the borings of the barrel on the rifle seized at the farm. If Faye had known nothing of the macabre burials at the neighbors' barns, how could so many witnesses now testifying say they had seen her at those sites frequently, accompanying Ray? That list of names that experts now said was indisputably in Faye's handwriting had X's in the same script beside the names of slain men. What other meaning could such a death roll have? Faye knew those men were dead.

The telltale souvenirs from the basement became props in a heartrending melodrama when prosecutors handed items that had belonged to the slain men to tearful relatives brought in to identify them from the witness stand. They spoke haunting biographies of their murdered kin. A pair of blue jeans with a special laundry mark, a M*A*S*H T-shirt bought as a little gift, and a plaid lumberjack shirt she had pressed many times were identified as belonging to Paul Cowart by his weeping mother, Edith Chilen. "He was very sentimental when it came to his family. He would call on my birthday and on his grandmother's birthday. He said he was going to get a good new job. He was going to set me and his grandmother up by sending us $100 every month. He was a dreamer, traveler, believer, and seeker of tomorrow," the young man's mother sobbed.

When she was notified that her son had been found in a lonely Missouri grave, Edith Chilen said she felt a sense of sad relief. "I know where he's at now. I don't have to wonder anymore. I may not like where he is, but I know he's not hurting," she told the jury, then added a bittersweet eulogy as she stared unflinchingly at Faye Copeland. "I know my son got his revenge. They matched the bullet in his skull with the gun. That's the way he paid back the person who did this to him. He got his revenge and maybe got revenge for the other men."

Faye Copeland's head was bowed. She did not meet the eyes of the mother who had passed a sentence of her own on the old woman.

The jury deliberated for three hours before finding Faye Copeland guilty as charged in five counts of first-degree murder. They met again quickly to determine if she should be sentenced to die by lethal injection.

Miller pleaded for his client's life. Consider her age, he told the jury, remember the testimony that described her bitter cup of life, her husband's ruthless dominance. "If you're too harsh, there's no going back. This is as final a decision as you are ever going to make," he quietly informed the jury.

The prosecution did not waver in its intent. "Mercy is for those willing to extend mercy. In this case, there wasn't any mercy," prosecutor Roberts rebutted.

The profits of the Copelands' business had been calculated from seized bank records. The lives of five men, perhaps more, had been taken for a meager $32,000.

Hulsof's final argument was scathing. He held up the letter Faye had written her husband, the one in which she expressed the belief things would cool down and made the wry observation about the failed effort to find additional bodies. "Nothing found, nothing gained."

Hulsof glared at Faye Copeland. "I'm sorry, Mrs. Copeland, but things haven't cooled down. We have exposed you and your husband in this vile little game and things have heated up. "Something found, everything gained," the prosecutor rebuked.

Hulsof's riveting eloquence visibly affected the jury. "This case is really about greed. They lured them, they deceived them, they recruited them, they betrayed them, and then they murdered them. Their lifeless bodies were littered about this county like so many pieces of wadded paper."

The death sentence was returned.

Faye Copeland cried out, "Oh, God. I never did nothing."

In the months that followed, the courts ruled Ray Copeland was competent to face charges and that his health could not be used as a reason to circumvent justice. Ray, too, was found guilty and sentenced to die. The Copelands became the first husband and wife to be sentenced to die since the resumption of capital punishment. Faye Copeland also became the oldest woman on America's death row. Her sentence and that of her husband's are being appealed.

Idaho cowpuncher Jack McCormick was awarded $500 for the tip to Nebraska police that cracked the Missouri murder case. He was fined $500 for stealing the car he'd taken for a test drive and never returned.

"The damn thing had a bad fuel pump, but I fixed it," he laughed. About the $500 he was philosophical. "I thought about the alternative. I could have been buried out there somewhere with those poor other guys. I figure I came out all right."

McCormick hit the road again, maybe heading back up Idaho way.

7

Maxine Walker

MAXINE WALKER FROWNED, THEN SCOWLED HER PLAIN face in flushed irritation. She peered out an open kitchen window into the soft twilight that had come to gather up the day in Sylacauga, Alabama.

He was out there again. *Damn that pesky hillbilly fool!* She had heard the wheezing of his gone-to-pieces junkyard hundred-dollar car. Did he really think he could slither up to her house in that noisy old bucket of bolts?

"Charles, come yonder!" she barked in an exasperated voice. "W. C. is out there again. You go tell that sneaky polecat if he ain't gone in one damn minute, I'm comin' out there and wring his dirty neck like a chicken!"

"Hell and damn," Charles Lawhorn snorted angrily. "How many times do I have to whoop that dumb cracker 'fore he gets the idea he ain't better come around here no more? You stay put, Auntie Max. I'll fix that old boy's hash. I'm gonna whoop him this time so's he's never gonna come sniffin' around here again ever!"

Maxine's young nephew stalked to the kitchen's screen door in a gathering boil. Lawhorn was big, tough, and young—nobody to fool with when he worked up a mad. W. C. Berry had already learned that bruising bit of southern Appalachian mountain lore to his still-smarting sorrow. Maxine Walker's hard-eyed nephew had cornered Berry once before to warn him to stop pestering his aunt. Outside a convenience store, the burly mountain youth had thrashed the living daylights out of forty-two-year-old Berry. The older man was no match for Lawhorn. Other of Walker's kin had also warned Berry to leave her alone, threatening him with more of the same.

Berry wasn't about to get himself caught so disastrously again. He saw Lawhorn send Maxie's screen door flying. The young man moved with rage and steam and a gathering menace toward his car. Berry had prudently kept the engine running. He hoped he could time his exit just right. He prayed the clunking old engine wouldn't conk out. Charles Lawhorn was now mere feet away. Berry leaned across the passenger seat and shouted through the car's open window. "You tell that old bitch dog in there that W. C. Berry is gonna burn her goddam house right down to the ground with her in it. You tell her that, y'hear me, you big sack of coon shit?"

The chilly sweat that had gathered on Berry's forehead retreated as the old car's motor responded, sending gravel flying and carrying him safely away from Charles Lawhorn's ham-fisted wrath.

A frustrated Charles scattered a fiery stream of curses ahead of him as he made his way back to Aunt Maxine's comfortable kitchen. A hot cup of fresh coffee had been poured for him and a hungry man's slab of pecan pie was waiting. Maxine Walker knew how to treat a man who did her a kindness. She was waiting for him, her eyes filled with anxiousness. She dabbed away the kitchen's humid dew from her face with a soft kitchen towel. "Did you talk to him, Charles? Is he gonna leave me alone?"

"I don't think that damn flea-brain is ever gonna stop plaguin' you, Auntie. Not 'til he's damn well dead and under six foot of dirt," Lawhorn answered disgustedly.

"Lord, what a blessin' that would be," Maxine Walker said.

Lawhorn looked up quizzically from his half-eaten pie. His aunt's voice had sounded strangely different just then. She slid soundlessly into the chair across from him at the old pine kitchen table. Her eyes had not left his. "Could you see to that for me, Charles? Could you fix it so's W. C. was six foot under the ground and not vexin' me every other minute?"

Lawhorn did not flinch. "If you'd like me to, I could, Auntie Max. I sure could do that small thing for you."

She reached across the table and tousled his wiry black hair, then let her hands smooth and lightly set right the gentle damage her intimacy had created. "You know I wouldn't ask this of you if there was some other way, but that crazy man is going to hurt one of my children and me, too, if somethin' don't get done with him. I can't think what else to do about him anymore," she said softly.

"You're a good boy, Charles. You and your brother Mack are like my own sons. You're my sister's boys, but I swear I love you just like you was my own. Ever since the mister died and I got mixed up with that fool W. C. Berry . . . well, you know. It's been a bad dream. That's why I asked you to come stay with me for a bit. I've been plumb scared. It was awful good of you to oblige me."

"We're family, Auntie Max, and we're mountain people. That still counts for somethin'."

"I could pay you some to take care of this business for me," Maxine Walker told her nephew. "Maybe Mack could do a piece, too."

"Well, I'd sure hate to take any pay, Auntie Max, but truth to tell, I am a bit short of money. Mack is, too."

"Would fifty dollars each be 'bout right? I could give you some more later on . . . after . . ."

"That seems fair enuf," Charles responded. "Hell, Aunt Max, you know we'd be pleased to do it for nothin'."

"The laborer is worth his hire. That's what the book says," Maxine Walker said piously by way of sealing the deadly bargain.

"I guess we just need to figger out how to do it then," Charles said.

"I've been thinkin' on it a mite," the stocky, bespectacled forty-three-year-old woman replied. "I've got a scheme or two in mind."

William Charles Berry had scurried his way back, heart still thumping, to the doubtful security of the run-down house he shared with his brother James. Just about everyone in the small Coosa River Valley town of Sylacauga knew old W. C. He was the slightly peculiar, none-too-bright, but pleasantly obsequious little man who mowed their lawns when he needed some pocket money. He patched their screen doors if he wasn't too busy doing nothing. He also retrieved kittens out of trees for tearful little girls. "I wouldn't think of takin's a penny, ma'am. I'm just right pleased to see the little lady smilin' again. Well, thank ya, ma'am. My brother James does need a dollop of his tonic agin."

To most, W. C. Berry was a mildly comic figure, the kind they loved to razz down at the barber shop and make the victim of pranks. But some knew his darker side. There had been an incident of violence in his past. Twelve years earlier, in 1976, a pretty young teenager from the valley had been found choked to death and dumped in a remote backwater creek. Her killer had been another of William Berry's brothers. He was found guilty of the slaying and sentenced to life in prison. W. C. had been involved. He was charged with manslaughter and had done time for his part. There were some people in Sylacauga who didn't want W. C. Berry to retrieve their daughter's kitten from a tree.

Berry was an object of back-fence talk for yet another reason. He was said to be married to Mary McDaniel, sometimes a butt of gossip in her own right in the clannish deep-Dixie community. Some said they weren't really married at all, that a love-struck Berry just handed over a substantial part of a disability check he received each month to her. Some said they knew why, what he got in return.

Berry was a familiar sight idly strolling the rural valley's back roads, out near the marble quarry some days, trudging with no apparent destination. On other days he might be seen walking along the edges of the sprawling Talladega National Forest in the company of his brother James, waving a friendly salute to dusty pickup trucks that passed, acknowledging the horn honk of greeting.

"Looks like old W. C. is headin' out to the woods early this mornin'," a passing driver would say.

"Must be he heard them turkeys gobblin' and he's fixing to shoot hisself one."

"Well, he ain't the brightest old boy in Talladega County, but he's probably the happiest. And he don't bother nobody," some would say.

Maxine Walker had been having a troubled time getting over the sudden death of her strapping husband, felled in his prime by a crushing heart attack. He'd been a hard worker and a good man. He'd provided well. The shiny new white Ford pickup he'd bought just before his untimely death brought admiring, envious glances from neighbors. It was proudly parked in front of the pleasant home where Maxine now lived with her two youngest children. Another son was grown. He had moved out but lived only a country holler away in nearby Goodwater. He was a fine young man. There had been a nice insurance policy, too, from her husband's job at the pulp mill. Maxine Walker could go on being a homemaker if that was what she wanted. She was well thought of in the town. Being a widow brought some new freedoms into her life. But then again, she confided to a close friend, it was awfully lonely. She missed the comforting presence of a man around the house, someone to do for and someone to do for her.

W. C. Berry softly knocked on the door of widow Walker's comfortable house a little earlier than good manners might have dictated, shortly after the death of Maxine's husband. His awkward but sincere condolences seemed, however, to make that breach of small-town etiquette innocent enough. "I know how hard it must be for a lady of your quality to take care of things with your man gone," W. C. Berry soothed. "If I can ever be of service to you, ma'am, you've only to let me know."

Maxine Walker opened the kitchen door and beckoned Berry to come in, sit a spell, and join her in a frosty glass of homemade sweet tea. Over the next few months she opened her heart to him, too. It was not long before they had come to a quiet, comfortable arrangement. Berry would discreetly stay at the widow Walker's home. They would need to keep their growing fondness for each other a secret.

At night, when the children were asleep, Berry

would find his way into Maxine Walker's tidy bedroom, and they would make furtive love to each other, quick, timid, Bible-belt love. It seemed to slake a thirst in both of them and to work a growing change in each as well.

W. C. at first proved to be a laborer worth his hire. All the small odd jobs that her busy husband had not been able to get to were taken care of around the property. Berry's clothes were freshly laundered now, and he took more care in his appearance. He still did other odd jobs around the county, but now he went to and from those jobs in a shiny new Ford pickup truck. He drove it with peacock pride. He loved to take a route that passed by the barbershop and make the locals gawk as he slowly cruised by.

"Was that old W. C. in that pickup?" someone would ask.

By God, it was. He'd turn the spunky Ford around on a dime and come back by to give them another look at a man behind the wheel of some real iron. This wasn't someone in a hundred-dollar car, someone to poke fun at.

Sometimes the Ford might be glimpsed down by the house of Mary McDaniel even though Berry was careful not to park it too close by. It wouldn't have done for that to get back to Maxine Walker.

Friends and relatives of Maxine could not help but notice a change in her, too. Although they made knowing guesses about the reasons to each other, none tried to make it their business.

The small mirror in her bedroom had become an encouraging friend. Maxine Walker knew she would not be chosen Miss Coosa Valley in any local beauty pageant, but her hair was nice. Maybe the thick, large-lensed eyeglasses she wore could be put aside for something more flattering. It also wouldn't hurt to lose a few pounds and shop for a new dress or two, not the feed-bag-looking housewife kind she had always chosen before, but something a bit more like the ladies wore up in Talladega.

Even without a whole lot of gussying up, Maxine Walker knew that other men had started paying some notice to her. Trips down to the store had become almost skin-tingling adventures now. Some man or other would always politely inquire as to how she was getting on. They'd offer to stop by and take care of chores at her place. No trouble at all, ma'am. I knew your husband, a right fine man. There always seemed to be an exciting undercurrent of warm, dreamy possibility beneath their words. A new, yet somehow familiar tremble of feelings began to rush on the shores of her ordinary life. It felt good. Maybe other doors might be opened, not just the screen door that led to her cozy kitchen.

If her dowdy image in the mirror had changed for the better, some of the things Maxine Walker had lately come to see were not quite what they had once seemed. W. C. Berry metamorphosed in ways that had at first been only mildly annoying, then downright irksome.

"Why're ya allus going down to the grocery every little stitch?" he started to demand.

"Why was you jawbonin' so long with that Wilson fella? He's plain trash; thinks you come inta some cash he could get holt of."

"They ain't no gas in the pickup agin. You fixin' to lock me up in the henhouse next?"

"Why's them kits of your'n always looking so sideways at me? What you been tellin' em?"

The glow of love was flickering and dimming in Maxine Walker's heart day by day. She had discovered some things she had not known before about W. C.

"Folks say you're married to Mary McDaniel. Are

you?" she demanded. "How is it my truck seems to go down to her place all the time these days?"

"Tell me about that girl people say you helped your brother kill . . ."

William Berry would explode. "Me an Mary ain't none of your damn lookout, nor none of your fancy friends!"

"Maybe I did have a hand in killing that little hoor and maybe I didn't. Maybe you're gonna damn soon find out if you don't mend your ways. Maybe they're gonna find you and your brats out where they found her," he fumed.

There was yet one other horrifying corruption her affair with Berry had visited on Maxine Walker. She had begun to suffer from a disgusting rash and discharges from "down there." A humiliating visit to a medical clinic in nearby Clay County confirmed her fears. She had contracted a venereal disease. There was only one place she could have come by that. Only one low-down, sneaky woman-chaser could have brought that secret shame to her.

"Pack your trash up and get out of here and don't ever dare to show your weasel face around here again," she bellowed at Berry when she returned from the doctor's visit.

The little yardman seemed to shrivel under her fury. He meekly did as she had ordered. But first he made his apologies and a plea. "I'm plain sorry for your trouble, Maxie. You know I wouldn't want to cause you any hurt. You're righteous mad now, but I say we was good for each other. I'll just stop by later when you're feeling some better about things."

Berry walked the backroads again from Maxine's house near Goodwater back to Main Street in Sylacauga where his brother greeted him indifferently and his old car waited just as trouble-filled as the day had proven to be.

149

The next few weeks were dark ones for Berry. When he coaxed his ancient, dying car down the road to Maxine's house, she met him outside the door with a livid spleen that put him to flight again. Her anger had not cooled nor her determination that she wanted nothing more to do with him.

There were no more showboat excursions down past the barbershop. Berry didn't need to face up to the razor-edged country hazing he knew was waiting there. Then Maxie had her son, Roger Kilgore, pay a painful call on him, saying that Berry would get another sound cuffing every time he showed himself at Mrs. Walker's home. Quickly, she had one of her sister's boys, Charles Lawhorn, move into her house —*their* house only weeks before. The thumping Charles had given Berry was a dear price for continuing to ply his suit with Maxine.

Worst of all, Maxie had begun showing up at some of the county dance halls with her whang-leather-tough nephew in tow. She'd spend the whole night dancing with other men while the fiddles sawed out mountain tunes. She looked very pretty. She wore a new dress. Berry kept a seething watch on this heart-breaking turn of events from the safety of the parking lot, peering in windows to take in the sluttish betrayal of their once ardent love.

Once, when Maxine stepped out of a dance hall alone to catch a breath of air, Berry's jealous rage brought him out of hiding. "Why're ya sneaking around with that hilligan nephew of your'n? Is he on your pillow now 'stead of me?"

Berry continued what he believed he needed to do to win back Maxine's love. He seemed unable to accept the finality of her rejection. As she drove her fancy pickup down quiet streets, Berry's rattletrap car would soon appear in her rearview mirror. Her phone rang constantly. Sometimes no one spoke. Other times Berry's voice would be pleading or cursing and threatening.

Maxine Walker refilled her nephew's coffee cup. They continued their conversation. "I could just give him another real whooping," Charles Lawhorn said. Perhaps he was testing the depth of his aunt's resolve.

"No, Charles. That ain't gonna do it, not for good and all."

Maxine Walker laid some other suggestions on the table. "He takes some kind of medicine. I don't know what it is, but maybe you and Mack could get him down and pour some down his neck. That could do it." Charles rejected the idea.

Maxine had another at the ready. "What if it looked like he done himself in? He's got reasons. Nobody would think much of it." Charles said he didn't think that was the answer.

She was full of suggestions. "That shack where he lives wouldn't be no problem to sneak into of a night and just shoot him in his bed, *bang, bang.*"

"Shootin' him sounds right, but not at his house. We oughta' get him out in the turkey woods. Shoot him there and leave him for the buzzards," Charles Lawhorn said.

"I believe you've come on it," Maxine Walker said with a nod of relieved agreement. "And I know just how to get Mr. W. C. Berry up into those woods. Yes sir, I do."

W. C. Berry didn't know exactly what to make of it when his brother handed him the phone and told him it was the Walker woman calling. Was he going to catch hell and damnation again from her acid tongue? He smiled broadly when he heard the reason Maxine Walker had called. *They were all the same when you got right down to it,* he reflected to himself. Every damn one of them panted and snorted after the same thing. So the fancy lady needed a little of the real man's service, did she? Those dance hall hillbillies just couldn't give the widow what she wanted. Well, by God, old W. C. could, but she'd have to do some real sweet talkin' to get it. Yes, sir, by God, she wouldn't be so high and mighty pretty soon. He'd go with her up in the woods, to the same road in Talladega National Forest where they'd done the thing a few times before. No one would be around, not with 200,000 acres to wander. He knew the lay of the land. He'd sniped more than his share of wild turkeys right up there. It was a good place to let her eat a little humble pie. He would be on his turf in more ways than one.

Berry whistled a tune as he chugged toward Collier's Trading Post on Highway 148. The mountains loomed on either side of him as he made his way to the rendezvous. She'd said to meet her at the Post. They'd drive the pickup on up to the woods.

Maxine Walker was coming from another direction. She thought of how the damn little rooster was just like all of them; tell them they could have a little of what was down there and they'd come running like some old coon hound, stepping on their tongues and howling every inch of the way. Maxine would have to make a detour. There was an errand to perform before she picked up Berry.

Charles Lawhorn sat in the pickup waiting. He snapped open the carefully oiled, single-shot .12-gauge shotgun and expertly slid a red-jacketed shell inside. It was a double-ought load. One could handily blow away a young pine with one thunderous charge from its long black barrel. "We best hurry to pick up Mack," he said as Maxine got behind the wheel.

Mack O'Neal Lawhorn waited impatiently at Mike's Big O, a local bar in nearby Alexander City. Beneath his belt he carried a .25-caliber automatic pistol. Charles had told him they might not need it, what with him carrying the big shotgun. But better safe than sorry.

"We need to take care now that no one sees us," Maxine Walker cautioned as they drove toward the woods. The plan was simple. Maxine would drop her nephews off near the proposed trysting site. The brothers would take cover in the heavy pine and oak stands along the lane. Maxine would tell Berry she needed to get out of the truck before they made love to answer a call of nature. Charles and Mack would then rush up and slay the waiting W. C. Berry in a fusillade of shotgun fire.

Grover Williams was shifting heavy loads of topsoil to fill a wash on his property when he looked up that morning and saw a white Ford pickup turn on to Wiregrass Road, heading for the forest. A woman drove. Two men accompanied her.

At the trading post on 148, Berry had arrived. The small general store was closed, but a soda machine stood out front. He fumbled change from his pockets and bought himself a cool drink, popping the lid and swallowing a draught just as the white Ford pickup pulled up in front of the store. He smiled as he got inside, giving Maxine a small peck of greeting.

Mona Lisa Jones, who lived on Brickyard Road, stopped her car at the store momentarily, thinking it was open. Getting back in her car, she found herself following the pickup that had pulled away moments ahead of her. She could see its driver and passenger.

The simple plan Maxine and her nephews had agreed upon did not come off without some serious hitches. Maxine exited the truck offering the ruse that

she needed to relieve herself, and Berry waited unsus-
pectingly at first, eager for her return. But then he
heard a sudden clamor from the woods. Twigs broke
and voices reached his ears. The Lawhorn brothers
were willing but not exactly adept at murder by
ambush. Berry hurriedly exited the truck. In a panic
he started to make his way back toward the blacktop
highway.

Maxine Walker cussed. She shouted to her nephews,
"Get in the back of the truck, dammit! Don't let him
git away."

She leaped into the vehicle, keyed it to life as
Charles and Mack scrambled into the back. Maxine
pointed the truck in Berry's direction, quickly caught
up to him, then slowed.

"Now," she shouted to her nephews.

Charles Lawhorn took as steady an aim as he could.
The .00 buckshot freight-trained its way into the
shoulder of the frantically scrambling victim. For a
moment, the impact stood him stock still. Then he
spun and flapped like a scarecrow in the wind. The
truck was still moving, and Lawhorn fired from a
different angle. That white-hot fistful of lead pellets
tore into Berry's stomach. He clutched at some part of
himself no longer there and fell to the ground.
Lawhorn shot again, then again and again. The grisly
heap that once had been William Charles Berry was
butchered beyond recognition. Mack Lawhorn joined
in the bloody frenzy. He pumped round after round
from the pistol into the mutilated hulk.

Maxine Walker could not look. She did not imagine
it could have been like this. She immediately wanted
to get away. Charles jumped back into the seat. Mack
was ordered to lay down in the back. They would
sneak him back to Alexander City.

* * *

Wayne Martin was a woodsman, one of the better turkey hunters in the valley. On April 2, 1988, shortly before Easter, the urge to take a few of the wily birds came over him. Well before daybreak, Martin drove up into Talladega National Forest. He went down to a spot that was a favorite of his, down by an old lovers' lane the kids from town headed for at night. He settled down to wait for daybreak. When it came, he began a stealthy reconnaissance in search of that prized Appalachian dinner: the elusive and cunning eastern wild turkey.

What Martin stumbled across instead made him hurry back to his car in shock and horror. He found a phone and called the Talladega County sheriff's office.

"I wasn't even sure it was a human. I could hardly tell," he explained to Captain Frankie Wallace when he and a crime scene crew arrived. Wallace looked at the fly-covered corpse and agreed with Martin.

Within minutes, lights flashing, the car of Sheriff Jerry Studdard arrived on the scene. He took in the grim tableau: "Anyone know this man?" he asked. No one did. "Anyone gone missing around these parts? This boy's been here a day or two!" he added.

Berry's body was taken to a hospital in Birmingham for autopsy. Someone would soon report a missing person. James Berry tearfully identified the broken remains as that of his brother, W. C.

Wallace, a team of deputies under his command, and cops on loan from Sylacauga police worked around the clock to find who had so brutally murdered this man. He'd been shot down like a wild animal.

Maxine Walker's affair with Berry was not as secret as she had thought. The troubles she had lately had with the scorned boyfriend had been talked about much more than she knew.

The countless man-hours of investigation Studdard had set into motion and the quiet, determined methods Captain Frankie Wallace oversaw from the department's southern county division in Sylacauga had begun to draw suspicion to the kitchen door of Maxine Walker.

"She's had Charles Lawhorn, her nephew, living with her for a time to keep Berry from bothering her," Wallace told Sheriff Studdard at a morning briefing several days into the investigation.

"Him and his brother are from over in Talapossa County, and they're kinda wild boys. They think they're badder than they are, but they've done a little time, burglary mostly, nothing violent, but they may have thought they were hot enough for something like this."

"You ready to have a talk with 'em?" Studdard queried.

"I believe we need to bring Charles in for starters," his deputy responded.

Charles Lawhorn told Wallace he had no idea about what had happened to W. C. Berry. He admitted he had gotten tough with the pesky handyman when he wouldn't leave his aunt alone, but he hadn't seen him for some time. The runt must have finally understood his aunt's family wouldn't put up with him.

Wallace told the rugged suspect that he believed differently. "You've been sittin' here lying to me. We've got some witnesses, Charles. You and your brother killed W. C. and you're about to be in a world of hurt."

Charles Lawhorn suddenly blinked back tears. "My brother didn't have nothin' to do with this. I did it for my aunt. Mack never knew a thing about any of it."

Wallace ordered Maxine Walker brought in next. She had not seen Berry in months, she insisted. Her nephew shoot a man? That boy wouldn't think of it!

Wallace told her that her favorite nephew had confessed and implicated her.

"You were driving the truck. No good to tell me you weren't," Wallace told a now sobbing and crumpled Maxine Walker.

"He wouldn't leave me alone," she wept. "He said he was going to hurt me and my children. What could I do?" she asked, pleading eyes behind the unglamorous spectacles she still hadn't gotten around to replacing.

"You might have come and told us what was going on, Maxine," Frankie Wallace said. "That's what we're here for."

"No. That's what family is for, Captain. "We're folks that take care of our own business," she replied.

In a crowded courtroom, Maxine Walker seemed quaintly out of place as she watched and heard the skein of patiently gathered evidence drawing her to her fate. A farm-town housewife, she had difficulty following the pin-striped legal arguments swirling around her. She seemed embarrassed when the jury heard the twenty-minute taped confession she had given to Wallace. The part that seemed to bother her the most was when she had told about the disease she believed Berry had given her.

Her defense was largely a plea for understanding. She wasn't some fancy or slyboots woman. She was mountain stock. When someone threatened her home, her family, she knew what had to be done. She had done it.

Many of the jurors who heard the case knew what Maxine Walker was talking about. Some part of the Coosa River still ran through their veins. Some part of their beliefs had come down from the pine-wooded Appalachians, too. But things had changed. It took them only fifty minutes to find her guilty. Their recommendation to Judge Jerry Fielding was that she be sentenced to death in the electric chair.

Maxine Walker spoke to that judge before he passed his sentence. She asked that God forgive her, but she didn't believe her trial had been fair. Whether or not they wanted to admit it, she believed there wasn't a body in the courtroom that would not have done what she did.

Judge Fielding followed the jury's recommendation. He ordered execution as the punishment for her crime. As required by Alabama law, the sentence was suspended to permit an automatic appeals process. In the fall of 1992, one of those appeals was successful. It had been determined that the makeup of Walker's jury was not racially balanced. Maxine Walker remained in prison but would be given a new trial. She did not mind her confinement. She told a local newspaper reporter her isolated death-row cell was as good as any place to live. The guards were friendly, real gentlemen, not like someone else she could mention.

Within weeks, it was the turn of Charles and Mack Lawhorn to face Alabama justice for their roles in the slaying of the handyman. Charles was sentenced to death. His verdict is also on appeal. The participation of Mack Lawhorn was viewed as more spontaneous than premeditated. He was given a term of life in prison with no possibility of parole.

8

Blanche Taylor Moore

ASSISTANT DISTRICT ATTORNEY JANET BRANCH SEEMED TO take no notice of the courtroom's gathering silence. The last question had been asked and answered. It was time for the next. But the approach of some telling, pivotal moment had enveloped her in that quiet. The young prosecutor appeared as if she were harvesting some stillness before a storm.

Branch slowly rose from the mirror-polished prosecution table. Her reflection was captured there as she surrendered a yellow legal pad to the table's face, then caught a glimpse of her own—a vibrant thirtysomething, fresh scrubbed, and mountain morning pretty. She was trimly athletic, chicly but circumspectly dressed, firmly footed on a fast professional track. Friends enjoyed her waggish, wry sense of humor. But on that morning, Janet Branch was as serious as death by lethal injection.

Watching her approach with coiled, wary intensity, seated primly in the witness chair, Blanche Taylor Moore fidgeted uncharacteristically—only for a moment—with the precisely measured and gathered moon-glow-pale strand of pearls accenting her fashionable choice of apparel. This day it was soft, flatter-

ing silk teal, deftly collared at the throat to blur a
failing, late fiftyish jawline. Minister's daughter, now
wife of a man of the cloth as well, her righteously
poised, almost impatient air was as she believed it
ought to be: that of a respected, godly woman, good
mother and grandmother, falsely accused of unthink-
able crimes, beset by still another day of artfully
polite, yet mocking, cleverly baited attack by the
razor-minded, unyielding woman now stalking her
again.

"No older than my own daughters," Blanche Moore
mused, "but how different from them!" Missy Janet
Branch would never understand Christian charity of
the kind that had always been the wellspring and
bedrock of Blanche Taylor Moore's life. No, the slick,
cynical, big-city rules by which women like the flinty
young woman prosecutor lived could permit no real-
ization that some people—like Blanche—were put
here to help others.

Through months of pretrial hearings, weeks of
testimony, it had been as if some futuristic, cosmic-
lighted isolating force field had materialized each time
accuser Janet Branch and defendant Blanche Taylor
Moore circled each other in the courtroom setting. It
was suddenly as if the two women were starkly alone,
aware of none but each other in the crowded, confessional quiet of the North Carolina courtroom.

Janet Branch fixed the minister's wife, the preacher's daughter with a crafted, inquisitive mien. Then
she asked the question the prosecution had determined would be the gallow's trap: "During interrogation, Mrs. Moore, you have, on several occasions, told
police that you never—I repeat, never—brought food
to the hospital room of Mr. Raymond Reid and that
you never fed any such foods prepared or purchased
by you to Mr. Reid. Is that your testimony today?"

"Yes it is, Miss Branch," the woman in the witness

chair answered imperiously with near exasperation. "I believe I have said so repeatedly. I wonder that I am required to repeat it again."

Janet Branch's face did not register the elation she experienced at the answer so archly fashioned by Blanche Taylor Moore.

It had taken fifteen grueling months to come to that moment of truth—or untruth—in a Forsyth County courtroom. To recall to mind how it had come to be, Janet Branch needed only to quickly search the pews of spectators and seek out the ashen face of a country church pastor sadly averting the eyes of Blanche Taylor Moore. Witness after damning witness had unwound yet one more length of the enigmatic shroud that had hidden even from him the cold, murderous anger of the woman he had taken as his bride a little more than a year before.

Reverend Dwight Moore tensed his tormented body against the screaming roller coaster of pain that careened through him again. It felt as though his mottled hands and feet, his grotesquely swollen abdomen, even his bloated eyes, would explode with his next wildly racing heartbeat, scattering him across the heavens in some fiery, final pinwheel of death.

Patient gown soaked in sweat, lying helplessly in his minutely-monitored intensive care unit bed at Memorial Hospital in Chapel Hill, Moore prayed to accept God's will for him when brief moments of consciousness allowed. Concerned medical specialists were baffled by his illness. About one certainty they agreed—his chances of survival were perilously slim. Prayer had an appropriate place at his fevered bedside, doctors said. Dwight Moore's fate was more in His hands now than theirs.

Only days before, the Moores had cut short a honeymoon trip that included a stop in New Jersey to visit one of the minister's children by a previous marriage. He had begun to feel ill then but then he felt somewhat better on the couple's return home to Columbia and the cozy parsonage. It comfortably sat near his pastorate, the inviting, well-attended, solidly brick United Church of Christ.

The fifty-four-year-old graying, but normally energetic preacher knew it had come time for him to be much more prudent about his health. With a new wife and a growing flock, people depended on his full-time, vigorous leadership.

These past few years there had been two troubling health alarms. A debilitating, flulike bout that had hung on relentlessly had finally lifted. More serious was the painful bowel obstruction that had required hospitalization and extended rest. Thank God for Blanche being at his side to see him through—even before she had accepted his ring of betrothal.

Now she hovered near him again at Memorial, like some soothing, ministering angel. He remembered that when he had first met his wife-to-be, she had been volunteering the same exact, wondrously devoted Christian duty she was now performing so faithfully for him. What had the man's name been? Reid, yes, Raymond Reid. A quiet, shy, Bible-believing man. Blanche had been like a sister to him, right up to the hour of his sad death. They had known each other from work, he believed she had told him.

Outside Dwight's hospital room, Blanche Taylor Moore had been gently summoned away from her endless vigil. She seemed to be listening with brave calm as attending physicians, gathered in the cool corridor, told her of the diagnosis of her husband's illness. Within the hour, they said, they had received the results of a sophisticated urine profile performed on specimens taken from Dwight Moore and analyzed in the hospital's pathology lab. It had revealed a most unusual—actually incredible—condition. Present in his collapsing system, they believed, was the highest concentration of the deadly poison arsenic ever recorded in a still-living human being!

Had the pastor been working a great deal in the yard or garden lately? Had he or she purchased any strong chemical compounds for cleanup around their home or for pest control? Blanche tried to remember. Why, yes, she said, Dwight had been doing some work on the lawn on the day he had become so suddenly ill. If she recalled correctly, he had come in, had a bite of lunch she had prepared, but before he could return to his tasks, had been stricken by what appeared to her to be a heart attack. Her first husband, James, had died tragically of just such a condition.

Hospital staff asked that all cans of weed killer, hornet spray, rose dust, or any other pesticide at the Moore home be brought into the toxicology lab for examination. Still doctors said it seemed unlikely her husband could accidentally have ingested so huge an amount of arsenic as the tests revealed. They said they felt it necessary to advise local police of the strange lab results in the event, however unlikely, that someone had set out deliberately to harm the soft-spoken small-town minister. We live in a mischievous age, they said. Who knew what might actually have happened? Additionally, just as a sensible precaution, from that moment on, no one would be permitted to enter Reverend Moore's room alone.

Blanche Moore reached with her right hand to her left and distractedly twisted the large diamond and ruby ring she wore there. Was there a nearby pay phone she might use, she asked demurely, then excused herself.

From a modish designer handbag, Blanche Moore extracted a neatly organized cache of small change and dialed the first of several calls she would make asking that prayers be offered for her husband's swift recovery from near death. To several of her closest, devoutly Christian friends, those who had known her for years, she added a curious postscript to the conversation. "I hope this investigation into Dwight's condition won't bring up any ugly questions 'bout dear Raymond's death," she said.

Reverend James Rossner was a sympathetic minister and friend. He had recently joined Blanche Taylor and Dwight Moore in marriage in his church. Now he hurriedly offered the attractive, youngish fifty-seven-year-old grandmother the reply she apparently had hoped to elicit. "Don't be silly, Blanche. Who could ever think you had done anything to harm Raymond Reid?" He pledged his wish and prayer that Dwight Moore would speedily be returned to health now that his physicians had determined he had somehow—carelessly, unknowingly—ingested arsenic.

How odd, some of those friends later wondered, that Blanche Taylor Moore, a respected minister's wife, would suffer even a moment's apprehension that someone might imagine a link between the freakish incident that hospitalized her husband and the death of pleasant church-pillar Raymond Reid who had succumbed to a nervous system disease in 1986. No one had shown more true Christian love and compassion to a dying Raymond Reid than good-hearted Blanche Taylor. What a shame it was that he had not lived to marry widowed Blanche, as gossips wagged he would. She had been alone far too long after the sudden death of her still-young first husband, James Taylor. He had been—what?—forty-five when he passed on to his reward?

Intensive care unit nurse Wanda Moore was not prepared for the disheartening scene awaiting her as she stepped into the room of one of her favorite patients. Only a few days before, when she had left for her weekend off, Raymond Reid had been making a steady, encouraging recovery from the dangerous, but not usually fatal illness his doctors had diagnosed as Guillain–Barré syndrome. Now, tears welled in her eyes as she looked down on him. He'd been rushed back to the intensive care unit at North Carolina Baptist Hospital. She shuddered at how cruelly the disease had regathered its strength and again struck the friendly, easy-going fifty-year-old supermarket chain executive. Reid was monstrously swollen. His slight frame had taken on an incredible sixty pounds of water from fluids retained when an emergency intravenous procedure was ordered to stabilize his plummeting blood pressure. Kidney failure had added to that grotesque enlargement of his trembling body. He writhed in a pain no medication could quell. He thrashed as though possessed by a host of demons. His eyes appeared to have been scorched by fire. Nurse Moore reached for a cooling basin and towel to apply to his face.

Raymond Reid's awful eyes followed her in recognition and pleading. Soundlessly, through parched lips, he formed mute words that burned themselves into the nurse's sad heart. "Help . . . me . . . or . . . I'll . . . die," he painfully mouthed.

Raymond Reid and Blanche Taylor—not yet Moore—had known each other for about twenty years. Sometimes they had worked in the same supermarket in the giant Kroger chain that dominated food trade in the Carolinas. He had always been attracted to the comely, outgoing, hard-working woman who did her work as though she was grateful to have the job. He knew it provided the nice, elegant little things for herself and her two pretty young daughters that her husband's employment as an antique furniture refinisher didn't pay enough to provide.

Blanche Taylor seldom openly complained about the life her husband, James, had made for the family in the twenty years of their marriage, but friends and co-workers like Raymond Reid came to know her well enough to understand that James Taylor was a disappointment to Blanche. Of all of his brothers and sisters in a family that numbered eleven, James was the only one of his siblings who had not managed to provide his family with a house of their own. They were renters, a galling reminder to Blanche of her bleak childhood when her family had lived in boxy, cramped, four-room clapboards owned by the textile mill in Lexington. Both of her parents had worked at low-paying, back-breaking jobs. Sometimes a few extra dollars were thrown in when her father, Parker D. Kiser, Sr., was able to ply his part-time trade of backwoods, itinerant preacher. The clear, sweet voice of little Blanche would rise heavenward behind him in songs of gospel praise when the collection baskets were passed.

Then, too, James Taylor had more than one sinful habit. She bore them quietly, even though they stole precious pennies from her plan to raise her family's fortunes a notch or better.

It was evident that Blanche Taylor had barely enough of her own. Reid respected the way in which the industrious mother of two still found time to help out, when she could, others with problems worse than her own. She was a devout churchgoer and worker. Reid knew that in her modest home, unlike his own, the Bible was read to the children every evening. When Reid's wife was pregnant with a second child, it was Blanche Taylor who hosted the charmingly decorated, perfectly planned baby shower for Linda Reid.

On that October day in 1973 when James Taylor died in his bed of a massive heart attack, Raymond Reid came to the house to pay his sincere condolences to the widow and her young children. He and his wife had divorced two years earlier. In his own fumbling way, he had tried to let Blanche Taylor know that strong feelings for her stirred within him, far beyond those of friendly co-workers who had known each other and shared small secrets over many years.

Later—it seemed only after repeated prompting—Blanche Taylor confessed to Reid that her husband's death had faced her with dire financial circumstances. "He left us about $2,000," Blanche softly wept. "It wasn't even enough for the funeral, let alone all those medical bills." Raymond Reid insisted that he be allowed to help. He had advanced on the food chain's management ladder and could well afford to do a small kindness for someone about whom he deeply cared. With reluctance, Blanche accepted loans of about $10,000 over the next few years.

To Raymond Reid's delight, Blanche Taylor seemed to be returning his attentions, in a proper way, befitting her recent sorrow. Their first date, Blanche noted in a diary, came after Reid had admired a grave wreath Blanche had handcrafted to place at the small headstone of her late husband. Reid prevailed on the widow to make a similar one for his parents' resting place up in Danville. She did. They drove together to the cemetery to place the wreath, then stopped at a roadside inn for a pleasant lunch.

Then Blanche Taylor did something Raymond Reid found hard to understand. There had been times before when she had made the coquettish claim that men had always seemed to find her an object of intense sexual interest; she couldn't quite explain why, she would blush. She had recounted a time, not long before, when a fire had mysteriously broken out in her home. When she returned, the fire had been doused and was being probed by investigators. Her bedroom, she pointed out to them, was in wild disarray—not the way it had been when she had left that morning. The contents of her lingerie drawer were scattered about. And, ominously, a scandalously suggestive pair of red panties was missing. They had been given to her by one of her daughters as a gag gift.

But now, Blanche told an astonished Reid, a man they both knew, Robert Hutton, a long-time Kroger zone manager, had lain in wait in the rear of a store where Blanche was working. As she approached, on a break, Hutton had appeared from behind wearing not a stitch of clothes, exposing himself to her. After roundly berating him, Blanche said she snatched up Hutton's trousers and underwear and fled the frightening scene. She had kept the executive's clothing for evidence in a multimillion-dollar sexual harassment suit she planned to file against him and the Kroger Corporation. She told a stunned Reid that perhaps it would be best—considering his future with the company—if it appeared they were no longer seeing each other, even better yet, if they each dated others.

Raymond Reid argued against such a harsh necessity, but Blanche firmly insisted. They did not see each other for some time. Blanche began consulting with Dr. Jesse McNeil, a Burlington psychiatrist, as she began preparing her suit against Hutton and Kroger. She discussed with Dr. McNeil her relationship with Reid and another man she had become acquainted with while attending an Easter Sunday church service: Reverend Dwight Moore.

"Raymond Reid is not the man I really want in my life," she told McNeil. "Dwight Moore has more of the qualities I am accustomed to."

Raymond Reid never learned of that conversation, but he felt Blanche's new coolness. He wrote her a touching letter. In the event anything ever happened to him, Reid said, he wanted Blanche to be the executor of his will and estate. He also revealed that will provided that all proceeds be equally divided among three people: his two sons and Blanche Taylor. "Remember me in your prayers," he added in the fine, firm hand with which he closed the letter.

Blanche occasionally began to see her friend Raymond Reid again. Because his advancements meant longer work hours, and she had more time to spare since leaving Kroger, Blanche thoughtfully prepared some of Raymond's favorite meals in her kitchen and left them at his house so he could warm them in the microwave no matter what time he got home.

Meanwhile Pastor Dwight Moore was enjoying getting to know Blanche Taylor. They enjoyed pleasant breakfasts together. His disappointment when she would check her watch and announce she had to run was always softened when she explained she had some errand of kindness. Frequently, she spoke of a hospitalized friend, someone she'd once worked with, who was quite ill. She'd promised to visit and bring him a special treat, some of her homemade banana pudding and perhaps a peanut butter milk shake.

Could he be of help in some way? Moore asked. Blanche wrinkled her forehead into an appealing, harried frown. Yes in fact, if he didn't mind, what with all her comings and goings, she'd forgotten these last few days to pick up a bottle of ant poison to rid her house of those pesky red devils that could bite so cruelly. She'd gone to Ken's Quickie Mart on Hopedale Road to find the product she'd once found effective, but Ken Wolfe said he didn't stock Anti-Ant. She'd told him he ought to. It worked very well. Would Dwight mind stopping someplace to see if he might find a bottle? Reverend Moore said he'd be happy to do so. He found it that very day.

In the intensive care unit, nurses Wanda Moss and Lisa Hutchens were pleased when the elevator opened to reveal the arrival of Blanche Taylor, carrying her

cute tote bag brimmed with Tupperware filled with
goodies. Sometimes she'd surprise the nurses by pro-
ducing out of her bottomless bag a small, delightful
brunch for them. But always, there were daintily
prepared snacks for the patient she visited so faithfully, Raymond Reid. When he had been feeling better,
Reid would brag about his friend Blanche's kitchen
skills: "No one in North Carolina makes banana
pudding the way Blanche does," he would beam.

Visiting hours were made generously flexible for the
thoughtful Mrs. Taylor. Sometimes she came twice a
day bearing treats. Nurses on every shift noted that
Raymond Reid suffered anxiety on the few days when
Blanche failed to appear. They made notations in the
chart kept at the ICU nursing station desk. "4:30 P.M.,
August 31, 1986. Ms. Taylor in to visit . . . took good
supper and Ms. Taylor feeding."

On another day, as Reid's health continued to
decline, his chart reflected: "Offered pureed lunch.
Sick on stomach. Took less than one-third of diet and
continued complaint of sick stomach."

By mid-September, Raymond Reid was gravely
close to death. When one of his oldest friends, Bill
Odham, came to visit, Reid could communicate only
by blinking his tortured eyes and clicking his swollen
tongue. Three tubes ran into his frail body, a large-
bored heart catheter drained deadly fluids from his
chest. He was still able to move his hands but not
without pathetic trembling. He was barely capable,
nurses remembered, to affix his signature to the legal
documents Blanche and a lawyer brought one morning for him to sign.

When he finally expired on October 7, the cause of
his death, at age fifty, was still not entirely understood. Doctors suggested an autopsy to provide some
of the missing answers. Weeping softly, steadied by
the consoling hand of the hospital chaplain, Blanche

revealed a flash of unbendable iron beneath her grief. "Raymond would not have wanted to be cut on like that," she said. "An autopsy can't bring him back, can it?" Blanche Taylor added. No autopsy would be performed. The decision was hers as executor of Raymond Reid's estate.

Sheriff's investigator Phil Ayers had become a frequent visitor to the hospital room where Reverend Dwight Moore now battled to regain the use of his numbed limbs. His recovery from the arsenic poisoning was slow, aching, discouraging. Ayers sympathetically prodded the minister to recall every small detail that led up to his hospitalization. He had already taken statements from Blanche. She had been unable to add anything more than she had told doctors treating her husband. Now, Ayers, purposely alone in the hospital room with Moore, asked another question his cop's mind had inevitably steered him toward. "Has anyone in your family—or Blanche's— ever died under odd circumstances?" the investigator asked.

Moore reflected on the query for long minutes. Then he answered as though what he was recalling might not really be important enough to mention. "I can't think of anyone in my own family who fits what you're asking . . . but Blanche did have quite a good friend who died a few years back and the doctors weren't quite sure what caused it. I think, in the end, they called it some kind of syndrome . . . Gillian something or other?"

Phil Ayers felt a sudden, jolting voltage of discovery pass through him. It wasn't Guillain–Barré syndrome, was it?

That sounded right, Moore affirmed.

The investigator left hurriedly to return to his office. There was a recent law enforcement bulletin that had been circulated all across the state. It had to do with the death of a woman whom doctors had first believed had succumbed to Guillain–Barré syndrome. An autopsy showed that, instead, her death had been due to massive arsenic poisoning. Phil Ayers wanted to read that bulletin again very carefully.

The strange illness that had struck down Reverend Moore was a topic of wide community interest and concern. The odd statements Blanche Moore had made about the possibility that her new husband's near demise and the death of Raymond Reid might maliciously be connected had fueled small-town gossip. It came to the attention of the Taylor family, many of whom still made their homes in the areas of Forsyth and nearby Alamance Counties. Some of them began to wonder about the death of James Taylor, taken at such a young age by a shattering heart attack, a medical problem that was not especially recurrent among them.

The Taylor family knew that the marriage of their brother and the former Blanche Kiser had not always been a perfect one. She had only been eighteen when they were wed. He was twenty-six and perhaps not quite as ready to settle down into family life as the serious, ambitious teenager he had made his wife. Some of the young family's disharmony had come from his continuing habit of betting—and mostly losing—on sporting events. His average-paying job wasn't enough as it was to secure the nice things Blanche wanted. She carefully managed her own small salary as a checkout girl at Kroger. Often, when he had a gambling debt he could not cover, James Taylor would demand that his wife hand over some of her rainy-day savings. Once, when she had rebelliously refused, Taylor had snatched a bowl of cooling rice pudding from a kitchen counter and threw it into

Blanche's face. Several of Taylor's sisters upbraided him. Blanche said she prayed every day that the Lord would lead her husband down more righteous, more responsible paths.

Toward the end of their twenty-one-year marriage, it seemed as though God had heard her prayers. James Taylor joined the church, even became energetically active, and took on the task of aiding foreign mission outposts supported by his congregation. On the night he died of what doctors determined was a massive myocardial infarction, James Taylor had been preparing teaching aids to be used in the mission schools. The work exhausted him. He had not been feeling well lately.

Fourteen-year-old Cindy Taylor was frightened the morning of October 2, 1973. She had been awakened by the screams of her mother. "Oh, my God, he's dead!" she had heard her mother's voice wail from the bedroom next to hers.

Barefoot, terrified, Cindy padded into her parents' bedroom. Her mother tried to shield her from the sight of her father, dead in the rumpled bed, the notes he had been working on scattered about him.

"Call your cousin Vickey," Blanche ordered. "Hurry now. She'll know what to do. Everything will be all right."

James Taylor's niece Vickey Bolden was a registered nurse. She rushed over to her aunt's home in response to the urgent call. She reached for the wrist of James Taylor and found no pulse. She listened for a heartbeat. There was none. Vickey Bolden gently turned her uncle's face upward from the pillow that had partly covered it. She recoiled at the sight. James Taylor's face was set in a mad grimace.

His eyes were frozen, widely open in a frightful death mask. The heart attack that claimed his life must have been huge, thunderous, she thought. She left the room to telephone James Taylor's doctor to tell him that his patient had died during the night. Then she wanted to console her aunt Blanche. She found her on the kitchen telephone, talking to someone. She believed it was a man named Raymond.

Blanche received dozens of sympathetic friends and relatives over the following few days. She tearfully told them how James had insisted she sleep with Cindy the night he died. The pretty teenager was feverish, coming down with a sore throat. How sad that circumstance had prevented her from being in bed with James. Perhaps she might have done something to save him. She recounted her heartbreak in the morning when she entered the bedroom. "I tried to awaken him. I said, 'Boy, wake up. It's time to wake up.' He couldn't. He was with the Lord," she softly cried.

Investigator Phil Ayers had been quietly at work for more than a month, after his last conversation with Reverend Moore. His quest for information had taken him to records bureaus and medical centers in two counties. He had interviewed doctors, nurses, toxicologists, and dozens of relatives about the deaths of Raymond Reid and James Taylor. He had made special note of what ICU nurses had revealed about Blanche Taylor's numerous visits to the bedside of Raymond Reid and the specially prepared snacks she so frequently brought her friend. Ayers had also sifted through banking and credit records. He had talked to Blanche frequently as his investigation progressed. His questioning had been general and down-Dixie polite. But the time had come for his questions to become a good deal more pointed. He also wanted an indisputable record of her responses. He attached a tape recorder to his office phone and called Blanche Moore.

How many times had she brought food she had made at home to Reid's hospital room during the four months he had been a patient? Ayers asked as the recorder preserved the conversation. "He especially liked your banana pudding and peanut butter milk shakes, I've been told," Ayers said.

There was a pause on the line. Then Blanche Moore slowly answered, "I have never in my life made a peanut butter milk shake. I wouldn't know how," she said. "The only food I ever fed to Raymond was hospital food. I don't know that he could have eaten anything else."

She had brought food to the hospital, Blanche confirmed, but only for the nurses. "On several occasions I was invited to eat with the nurses, like a little bruncheon. I brought some little things I thought they would enjoy. Just goodies. I took a tray of them." That must be what the investigator had heard about. Blanche had absolutely never fed Raymond Reid any food that she herself had prepared.

"Blanche, I should tell you that I may be obtaining a court order to exhume the body of Raymond Reid . . . and perhaps some others," Ayers said as the phone interview closed.

"I see," Blanche Moore said. She quickly ended the conversation.

Perhaps it had come time to seek some legal advice, Blanche Moore decided. Her financial situation was a great deal better now that she had received the proceeds of her one-third of the estate of Raymond Reid. It had amounted to nearly $45,000.

Reid's sons, Steve and Ray, Jr., had soon become introduced to a side of Blanche Moore they had never before encountered during her friendship with their dad. Within three days of Raymond Reid's funeral, Blanche had approached Ray, Jr., and said she intended to expedite distribution of the monies in his father's estate. She added another piece of information. "You know your daddy also wanted me to have a third of the insurance money," Blanche said.

The two sons were not aware at that time that the will made such provisions. When they received the insurance settlement of about $130,000, they gave Blanche one-third of that money—almost $45,000.

Ray Reid and his brother had not hesitated to see that Blanche received all the money their father had intended. They had visited his dying bedside. They had no intention of denying his final wish. "I want Blanche taken care of," he had told them.

What bothered the dead man's sons was Blanche's unseemly hurry to get her hands on her share. They felt her discussing the will within hours of their father's funeral was in poor taste. They were further put off by her daily calls that followed, asking if the check from the insurance company had arrived yet.

Then there was the settlement of the huge lawsuit Blanche had filed against Robert Hutton and the Kroger supermarket chain, rumored to have amounted to $275,000. The zone manager accused by Blanche of exposing himself had a different story about the incident. He said he had indeed removed the clothing Blanche had grabbed from him and dashed off with, but only because she had told him she wanted to have sex with him and had begun the motions of removing her own apparel. His admissions, over seven days in court, that he had other, more successful encounters with other female Kroger employees may have been the reason lawyers for the defense offered the undisclosed buyout of the $14 million suit.

There had been another interesting aspect to the case. To bolster her demand for the large sum asked in the suit, Blanche had consulted extensively with psychiatrist McNeil. He was prepared to testify that Blanche had suffered extreme emotional trauma as a result of Hutton's actions. It had rendered her incapable of forming new loving and trusting relationships. It had caused repressed anger toward the men in her life to bubble to the surface, beginning with her feelings toward her father. He had left Blanche's mother after a marriage of more than thirty years to take up with a younger woman. Blanche had also become aware and was deeply disturbed to learn that Dwight Moore had engaged in a lengthy affair with a church secretary, since moved to another state. But she was not so far away as to make some resumption impossible.

Blanche Moore began asking of friends their opinions of law firms in the county. Some recommended a firm in which criminal defense attorney Mitchell McEntire was a partner. Only days before, Dwight had asked her a most disturbing question. "Did you have anything to do with my becoming ill, Blanche?" he asked.

"How dare you ask that of me?" she angrily spat.

On June 13, 1989, the well-preserved body of Raymond Reid was exhumed by court order from Pine Hill Cemetery in Burlington. Within a week, Dr. John Butts, state medical examiner, said the grocery store manager had died of arsenic poisoning.

On July 6, the less well-preserved remains of James Napolean Taylor was removed from the same oak-shaded graveyard. An examination of body tissue, finger- and toenail clippings, and snips of hair revealed that he had perished from the same deadly poison as well.

Blanche Taylor Moore was arrested on July 18 by

authorities in Alamance County on counts of first-degree murder in those deaths. She was also charged with attempting to kill Dwight Moore. Later, another count of attempted murder would be lodged against her. Moore's earlier illness had been shown to also be the result of poisoning. Blanche Moore was ordered held without bail under North Carolina statutes that permit refusal of bond in some capital cases.

It would take months for the cases to come to trial. A shocked community soon began to hear why; more court orders for exhumations were being sought by lawmen and district attorneys in both counties. The body of Parker Davis Kiser, Sr., was taken from its grave in Oakwood Cemetery in Mebane. The balding, bespectacled, sometime preacher who had died at sixty-two of heart disease was found to have arsenic in his body. It was not enough to charge Blanche Moore with his 1966 death, but lab tests showed he had taken in significant amounts of the poison in the last week of his life.

Authorities next dug up the corpse of Isla Taylor, Blanche's mother-in-law, who had died after a week of rapid failure following five months of illness in 1970. Her body also showed high levels of arsenic, though it could not be confirmed as the cause of death.

Stunned friends with whom Blanche had worked at Kroger followed, with disbelief, rumors that the bodies of perhaps a half dozen co-workers with whom Blanche had been particularly friendly might also be exhumed. And there were yet other cases police were known to be investigating. One was the death at fifty-seven of Fred Vaughn, a bakery route driver who delivered product to a store where Blanche worked. Still another was John Reiber, an elderly member of Dwight Moore's congregation. In the end, only five bodies were removed from their graves, but the medical records of numerous others who had some close association with Blanche Moore were investigated. Among themselves, cops believed other charges could have been brought.

Blanche Moore had been a model prisoner during her stay in the Alamance County jail. She led a small Bible study class. She prayed with solid-brass street chicks with needle-pocked arms. She asked relatives and friends, still stoutly defending her, to bring small toiletry items and clothing for inmates less fortunate.

She had been catapulted into a ghoulish carnival kind of celebrity owing to the swirling media coverage of her arrest and the ongoing investigation. She wrote dozens of scripture-studded letters to supporters—more than forty to one elderly woman. She avoided reporters' questions when leaving courtrooms for numerous hearings and motions concerning her case, but she asked attorney McEntire to convey some of her feelings to the hotly inquisitive news media. How did she explain all those bodies and all that arsenic? reporters wanted to know.

"She says it's not normal," McEntire replied. "She says it's horrible . . . Everyone she has ever loved has been poisoned."

It was hard not to remark on how perfectly and elegantly turned out Blanche was at her every appearance. A sister-in-law, a licensed cosmetologist, was permitted to visit and do her hair. A local department store was providing the endless new, beautifully coordinated clothes she wore. Across the state, you needed only to say "Blanche." Everyone knew whom you meant.

One person followed the news accounts with an even deeper interest. Garvin Thomas was a small-time felon with serious alcohol and drug problems. At fifty-seven, he had nearly worn out his welcome with the few relatives still willing to have anything to do with him. He lived by himself, caring for a dozen cats he'd found on his wanderings, then brought home to his desolate lodgings in a condemned house. Severe pulmonary problems made it a gasping labor for him to breathe. His condition was complicated by diabetes and circulatory problems that caused his legs to swell painfully. Sometimes he would seek free treatment at a county hospital but would never stay the night. That would mean leaving his cats alone. He suffered another embarrassing medical stigma. Years of sucking on the cotton innards of medicated nasal inhalers for cheap highs had left him with a cruel disfigurement: He could no longer control his tongue. It lolled and wagged grotesquely when he tried to speak.

Thomas was fascinated by Blanche Moore. He told a friend, Jackie Williams, he believed he could scam a few badly needed dollars by getting messages through to the accused woman, conning his way into a friendship with her, then selling whatever exclusive tidbits that might surface from the relationship to news-hungry reporters and publications. Enquiring minds —much like his own—wanted to know.

He had already played a cunning opening gambit, Thomas told Williams. He had managed to persuade a jail guard to accept a small teddy bear as a gift for Blanche along with a gushy note that conveyed his best wishes and interest. He had asked the guard to pass on to Blanche another piece of information: Doctors had told him he didn't have a great deal of time to live. He very much wanted for he and Blanche to become friends before . . . well, while it was still possible. She would understand.

Chatty jailers had made Blanche Moore aware of

Garvin Thomas's attempts to reach her. Some who had become friendly teased her about her new "boyfriend." To cellmate Terry Edwards, Blanche chuckled that Thomas must be some kind of loony grandmother groupie but added that his overtures concerned her too. Men always had some perverse motive, she confided, and she, in particular, always seemed to fan their most lustful instincts though she did not intend to do so.

Cellmate Edwards smothered a grin. She let the matter drop. But she could not help but wonder about a small incident she witnessed in the jail's common room one day not long after. She had just finished reading the morning paper when Blanche sat down next to her and picked up the section Edwards had just finished. She watched as Blanche neatly folded and tore from a page a clipping from the obituary column. Edwards had been paying no special attention. Now she watched more closely. Blanche Moore extracted and pocketed the clipping. The obituary had been that of Garvin Thomas. So, he had died, Edwards found herself musing. And soft-hearted Blanche had wanted some small memento by which to remember him. People *were* strange, Edwards thought.

Defense attorney Mitchell McEntire read again the utterly amazing contents of the five-page letter he had just received at his office. He could barely contain his genuine joy about what the letter would mean to his client. He asked his secretary to connect him immediately with the office of the police chief. Within seconds, McEntire was relating to a stunned lawman the gist of the most incredible piece of evidence that had ever fallen into his hands.

"It's a confession from some man named Garvin Thomas. He said he's the person who did all the

poisoning . . . Blanche Taylor never even knew him
. . . or knew anything about what he was doing.
Blanche Moore is innocent," Mitchell McEntire said
in excited agitation.

The astonishing letter the apparently smitten, dying
loner had written fell from an undreamed of strato-
sphere with near nuclear impact onto the case of the
State of North Carolina v. Blanche Taylor Moore.

The date at the top of the letter indicated it had
been written on May 19. Thomas had died on May 22.
It was written in a shaky cursive hand, the language
sometimes hard to follow, the style choppy, sprinkled
with abbreviations and sparsely punctuated.

> My dearest darling,
>
> You do not even know me, but I have loved
> you for years.
>
> I only have a few days to live and I need to
> right my wrongs to you and others involved. You
> see I am responsible for these deaths. . . .
>
> I knew James from the antique shop and went
> there often. . . . Blanche, I was so jealous of you
> all the time and knew everything you did and
> you might say obsessed also. When he died and
> you were free I was so happy.
>
> Then there was Raymond and I hated him. He
> loved you too much. I used to follow you to his
> house in Kernersville. When he got sick I fol-
> lowed you to the hosp. Finally I could take no
> longer all the attention you gave him so I went in
> to visit him as a hosp. chaplain. . . . He was
> thirsty. I got him a coke and filled it with
> arsenic. . . .

Toward her current husband, Dwight Moore,
Garvin Thomas seemed to have harbored a special
dislike:

Later there was Dwight and I hated him even more so but you married the bastard. I still rode by that parsonage every day.

Thomas's letter said he had managed to slip heavy doses of arsenic into Pastor Moore's bedside ice-water pitcher when he had been hospitalized.

I just thought he would die like the others, but he didn't and this has gotten you in a lot of trouble and hurt you a lot. I can never make this up to you and your family. I love you too much but the plan failed me.

You see I have been obsessed and could not bear the thought of anyone having you. . . .

I have asked for this letter to be mailed after my funeral by a friend. God knows I pray this last request is granted.

I pray and asked for forgiveness so darling please forgive me. With me gone you can at least have a life . . . My baby I must go. . . . Please forgive me. . . . Now at least you know what happened. . . .

Garvin Thomas appeared to have made yet another blood-chilling revelation as he waited for his own death.

My final plan was to get everyone that has hurt you like both D.A.'s . . . the Reid family . . . Dwight Moore . . . even the man in your sex case. . . .

Goodbye my darling forever . . . keep those pretty brown eyes sparkling . . . love always . . . bye, bye baby . . .

183

The letter had reached its startling, confessional end but added a strangely gratuitous paragraph: an erotically explicit, vivid sexual fantasy coupling Moore and Thomas in torrid, uninhibited lovemaking. Maddened, it seemed, as he faced his lonely phantom-of-the-choir-loft death, Thomas could only reach out with a pen to quench his thirsty passion.

(In the courtroom, when the letter was submitted into evidence, jurors alone were permitted to read that concluding paragraph. It was passed among their ranks for study. Some of them snickered and rolled eyes toward the ceiling. Some quickly passed it on to the next, unwilling to appear to be dwelling on the molten obscenity it contained.)

There was yet one more curious passage in the letter. Garvin Thomas seemed to want to make it irrefutably clear he was the author of the letter in the event the handwriting in his thunderclap, providential confession ever became an issue: "This is the same handwriting . . . this time worse because I am sick," he had stated.

The prosecution team retained a calm public face when the blockbuster letter appeared in the ring. They had spent exhausting months gathering boxfuls of evidence all pointing in one clearly marked direction. It seemed improbable—no, wildly impossible—that everything that led to the door of Blanche Moore had been mere coincidence, chance circumstance that led them to fix blame on an innocent woman.

When their copy of the Thomas confession was handed to them, a sea of suspicious speculation had already begun to churn. "My first guess was that Blanche Moore had persuaded some friend or some new fan to write a letter she had dictated," prosecutor Janet Branch said. "When I read the crude pornography in the last paragraph, I was certain she had a hand in it. It fit exactly the ego fixation she had about her own sexual desirability. She truly believed men had some magnetic sexual attraction to her."

There was one thing, however, that assistant district attorney Branch had not prepared herself to believe: that Blanche Moore might have been reckless enough, arrogant enough, to have written the supposed Thomas letter herself in her jail cell, taking the desperate gamble her forgery would not be found out.

As a matter of routine, the question of handwriting would be raised. It would be an important issue. Branch received court permission to obtain the forty letters Moore had written to elderly Doris Pender, her pen pal. They were rushed by deputies to her home late at night. Branch wearily took the samples of Moore's handwriting to bed with her, spreading the letters around herself in a fan. The prosecutor knew she was not qualified to offer scientific opinions, but she was curious to form her own opinions. Near the Moore letters, Branch placed the admission from Thomas. Janet Branch began to read. Midway through, she bolted upright in the bed. Her sleepiness vanished. She read again, compared again. Then she filled her quiet bedroom with a piercing shriek. "My God, Blanche, you didn't . . . you couldn't have been that absolutely dumb. You wrote this damn letter yourself!"

Branch made an excited call to another member of the DA's staff, Vincent Rabil. They had worked together on the case. "Vince, you're not going to believe this . . ." she began. She told a whooping Rabil the details of her discovery. Over and over in the letters she had written to her friend, Moore had used the abbreviation "hosp." for hospital. The alleged Thomas confession used the same odd truncation. Eight times in her jailhouse correspondence,

Blanche used the short-handed rec'd for received. It, too, was found in the Thomas script. Blanche Moore favored a curious double-dotted letter *i*. How impossibly coincidental that Thomas used that same uncommon jot!

When the Thomas letter took on the stature of evidence, it was mercilessly torn to bits by handwriting experts. Other refuting evidence was introduced. Pages of a diary kept by Garvin Thomas showed that he wrote in neatly printed block letters. He signed his name in cursive only on legal papers.

A stepsister of the dead man was called to testify. Until the time he had confided his sappy plot to exploit Moore, he had never before mentioned her name. Strange for a man overwhelmed by obsessive passion. That he could have stalked and poisoned the men in Moore's life over a lengthy span of years was unbelievable to his relatives. Janie McCrickard said her stepbrother was being used as a dupe in his grave. "They found the perfect candidate to dump all this on," she said.

McCrickard added a wry sort of eulogy to the outsider life Garvin Thomas had lived. He had always enjoyed playing jokes on the establishment. "If Blanche had asked Garvin to write this letter, he probably would have, but he never would have killed anybody," McCrickard said.

The jury never heard another damning discovery investigators made. The envelope in which the letter had been mailed bore a marked similarity to an expensive type of stationery Blanche had bought at a local department store. It was not necessary. After the trial, jurors said they were totally convinced the Thomas letter was a clumsy fake written by Blanche Moore.

Defense lawyer McEntire fought back with expert

testimony of his own. A veteran handwriting expert who had trained some of the prosecution's professionals in their skills said flatly Blanche Moore had not written the letter. McEntire produced a minister who said a tearful Thomas had appeared in his study six months before his death and said he had committed a great wrong, that he needed to right it before his death. Thomas had also once visited McEntire's law offices, acting in much the same way. They had not known the importance of what the anguished man was trying to reveal to them until the letter had arrived after his death.

Prosecutor Branch called the defense contentions about the letter far-fetched. "I'll tell you who wrote that letter," Branch thundered. "The defendant's own best friend—herself!"

The state of North Carolina braided a noose of conviction from the threads of testimony offered by more than fifty witnesses as prosecutors Branch, Rabil, and their boss, District Attorney Warren Sparrow, continued to link Blanche Moore—and only Blanche Moore—to the deaths by poisoning of the victims who had so loved and trusted her. Finally, that day had come when the cool, unflappable, fashion-plate grandmother would take the stand on her own behalf to deny, often in icy outrage, that anyone had ever died by her hand.

Prosecutor Janet Branch was waiting. She could not believe it when the defendant denied ever having brought home-cooked treats to the hospital and fed them to Raymond Reid. "The nurses had seen her. She had heard them testify. She could just as easily admitted that she had prepared and fed those snacks to Reid. That would not have proven there was poison in them. Mrs. Moore could have simply said, 'Yes, so what?' but she thought she could bluff her way through. That proved to be her fatal character flaw;

her arrogant belief that no one could doubt her sick lies because of the false face she had presented for so many years."

The defendant was dressed in black widow's weed. She again began to sign her name Blanche Taylor. Her husband, Dwight Moore, had filed for a separation. The media had fixed on her stoic, glacial lack of emotion as she listened to the heart-wrenching details of the agonizing death of Raymond Reid, the painful horror that Reverend Moore had been put through, the cruel cutting short of her first husband's life. None of those recountings seemed to move her. Now, with a jury of six men and six women forming their final impressions, Blanche's tightly gripped calm seemed to waver. She wept as she spoke of Raymond Reid: "We planned to be married and we would have been married had Raymond lived," she wept. "Raymond, I can truly say, was the best friend I ever had. And after we were friends, we became romantically involved. I loved both James Taylor and Raymond Reid."

"And Dwight Moore?" Branch asked.

"I cared for Dwight," the defendant answered. "I know arsenic was found in these people, but I did not put it there."

And what of Anti-Ant, the poison that worked so wondrously well?

"I've never had any of it either in my home or in my hands," Blanche answered.

In the immediate weeks following Raymond Reid's death, Branch wanted to know what Blanche's financial condition was like. Was it true that her bank balance had dropped dramatically—one account holding a mere $102? "That's all the money you had in the world, wasn't it, Mrs. Moore?" Branch asked.

"You might say that," Blanche replied.

Why had she refused permission for an autopsy to be performed on Raymond Reid?

"I can't recall anyone speaking to me about an autopsy. I would not have opposed one," she answered.

She had even tried to persuade Raymond Reid from naming her in his will, Blanche Moore said. "I told him, 'Raymond, I don't think that's necessary at this time,' but he was persistent. He wanted a will done."

The ruby and diamond ring that Dwight Moore had given her as a token of his love had been a gift she had not really wanted to accept, Blanche Moore testified. "It was a pretty ring. He had offered it to me and I had refused it. As a matter of fact, I was angry with him for buying that ring."

Reverend Dwight Moore cast his eyes downward when his wife described what had been for him a supremely happy occasion: the ceremony that had united them in marriage. "Well, it was not really that much of a wedding," Blanche Moore said.

Attorneys completed their cases. It became time to sum up for the jury what had been heard over all those days in Judge William Freeman's packed courtroom.

Blanche Moore's cocounsel, David Tamer, came straight to the point. "There's no denying these people had a snootful of arsenic. . . . We would be conducting a defense in bad faith if we tried to challenge that," Tamer told the jury. "Our case is not predicated on what killed these individuals, but who killed them, and we just don't think the state has proven that," he added.

Mitchell McEntire responded in summation to Branch's contention that the possibility that the Garvin Thomas letter was too far-fetched to believe. "It doesn't sound as far-fetched as saying Blanche Moore, who's led a good and decent life, did it. She's not the kind of lady who does these things," McEntire argued.

The prosecution had produced not a single witness who could ever place Blanche Moore with arsenic in her hands, the defense team argued. A good-hearted woman, motivated only by her deep sense of Christian duty had visited the bedside of a man dying, whom she would be unable to marry because of his fatal illness. How could that conceivably make her suspect in his tragic death? "The only consistency the state has is that three men she loved best had arsenic in them. It's a greater tragedy for her than anyone. And they've compounded that by dragging her down and putting her in jail," McEntire said.

The prosecution painted the life of Blanche Taylor Moore on a different canvas in darker, more sinister hues. "Poisoning is a cloak and dagger kind of crime. What better cloak to wear than a cloak of appearing to be loving, appearing to be caring, and appearing to be kind? The fundamental picture is death by arsenic, the only link is the defendant." Arsenic poisoning is a signature crime, the prosecution hammered. "The probability that these crimes were committed by different people is zero."

And the supposed letter of confession from Garvin Thomas, what was the jury to make of that? "The defendant wants you to believe she was followed for eighteen or nineteen years by an obsessive lover who loved her from afar but never approached. That pathetic ploy was nothing more than the product of Mrs. Moore's jailhouse imagination," Janet Branch said with stinging sarcasm. "It takes a special person to do that. Someone who can look you in the eye and say to you, 'I didn't bring any food from home for Raymond.'"

Branch continued the scathing attack. "What a

desperate day it must have been for the defendant when she realized that the state was onto this hoax. Her only shred of evidence gone . . . decimated . . . blown away."

Branch pointed an accusing finger at the woman whose wrathful nemesis she had become. "She must be held accountable, no matter what kind of a facade she presents." Branch walked slowly to the defense table where Moore sat. She stood mere inches away, face-to-face with the accused. Their eyes sought each other out in another eerie moment and remained locked. "Living spirits are in this courtroom surrounding us all," the prosecutor said in rising tones. "All of those spirits are turning and saying it's you . . . it's you . . . it's you who's guilty. And out of those throngs of spirits steps the ghost of Raymond Reid, and he says, 'Blanche, you murdered me and all I ever did was love you. Why did you murder me?'"

Blanche Moore's eyes followed the prosecutor as she poised herself once again before the jury and spoke her final accusation. "If she had succeeded in killing Dwight Moore, the murders of James Taylor and Raymond Reid would have remained her sleeping secret. If she had left Dwight Moore alone, James Taylor and Raymond Reid would still today lie in their graves undiscovered. She poisoned one man too many. She outsmarted herself," Branch said and returned to the prosecution table.

The jury returned its verdict in the case of the slaying of Raymond Moore. Their judgment was guilty, the sentence, death.

Outside the courtroom, as Branch made her way down the long reach of steps, she paused for a moment to hear reporters interviewing Reverend Dwight Moore. Why had he come each day to the trial, hadn't he gone through enough pain already?

Moore steadied himself against the cane he held in a numbed hand. "I wanted to find out a little more about the woman I was married to," the small-town pastor answered. "I've learned a lot," he added.

Janet Branch walked on then. Tears had begun to fill her eyes. She did not want them to be seen.

9

Marilyn Plantz

TRINA PLANTZ FILLED THE LETTER WITH ALL THE LOVE AND loneliness—and all the confusion—that ached so terribly in her nine-year-old heart.

She knew her dad had gone to heaven after the awful accident that had made everybody cry so much. But now Mommy had gone away to some place, too, and Trina and her six-year-old brother, Chris, couldn't go to see her.

Grandma and Grandpa Plantz had tried to explain what had happened, but it was more than Trina could understand. Chris just cried. He wanted his big, laughing, rough-housing dad to come home from wherever he had gone and to hurry and bring Mommy back, too.

Trina put her pencil back to the sheet of lined notebook paper. This was a very special letter.

"Dear Mommy," Trina began, "I love you with all my heart. I miss our big family when we was all together." Then Trina asked her mom the question that was troubling her so. "Why was daddy killed? Tell me, please."

* * *

193

Marilyn Kay Plantz, twenty-eight, would never answer Trina's question. She said she didn't know why Jim Plantz, her husband of eleven years, had been beaten senseless by two teenagers armed with baseball bats taken from her children's bedroom. Her husband was then driven, still alive, in his pickup truck to a remote road outside Oklahoma City, Oklahoma, doused with gasoline, and set afire while his assailants watched and laughed as their battered victim desperately struggled to free himself from the engulfing flames. He spent his last moments on earth in a hellish, monstrous inferno.

Oklahoma City police detective Ralph Gibson said he knew why James Earl Plantz had been so cruelly slain: Marilyn Plantz didn't want to be married to Jim anymore.

She wanted him dead in a way that looked like an accident or fathomless foul play in order to collect on a $319,000 insurance policy. Marilyn Plantz wanted the money so she and her eighteen-year-old boyfriend could buy a little piece of land in Texas, someplace where it wouldn't matter too much that a white mother of two and a black crack cocaine addict just wanted to be in love and left alone.

Marilyn Kay Plantz was leading a life filled with secrets and dark shadows. No one is certain exactly when it began or why. Some who knew her best still find it almost impossible to believe. In 1986, Marilyn began cruising the tough urban ghetto strips of Midwest City, looking for excitement, for forbidden kinds of love.

Marilyn's racy striped Camaro became a familiar sight when night fell. The streets swarmed with hustlers, hookers, pushers and addicts, thieves and pimps, awakening to their night's work. As she would near ESA Park, near 23rd and Midwest Boulevard— the hardening heart of the dying neighborhood—

Marilyn would slow the sporty vehicle to a crawl, jack up the volume on her raucous radio, and roll down her windows—a signal of invitation to the needle park's sundown citizens that she wasn't just passing by, that she wanted something that dangerous place had to offer. For Marilyn Plantz, that something was the company, the flattery, the attention, the secret sexual thrills, she discovered she was able to buy from the muscular, streetwise young black men who would saunter over to her car to find out why the heavy-set, plain-faced white woman was making it so patently clear she wasn't just passing through the neighborhood.

Marilyn would drop off Trina and Chris with an obliging neighbor before foraying out. She would pick them up before dawn, arriving home sometimes only minutes before Jim returned to their comfortable Midwest City house from his job as a night pressroom supervisor for the *Daily Oklahoman* in adjacent Oklahoma City.

Neighbors like James Taylor thought Marilyn's nightly exoduses from the family home were a little unusual but not really any of his business. Besides, what Taylor saw when Marilyn, Jim, and their kids were together was as normal as a blue Oklahoma sky. "They seemed like a very happy couple," Taylor would later say. "If they were having any family problems, you couldn't tell it. The kids loved him like crazy. He built them a beautiful playhouse out in the backyard. They seemed very ordinary. They fit into the neighborhood nicely."

But nothing inside the Plantz home was as ordinary as it seemed. Marilyn could no longer account for how she spent much of the money her husband gave her to pay the bills. Large amounts of it had gone to buy crack cocaine, expensive gifts for teenage lovers, nights on the town on Midwest Boulevard, cheap motel rooms that added up through hungry desire. Then there had been a very strange burglary at the Plantz home. Several of Jim's expensive guns had been taken, but not much else had been disturbed.

"It seemed like they knew exactly what they wanted and went straight to it," Jim Plantz told neighbor Taylor. "How could they have known where to look? I had the guns all put away."

At least one neighbor knew a secret. When Jim Plantz had gone away by himself for a few days, Marilyn had a visitor who stayed with her. His name was William Clifford Bryson. He was eighteen, a black high-school dropout who lived with his dad on Midwest Boulevard. Marilyn called him Cliff. They had been lovers for eighteen months. He had a friend who also came by the house when Jim Plantz was away. His name was Clinton McKimble. He was also eighteen years old. He had been Marilyn's lover, too. Sometimes he still was.

Jim Plantz had gently but firmly told Marilyn she had to become a better manager of the family's money. Just a few months ago he had taken on an additional $100,000 in life insurance. They had to watch their pennies, he mildly admonished. Marilyn brooded darkly. She feared her husband might soon ask harder, harsher questions about where their money was going.

Cliff Bryson stormed out of the family house on Midwest Boulevard, still fuming from another argument with his father. William Bryson, Sr., was a conscientious dad, doing his best to raise a decent son on the mean rookery streets that surrounded them. Cliff had not been able to conceal from his father's watchful eye the unexplained new clothes, the extra pocket money, the frequent calls from school guidance counselors that telegraphed trouble. Finally, he had seen for himself the cause of his son's disinterest in the wholesome pursuits Bryson Senior tried to encourage. His heart sank when he saw Cliff at the wheel of the shiny sports car. His free hand was draped possessively around the shoulder of a dowdy-looking white woman clearly too old for his son. When the elder Bryson confronted his son about what he had seen, he was pleased that, at least, Cliff made no denials. He even told his father the woman was married and had two children. He added that he had been seeing Marilyn Plantz for more than a year.

"You're going to get yourself in a fine bunch of trouble," William Bryson warned his son. "It's wrong to fool around with someone else's wife."

"The bitch loves me," Cliff Bryson snapped back. "I can't do nothing to stop that."

William Bryson, Sr., wished he could have.

Some of Cliff Bryson's friends had started to worry about him, too. There were rumors on the boulevard that Cliff had approached several of the strip's toughest tough guys with a very scary proposition: He was looking to hire someone to take a contract on the dude that was married to his girlfriend. Cliff said it was worth $10,000, but there was one big string attached.

"What is it?" Rod Farris asked.

"She'll tell you, man. C'mon," Cliff Bryson answered.

Marilyn Plantz's sleek Camaro was parked at the side of a convenience store on 23rd. Clint McKimble was there with her as Bryson approached with an inquisitive Rod Farris in tow. Marilyn was business-like and straight to the point. "I want my old man offed," she said. "But there's one thing. It's gotta look like an accident or we only get half the money."

Rodney Farris was a player but not when the stakes were murder. He had come along to satisfy his curiosity about the rumors he'd heard, and he wanted to take a look at the woman people on the strip had started calling "the crazy white chick."

"I ain't in to icing anybody," Farris said, but he accepted an invitation to join the trio at Marilyn Plantz's house. They stopped and picked up forty dollars worth of rock before Marilyn peeled the big-engined Camaro on the boulevard and pointed the car toward her comfortable suburban home with the well-built playhouse in the backyard.

When they got there, Bryson and McKimble got high. If they couldn't find anyone to do Jim in, they'd do it themselves, they loudly boasted. McKimble had an idea: take Jim Plantz out on a fishing trip and then knock him out with an oar and throw him over the side of the boat.

"That could work," Marilyn Plantz said. "He doesn't know how to swim."

Farris smiled inwardly as the evening advanced when he watched Bryson and Marilyn Platz kiss and cuddle on a living room couch. "What's with all this?" Farris asked Bryson when their paths crossed during a beer call in the kitchen.

"She's crazy gone on me, man," Bryson answered. "When we get the dough, we're gonna boogey on outta here . . . head down to Texas and get a little ranch, one with a pond. Then we gonna kick back, relax, and do some super shit."

"You gotta be shuckin' me, man. You ain't gonna off anybody over that broad. Get real, man."

Their conversation was cut short. McKimble flew into the kitchen.

"Someone just pulled up in the driveway, man. It's gotta be Jim."

"We're gonna take him right goddam now," Bryson said. He threw open a kitchen counter drawer, rummaging through it until he found a large knife.

McKimble spotted a hammer on top of the refrigerator and quickly grabbed it.

A neighbor knocked on the door. Could Marilyn help out with the kids' school car pool next week, she wanted to know. Rod Farris exhaled a pent-up breath.

"I'm outta here, man," he said.

Late summer 1988 had come to the Oklahoma City metro area, and its half million residents were enjoying a brief break in the season's scorching heat. Up around Tecumseh, an hour's drive away, small-town people and farmers like the Earl Plantz family and Marilyn's folks, Jesse and Normanda Sellers were looking forward to a final family picnic on Labor Day before the grandkids had to head back to school. In each home, treasured photo albums told the saga of their children and their grandchildren. A white-bound volume with gold script on the front held the pictures of Jim and Marilyn's wedding. High school yearbooks showed them together. How wonderful it was, both families felt, that they had fallen in love so young, knowing that soon that each wanted only to be with the other.

Marilyn Plantz had taken her copy of that wedding album down from a closet shelf. She showed the pictures to Bryson and McKimble. She wanted them to fix her husband's face firmly in their mind. She had a plan.

Jim Plantz drove his white 1984 Nissan pickup truck along virtually the same route every day when he went to work. He used a shortcut that took him along a road that was usually lightly traveled.

"Tomorrow you steal a car. You follow him. You take this gun and you shoot him. The cops think he was robbed. Got it?" Marilyn told her two boyfriends.

They didn't. When Bryson returned from the

scrubbed attempt, he said there was heavy traffic on the road and that they had lost her husband's vehicle. Marilyn apparently wasn't so sure. Maybe Bryson and McKimble weren't as tough as they talked. She gave Bryson the humbling task of approaching Rod Farris again, this time offering him $50,000 to kill Jim Plantz.

"Tell him it'll just be him involved, not you and Clint," she told a smarting Bryson.

Farris couldn't be reached. He was in jail for stealing a car. Marilyn grew impatient. Bryson said he'd take care of the problem and he'd do it that night.

Trina and Chris gave their dad a big hug as he left for his job in the pressroom that night, Friday, August 26, 1988. Chris chased his pop with happy waves partway down the driveway. It would be near sunrise before Jim made his weary way home. The big presses would be straining, turning out the inside sections of Sunday's *Oklahoman* in addition to putting the Saturday paper to bed.

Marilyn Plantz waited until after dark that night before dropping Chris and Trina off with their baby-sitter for the night. She picked up Bryson and McKimble at ESA Park shortly before nine. They stopped along the strip and shopped for crack, choosing two large rocks. Another stop was made for beer. They drove to Marilyn's house.

Jim Plantz called home, a little after one A.M.

"Is it raining out there?" he asked. "I'll be home around five. I love you a whole bunch, honey," he added. "Kiss the kids for me."

Marilyn Plantz put the telephone's receiver back in its cradle on the drum table near the bed. She reached toward the hard body of the young man lying next to her. Her face grazed the smooth steel ribbons of his stomach. With the hand that wore her wedding band she threw back her hair and feasted on the warm, gushing essence of the boy who'd promised to kill for her before daylight came.

McKimble slept on the living room couch. He awoke pleasantly, enjoying the sensation of the smooth hand that silently entered his slumber, tugging his shorts down. He felt the pulsing wetness of a tongue flicking against his thighs in the darkness. He smiled at the sound of his friend, Cliff, snoring in the bedroom from which his visitor had just come.

Marilyn had picked up Trina and Chris after she had arrived home. They tumbled from their babysitter's warm bed to their own, unaware there were guests in the house. Marilyn walked to their overflowing closet. She picked out two baseball bats their dad had bought for them for backyard slow pitch fun. She carried them with her into the kitchen and laid them on the counter.

She woke Bryson and McKimble. "Get into the kitchen," she whispered. "He'll be here any minute."

Jim Plantz had stopped to pick up milk, the special doughnuts Trina and Chris liked on Saturday mornings, a loaf of bread, some lunch meat, and a few other odds and ends. He liked the ride home from work in the predawn stillness and dew. He loved to wake the kids and catch their first smile of the day and keep it in his mind, like the pictures in his wallet. Marilyn always looked especially pretty to him then.

He entered through the side door leading into the kitchen. With his right hand, he began to ease down the bag of groceries. With his left, he reached for the oval ring that held his pressroom keys. He reached toward a peg on the wall where he always hung them.

Marilyn Plantz's heart was pounding. Her throat was dry. She shakily made her way from her bedroom to the children's. She entered the room and closed the door behind her, her palms still pressed against it. She had told her teenage lovers she could not watch them slay her husband.

Jim Plantz was whistling. Cliff Bryson was waiting. He swung the baseball bat Jim Plantz had bought for his kids against Jim Plantz's head. Bones broke, blood spattered. McKimble struck with the other bat.

Jim Plantz cried out a haunting, heroic word, "Marilyn?" he said through the blood filling his mouth. He thought something terrible had happened to his wife and children and now their assailants were attacking him. He tried to fight off his attackers, desperately trying to make his way toward the bedrooms down the hallway.

Bryson and McKimble struck him more than twenty times. He fell to his back, no longer able to counter the attack. The two boys continued their rain of blows until it seemed impossible that brawny Plantz could still be alive. Marilyn Plantz came hesitantly into the kitchen. Jim could not see her. His eyes had been beaten shut, but he moaned.

Marilyn exploded in a fury at Bryson and McKimble. "For Christ's sake, he's still alive, and he doesn't look like he's been in an accident . . . He looks like he's had the crap beaten out of him," she snapped. "Get him out in his pickup. Take him some place out in the country and set the damn truck on fire . . . Get the hell going. I'll stay here and clean up the bloody mess you made."

Bryson and McKimble tugged Plantz's fractured body out the side door and heaved it into the back of the pickup truck. His blood was smeared on both of them. Marilyn Plantz rushed back into the master bedroom. She found two of her husband's jogging suits.

"Here, for God's sake, put these on," Marilyn said, thrusting the clean clothes at the murderers.

McKimble gunned the engine of Marilyn's Camaro. Bryson slid behind the wheel of the Nissan pickup. He motioned for McKimble to follow him. They sped. It was nearly five-thirty now. They wanted to finish their work in darkness. In fifteen minutes they had arrived at the thoroughfare that divided small-town Midwest City from bustling Oklahoma City. They had attacked their victim in one jurisdiction; they would murder him in another.

The remote street where they stopped was in a lonely, wooded, rolling-hilled area. No traffic passed at that early hour. The killers slid Plantz's groaning body from the truck's bed and half walked him to the cab. They shoved him behind the steering wheel, gripped his bloody hands to it, then slammed the door. They stuffed a rag in the gas tank and lit it, cursing when it did not blow up the truck the way it did on TV shows. Then they emptied a gas can from the truck's back onto the semiconscious man. Bryson lit a clutch of paper matches, poised to run as he threw them inside the cab. Both he and McKimble watched in fascination as Plantz rose up, wraithlike through the flames, turned to his left, and pushed open the closed truck door. His left leg moved slowly out the door. It came within inches of touching the pavement. Bryson and McKimble watched the macabre scene in mounting terror. They fled.

The pair made a stop before returning to Marilyn Plantz's house. With the eight dollars they had taken from Jim's pocket, they stopped at a 7-Eleven and ate their fill of ham and cheese sandwiches, washing them down with fresh-squeezed orange juice.

Marilyn fumed at their lateness. She could have used their help. The blood on the carpet that led from the kitchen had been impossible to clean up completely, so had the blood on the bats. Besides, the clock was running. Within minutes she needed to make the worried phone call to police, telling them her husband had failed to arrive home from work. That was very unlike Jim. He was very punctual, she would tell police. She was beside herself with worry. She dashed the murderers back to Midwest Boulevard. Back home, she called police at six-thirty A.M. Trina and Chris were up, waiting for Daddy and the doughnuts.

Marilyn Plantz's eye sharply roamed the kitchen one final time. "Jesus!" There, under the kitchen table, almost out of sight, was the ring with Jim's work keys. My God, there was blood on them. She shooed the kids toward the TV set, snatched up the crimson-flecked key ring, and hurriedly hid them in the first place that came to mind: the bottom of her lingerie drawer in the bedroom she and Jim had shared.

A passing motorist, sleepily heading for work, discovered the blazing white pickup truck. He stopped and made a 911 call. Firefighters from Oklahoma City rolled and quickly quenched the blaze that had almost destroyed the front end of the vehicle.

They discovered Jim's body, charred beyond recognition, grotesquely poised in his desperate attempt to escape his white-hot death.

Authorities put together Marilyn's report of a husband who had failed to return home at his usual time and the grisly find out near Sooner Road. Jim's dental records were quickly obtained by pathologists. They matched the horribly burned body in the autopsy room. The vehicle registration checked, too. Police had the sad duty of informing Marilyn Plantz of the reason her husband had not returned home on time. He had been the victim of some freak accident.

But as the medical examination of the case continued, doctors were troubled by some of the injuries to Plantz's body they discovered. The pickup truck had not been involved in a crash, yet Jim Plantz's corpse was covered with trauma wounds. A massive radial concussion had somehow been inflicted on his skull. His forearms were shattered at places usually found when someone being beaten threw their arms up to ward off blows. Tests used to determine the amounts of carbon monoxide present in the body showed a level of 26 percent. Jim Plantz had been alive when the flames enveloped him. What combination of events could have resulted in him being found seated behind the steering wheel suffering the incredible trauma wounds covering his body? Jim Plantz had clearly been the victim of foul play. The case was turned over to homicide investigators at the Oklahoma City police department.

Detective Ralph Gibson had spent more than a dozen years discovering that most of the mysteries that pass across a police investigator's desk do not turn out to be as puzzling at the conclusion as they do at the inception.

"At first glance, the Plantz case had all the earmarks of a real whodunit," Gibson recalled. "But that's the exact time when experience tells you to start looking for the most logical answers, even when there are a lot of tempting, exotic trails that someone has thrown out for you to follow instead of tracks that lead to them.

"When someone plans a murder, especially one they want to look like an accident, they never seem to understand that the victim hasn't read their murder script and probably won't do the things they had imagined when they were hatching their plot.

"Maybe the killers of Jim Plantz imagined they would kill him with one or two blows to the head with the baseball bat. Even then it's hard to imagine what kind of 'accident' that would appear to have been. But, as it turned out, Jim was tough enough to take numerous blows from the bat and still remain alive. Now the plan has completely gone out the window.

Now the killers have decided they'll take him some-where, put him in his car as though he were driving it, and pour a flammable liquid on him. The kind of 'accident' or even foul play they had originally imag-ined they could create to explain his death became so improbable in the end that you have to start looking first at the last people you might suspect: a suburban housewife with a happy little family, two cute little kids, and a supposed happy marriage. In this case, that was Marilyn Plantz."

The case was already two days old when it found its way to Gibson's desk. It was the matter of chance that it did. Gibson had been assigned to another complex murder investigation. A skillful, quick deduction by the veteran detective cleared the case in less than thirty-six hours. He was free to turn his abilities toward the still-baffling death of James Plantz.

Ralph Gibson reviewed the report from the medical examiner's office. He began to work the phones. From Jim Plantz's employer he learned of the large life insurance policies the slain man had carried. He especially noted they had just been substantially increased. He pored over the details of Marilyn Plantz's original report to police that her husband was missing. She called only about an hour and a half past his normal arrival time. What had made her think something terrible had happened? Why hadn't she called the *Oklahoman*'s pressroom to see what time he had left or if he were still there for some work-related reason? Odd, Gibson thought, that she should have jumped so quickly to the conclusion that it was necessary to alert police to a situation that really wasn't that unusual.

When Gibson went to the Plantz home, his antenna was risen again by the newly widowed woman's near complete composure as they spoke about her husband's horrifying death. It seemed apparent to Gibson that Marilyn Plantz wanted to make the detective's visit as brief as possible. Was there something in the house she was afraid his trained eyes might discover?

Gibson made it a point to take in the room with an investigative eye. He noticed the furnishings of the living room where they sat were comfortable but not new. One item in the room, however, did have the appearance of newness. An eight-by-ten area rug covered the wall-to-wall carpeting near the kitchen's entrance. The living room carpeting, while again, not brand-new, seemed clean and in good condition. Gibson wondered what "accident" the area rug might be covering. Perhaps some food was spilled as it was being carried from the kitchen to the living room. Then again, perhaps the new rug was covering something else.

Why did she call the police so quickly, Gibson asked. Hadn't Jim ever been late arriving home before without necessarily letting her know?

Gibson's questions seemed to be making Marilyn Plantz very uncomfortable. Neighbors had told investigators they saw her leaving just about every night shortly after her husband had gone to work. Where did she go?

Marilyn said she was an inveterate shopper and enjoyed browsing through the malls. What malls were open at three o'clock, four o'clock, in the morning, Gibson wondered. There were none.

Not long ago, when Jim had taken a short trip by himself, had she had any houseguests or someone doing odd jobs, specifically a young black man?

No, Marilyn Plantz replied, she would never have anyone in her house when her husband was not there.

"Have you two had any quarrels recently? Is your

marriage a good one? Could your husband have been involved with some other woman?" Gibson queried.

"We've been very happy. We've been married eleven years. Our sex life is great. I don't think Jim would need to see any other women," Marilyn Plantz answered.

Ralph Gibson left the house wondering about two important things. Did the new rug in the Plantz house have any sinister meaning? Why had the young widow denied that a black teenager had been seen at her home while her husband was away on a trip? He began to pursue both of those troubling questions. Street unit cops were asked to put their ears to the ground in the rough neighborhoods around the strip. Perhaps the kid who had been seen at the house could be turned up. Gibson requested the courts to give him permission to examine checking account records of the Plantzes'. He had a hunch about that rug. He wanted to know when it had been purchased. What he discovered confirmed a growing suspicion.

Marilyn Plantz had written a $44.96 check to a nearby Wal-Mart discount store only minutes after they opened at nine A.M. on August 26, only a few hours after her husband's savage beating and monstrous death by fire. Records showed it was the very first sale of the day. Marilyn Plantz had to have been waiting outside the store when it opened. Only scant hours earlier, she had been on the phone to police telling of her husband's failure to come home from work. What could possibly have taken her away from her worried vigil at home? The sudden, strange urge to buy a cheap area rug?

Ralph Gibson returned to the courts. He wanted a search warrant for the Plantz house.

Gibson believed the unknown black youth who had been seen at the Plantz house held a key to the mystery. The earlier rumors that had made their way up and down the boulevard about the pudgy white woman who wanted to hire a gun had circulated widely. More astonishing was the carelessness of Cliff Bryson and Clint McKimble once they returned to the neighborhood. They recklessly began talking about— even bragging—that they had decided to commit the murder themselves. From the shadows, from informants, plainclothes cops soon began to pick up on those swaggering confessions. Rod Farris was brought downtown. He told Gibson about Marilyn's attempt to hire him. Two other 23rd Street regulars to whom the killers had boasted were also located. They told Gibson what Bryson and McKimble had told them in the early morning hours of August 26.

Michael Kendrick ran into Bryson at about seven that morning. Bryson's tennis shoes were flecked with blood. So were his hands. "He told me he did it . . . he killed Jim," Kendrick said. "He said there was a bundle of insurance money . . . him and the woman were going to go to Texas and get married."

Rod Farris expressed shock. "I thought she was serious, but I didn't think them two would do it."

Ralph Gibson placed the search warrant in his jacket and headed back to the Plantz home. This time he was accompanied by crime scene technicians. Marilyn Plantz expressed surprise and shock when the area rug was rolled back to reveal the large blood-stained areas of the carpet that she had been unable to wash away. When the inch-by-inch search turned up the ring holding Jim's work keys hidden at the bottom of her lingerie drawer, Marilyn Plantz said she had no idea how that blood-spattered item could have gotten there.

"You said Jim didn't come home that morning. How could the keys he needed for work have gotten here then, and why would they buried beneath your underwear?" Gibson asked.

"I have no idea," she answered.

"Do you know two young men named Bryson and McKimble?"

"No . . . I've never known anyone by those names," she responded.

"They say you hired them to kill your husband. They also say they've both had sex with you."

"They're lying, or they're crazy," Marilyn Plantz said.

Ralph Gibson arrested the now frightened house-wife whose clandestine life had suddenly been laid bare. Bryson and McKimble were arrested within hours. Both denied any involvement in Jim Plantz's killing at first, but when McKimble was told how much evidence had already been gathered to prove they were lying, McKimble wanted to know if the cops wanted to cut a deal. They'd talk to Bob Macy, the DA, Gibson promised. He'd see what he could do.

Ralph Gibson's interrogation of Marilyn Plantz was not going well. Over the years, the investigator had learned the delicate, difficult art of creating an environment in which suspects understood that he was just a man with a job to do, not someone who was shocked or horrified by the suspect's actions. He appeared to be an understanding friend, someone they could tell how they had been led to the desperate corner they now found themselves.

Marilyn Plantz wasn't buying a nickel's worth. "She was the coldest, strangest woman I ever encountered in this business," Gibson recalled. "Her stock answer was that she didn't know what I was talking about— even after we had Bryson and McKimble's confession, the bloody rug, and the key ring. Her attitude was that none of that made any difference. She didn't kill her husband and had no idea who did.

"In most interrogations, a suspect would want to try to tell you something . . . to convince you, at least, that they weren't the kind of person who could do something evil. She never bothered with that. "I have to say this was probably the most interesting murder I'd worked on in my career," Gibson said.

Less than a week after Jim Plantz's murder, the DA's office worked out a plea bargain with Clint McKimble. In exchange for his testimony implicating Marilyn and his friend Bryson, he would be allowed to plead guilty and receive a life sentence rather than facing death.

When Bryson learned his friend had snitched, his bravado failed. He tried to hang himself with the shoelaces from his sneakers in the holding cell at the county jail. He next tried to drown himself in the cell's stainless-steel toilet bowl. He was transferred to a jail area that was monitored twenty-four hours a day. Apparently calmed, Bryson made another cocky mistake. He told cellmate Ricky Dunn, a trusty, that he had murdered Plantz.

Dunn told Gibson. "He said he was in bed with that guy's wife . . . when he came home . . . He said he was waiting behind the door. He beat him with a baseball bat, put him in the truck, and took him out and burned him. He said it was for a $300,000 insurance policy . . . He didn't show any remorse or nothing."

A video camera was rolling when Gibson interviewed the teenager again. This time Cliff Bryson admitted his crime and described the awful moment. "We was hitting him everywhere . . . just swinging," Bryson said. "Marilyn was in the bedroom. She said she didn't want to see her husband when we did that to him."

District Attorney Robert Macy told reporters he would demand the death penalty for Marilyn Plantz and her young lover. "This was a murder for hire . . . We'll put the defendants on notice that we'll be seeking the death penalty," Macy said at a preliminary hearing. "If there is any type of murder you can deter it's one where they sit down and coldly plan it out. You've got time to think what the consequences are going to be."

Macy added he had been hesitant to spare McKimble's life but knew the state would not win conviction of Marilyn Plantz without his testimony.

Bryson's lawyers would argue that the youth was not competent to assist in a defense of his life. He was delusional, his condition accelerated by his use of crack cocaine. Marilyn Plantz's court-appointed lawyer, Ron Evans, fought to win separate trials for his client and Cliff Bryson. He had confessed to the killing; their defenses were "mutually antagonistic," Evans insisted. Judge Charles Owens turned aside the argument. The pair would be tried together but would be permitted separate defense tables.

Ron Evans recalls the trial that proved to be the most difficult of his career, Marilyn Plantz, his most difficult client. "She was nightmare to represent," Evans recalls. "She never took me into her confidence. The empathy a lawyer hopes to have for his client just never came to be. All of my conversations with her were the same. I would go over the prosecution's evidence with her and her only answer was denials. If I showed her the check to Wal-Mart and asked her why she bought the rug, she would say she didn't know. If I asked her what Bryson and McKimble were doing at her house, she would say they had never been there. It was only in the last few days before we went to trial that she would admit to me that she did know Bryson.

"What was I going to tell a jury about all of these

things the police had discovered? She said to tell them that someone was setting her up. Who would want to do that? Marilyn said she didn't know," Gibson said.

Marilyn Plantz never took the witness stand to deny her masterminding of her husband's cruel death. Her defense was brief, the verdict almost certain. The jury openly glared at her and Bryson as McKimble told the horror story of Jim's death. When photos of his ghastly corpse were shown, Marilyn doodled geometric designs on a yellow legal pad. *Daily Oklahoman* reporter Nolan Clay watched. "She came across to the jury as colder than an iceberg. I can't imagine what she was thinking. She was on trial for her life," Clay recalled.

"In retrospect, I probably should have put on psychiatric testimony that explored her childhood, her marriage, how she thought about things. Maybe I should also have been a lot tougher with her than I was and less deferential. Maybe she needed to be jolted into understanding how desperate her situation was, that she couldn't just try to stonewall her way through this," Evans said.

But there had been problems, he added. Funds to hire an independent investigator had been denied to the defense. Obtaining a top-flight psychiatrist did not seem a request the court was likely to approve.

"If you had gone out looking for a likely candidate to have committed this terrible kind of crime, the last person you would have picked would have been Marilyn Plantz, at least on the surface. There had to be things about her that defied ordinary understanding. I know that I never understood her then, and I still don't," Evans said.

Evans was not alone. Marilyn's family could not believe she had been living some seamy double life. She had never given the smallest hint that she wasn't

213

exactly who she appeared to be: a good mom, a good wife living on the comfortable rung of a good marriage and a secure future.

"We believe in our hearts that she's not guilty of it and that's the way I believe, and I love her with all my heart. I loved her when she was a child and I love her now," her dad, Jesse Sellers, said.

Marilyn's sister-in-law, Karen Lowery, had also been stunned by the revelations. "As far as we knew, they never had any problems, they never fussed, they never argued. It's still hard to believe. It seems like I'm going to wake up from a bad dream any time," she said.

The jury took less than three hours to return what had seemed to courtroom spectators almost a foregone conclusion. Marilyn Kay Plantz and William Clifford Bryson, Jr., were found guilty. At last, Marilyn wept as she was led away to await sentencing.

Ralph Gibson had been watching when the jury returned. "That was the first time anyone had seen her shed a tear," he said. "I was sure about one thing . . . The tears weren't for her dead husband or for those two poor little kids."

The sentencing hearings were brief as well. Marilyn said she did not want Trina and Chris to testify about what kind of mom she had been. "I think they've been through enough," she told Judge Owens.

Instead, the sweet letter that Trina wrote her was read into the trial record. The last paragraph was a poem the nine-year-old had made up: "Roses are red, violets are blue. You are the sweetest mom I ever knew." Trina then added, "I always pray for you!"

Judge Charles Owen followed the jury's recommendation. It had taken them five hours to report it back to him. Marilyn Plantz and Cliff Bryson should die for their crimes. That was the sentence he imposed. Owens added prison sentences of 125 years each for the pair's solicitation of others to commit murder and fined each $15,000 for conspiracy and for arson.

Cliff Bryson found some embers of bluster when Owens passed sentence. He laughed at the prison term and the fines. "That was kind of stupid, don't you think?" he flippantly said to the judge. "How am I going to do 125 years if I'm dead . . . How can I pay you $15,000 if I'm dead?"

Marilyn said nothing when her sentence was passed. She was led away softly weeping.

Her mother, Normanda Sellers, perhaps spoke for all of those who believed they knew Marilyn Kay Plantz best and still believed they did. "She's got another judge and that is Jesus Christ. She's put her trust in him."

10

Karla Faye Tucker

THE DESPERATE, SEEMINGLY ENDLESS LEGAL JOUSTING went on for a full six weeks before a jury was finally seated in Judge Patricia Lykos's packed Houston courtroom. After six days of shocking testimony that jury reached the conclusion that the angel-faced, heart-stoppingly pretty twenty-four-year-old defendant was a monster behind a girl-next-door's sweet mask, a sex- and drug-crazed Jezebel guilty beyond a heartbeat of doubt of the unbelievably cruel, violent, and senseless murders with which she was charged.

Karla Faye Tucker had taken a pickax and given Jerry Lynn Dean twenty fatal whacks. She knew someone was watching what she had done, so she gave the witness twenty-one. Later, she bragged, the killings were fun.

There was a tomb's quiet when Karla Tucker's attorney rose to present his closing argument to the eight women and four men who would leave the chambers within minutes to deliberate on their verdict. Mack Arnold rose slowly. He weighed his words once more in his mind. What he said broke that silence with a thunderclap of shock and surprise. It was the last card the worried defense lawyer could play for the client who now wept softly at the defense table.

"The evidence is overwhelming that my client is guilty of capital murder," Mack Arnold began. Stunned reporters rushed for pressroom telephones. "It would be an injustice for you to arrive at any other verdict but guilty," he added.

What they had heard about the bloody pickax murders of twenty-seven-year-old Jerry Dean and the unfortunate woman who was sharing his bed that hot June 13, 1983, night was true, just as prosecutor Joe Magliolo had told them.

"I could tell you all kinds of things for an acquittal or conviction on a lesser charge . . . but we are here to find the truth," the veteran courtroom warrior said.

The woman who had committed those savage slayings was not in the courtroom now. The murderer had been a Karla Tucker who had surrendered her ability to reason to a tragic life. She had been heartlessly guided into a sick, twisted, and perverted world. She had become a steady user of street drugs by age ten, turned onto prostitution at the innocent age of thirteen by her mother. The woman instructed her daughter in the most customer-pleasing ways to perform oral sex.

It was a wretched, wanton, wasted life in which sleazy rock promoters paid her way to travel with bands in exchange for the budding beauty of her body. They fed her rivers of drugs and booze and turned her into a mindless, conscienceless no one. This was how she became capable—in her hopeless confusion—of her crimes. It was now up to the jury to decide whether she should live or die.

Away from that desperate and debauched world, said Mack Arnold, was a Karla Tucker who would never harm anyone again as she lived out her remaining years in prison. This Karla Tucker would no longer be so easily swayed by men she wanted desperately to please, men like Danny Ryan Garrett, the thirty-seven-year-old lover whom she had accompanied to the home of the murder victim and with him swung the fatal blows of the deadly pickax.

The jury left. There had been no way to accurately gauge the impact of Arnold's bold, astonishing summation. But outside, the Houston press corps was wild with the drama the lawyer's desperate gamble had stirred.

"I think had I walked in there in the face of that evidence and told them I thought she was not guilty and tried to argue that, I would have lost all credibility and a jury would never have listened to me again about anything," the defense counsel explained to the noisy throng of TV and print reporters.

Why had he wasted the court's time, the jury's attentiveness, if he now calmly confessed his client's guilt, a reporter asked.

"We were not wasting the jury's time," Arnold shot back. "We were exercising Karla Tucker's rights."

Had his client given him permission to make his damning admission to the jury?

"Of course," he said but would add no further detail. He remembered that conversation far too well. He had told Karla Tucker days earlier that the verdict was almost certain to be guilty. "This is the only choice I have left to save your life," he had told Karla Tucker. She had agreed that his strategy was her only hope. The grim, unforgiving eyes of the jury had locked upon her own in frank horror a hundred times each day.

The daring move that Mack Arnold made added yet more fuel to the blazing front pages of Houston's daily newspapers, already giving the sensational trial soap opera treatment.

Reporters scrambled for reaction from the city's tight-knit but not so tight-lipped legal community. Everyone, it seemed, including Arnold's courtroom opponent, had an opinion. "It was the best thing for the client," prosecutor Joe Magliolo said. "But it takes some courage to get up and do that."

The county district attorney and Mack Arnold's one-time boss, John Holmes, said, "I think it's a damn good tactic. I'm surprised more lawyers don't do it. Sometimes you have to tell a jury 'Okay, she did it. Have mercy on her soul.'"

Not all the reviews were favorable. Lewis Dickson, who had also previously served as an assistant DA, chided his former colleague. "That's just not advocating. As a practical matter, a lawyer is on trial with his client, but he's not the one that's going to face the death penalty. It sounds to me like he doesn't realize he left the employ of the district attorney's office," Dickson added.

The six days of testimony to which the jury had listened in rapt silence had indeed been overwhelming. Karla Tucker had taken a bloody hand in murder. Worse, she later plotted to kill two other persons she believed might go to the police with information. Worse yet, she had laughingly confessed to a microphone-wired police plant that she had experienced pleasant sensations of sexual arousal as she struck each ghastly blow of the pickax into her pleading victims.

It had been a crazy drug- and booze-driven crime, a fatal falling out between aimless living-for-party-time rounders. Their addictions and the need to satisfy them led from one fracas to another in Houston's subterranean late-night precincts of hazy-eyed hopelessness and two-bit treachery.

Jerry Lynn Dean was a biker, a hanger-out in mean bars frequented by junkies and hookers, people like Karla Faye Tucker and her sister, Kerri.

A smoldering feud had erupted between Karla and Dean. It began when Dean's ex-wife managed to keep a bank card belonging to him after their divorce. At her urging, Karla and Dean's ex had cleaned out the biker's bank account. Dean threatened to turn them both in to the cops. But in retaliation, he instead got his hands on Karla's most cherished possession: a tattered photo album filled with the only remaining pictures of Karla's mom, her dad, and her intact family before their breakup when Karla was still a child. Dean had taken his revenge on the most loved photos, those of Karla and her mom, who had since died an aging prostitute's death. Dean used a knife to slash at the faces of Karla and her mom, sullying those memories that had meant so much to her. Karla's fury was fierce. She told friends she intended to kill Dean to even the score.

Danny Garrett, her latest outlaw lover, had a better idea. He knew that Dean's apartment housed expensive motorcycle parts that could be stolen and sold. He, Karla, and maybe one other friend who could supply additional muscle would sneak into Dean's apartment one night, using Dean's ex-wife's key. They would rough Dean up after they had surprised him. They would demand money and steal and sell the valuable cycle parts. The proceeds would come in handy, Garrett bragged to Karla. They would use it to buy guns and then take up the serious work he had in mind for them: knocking over drug houses. This was all dependent upon whether Karla had the guts and nerve for the enterprise. She eagerly said she did.

Jimmy Liebrandt, another street friend, said he'd go along to help put the fear of God into Dean. They had been doing speed in heavy gulps for more than three days. Karla had turned some tricks. She couldn't remember the last time she had slept.

It was early morning when the trio pulled up in front of Dean's residence in the 4000 block of Watonga. Liebrandt had dozed off and could not be woken. Karla and Garrett cursed him roundly and decided to go in on their own.

"I followed Danny into the bedroom and the light was out," Karla testified under Arnold's gentle prodding. "There was a little crack in the curtains with the light coming through. I could see the silhouette of a body sitting up . . . I knew it was Jerry. I went to him, sat down on top of him, told him to shut up . . . He said, 'Karla, we can work it out. I didn't really file charges.' He grabbed my arms. We started wrestling . . . Danny came up and got in between us . . . I saw the silhouette of Danny beating Jerry in the head with what appeared to be a hammer . . . I could see the outline of everything like a shadow on the wall," Karla Tucker related.

The defendant said she got up and turned on a light. Garrett had stopped bashing Dean with the hammer. The victim was making a torn, pathetic noise as he reeled from his wounds. "It was a gurgling sound . . . I kept hearing that sound. All I wanted to do was stop it. I seen a pickax up against the wall . . . I reached over and grabbed it. I swung it and hit him in the back with it.

"He kept making that noise and Danny walked back in. I told Danny to make him stop making that noise. Danny took the pickax and swung it several more times in the back . . . then he pulled him over on his back so he could hit him in the chest . . . The noise stopped," Karla said.

Danny Garrett left the room again. Karla Tucker

made a frightening discovery. There was another person in the bedroom trembling in terror, desperately trying to hide herself.

"I noticed there was a person underneath some covers laying against the wall by the door . . . Her head was under a pillow and her body was shaking.

"My mind . . . I don't know where it was at . . . I picked up the pickax and swung it again. I tried again and a second time and when I did the person came up from under the covers . . . and it was a female. She grabbed the pickax."

Karla said she fled the bedroom where thirty-two-year-old Deborah Thornton now writhed in agony from the blows Karla had struck. She summoned Garrett to help her and paused, exhausted, outside the bedroom door. She went back in.

"I walked into the bedroom and this girl was sitting down and the pickax was real deep in her left shoulder . . . She had her hands on the pickax. She said, 'Oh, God, it hurts. If you're going to kill me, please hurry up.'

"Gary hit her again and put the pickax right in her chest," Karla added, tears streaming down her face.

As ghastly as her story had been, an eyewitness would add an even more macabre and damning recounting of that carnage. The would-be accomplice Karla and Garrett had brought along woke from his sleep in the car. He entered Dean's apartment in time to see a shivering sight. "Karla had a pickax buried in a body that was covered with a sheet.

She was frantically tugging at the heavy ax, trying to wrest it free from the moaning body of Deborah Thornton.

"There was a gurgling sound coming from the body. It was like an aquarium pump that was broken," Jimmy Liebrandt testified. "She finally got the ax out . . . got it up over her head . . . turned and looked at me . . . smiled . . . and brought it down again."

Liebrandt looked in horror, then turned on his heel and fled the scene. "I hadn't gone for that. I was just supposed to be intimidating someone to collect some money. That's not my way."

Liebrandt's other explosive recollections would further harden the hearts of the jury. After Dean's apartment had been looted, Liebrandt met again with Karla and Garrett. They were furious about his cutting and running from the murder scene. But, typically, the drugs that were passed around mellowed the crisis, temporarily at least. Karla flicked on the TV set to catch the evening news. The lead story described the discovery of the bodies of Dean and his lady friend. "Karla was estatic," Liebrandt told the jury. "She was very proud of what she had done. She thought it was spectacular."

Others in the drugged dream world in which Karla and Garrett lived were also soon aware that it had been the pair who were responsible for the slayings. Within hours following the murders, Karla and Danny Garrett boasted to Karla's sister, Kerri, and her husband, Danny Garrett's brother, that revenge had been taken on Jerry Lynn Dean. "We offed Jerry Dean last night," Karla told her stunned sister and brother-in-law. "Danny hit him with a hammer and I picked him."

Karla added another eerie admission that sent shivers up the spine of Douglas Garrett. "Hitting them with that pickax made me get off," she giggled. "I mean really get off . . . it was a trip."

Then the subject turned to an even more sinister direction. Karla and Danny wanted Kerri and Douglas to help them kill Jimmy Liebrandt and another friend they had also approached about ransacking Dean's apartment.

"You could pick a fight and kill them in self-defense," a drug-groggy Danny Garrett told his brother Doug.

Kerri and Douglas Garrett left the apartment hurriedly, remaining noncommittal about what they had heard. For the next several weeks, they took turns sleeping and standing guard in their apartment. They kept a gun on a nightstand. Kerri didn't want to believe it, but Doug feared that Karla and his brother had now become crazy enough to kill them, too.

Doug Garrett had a friend in the Houston police department with whom he'd remained friendly since their days in junior high. He went to Detective Sergeant J. C. Mosier and told his friend that Karla and Danny were the persons Houston cops were seeking in the pickax murders. Doug Garrett told Mosier of his fears for his life and his wife's but added a startling twist. "I think the devil has taken possession of both of their souls and I think he's going to make them do something crazy again. Karla likes what she did. It made her horny," he told the cop.

Sergeant Mosier conferred with the task force hunting for the pickax killers. They had a suggestion. Would Doug Garrett wear a wire, go back to Karla and Danny's apartment, bring up the subject again, and record the conversation? Doug Garrett said he would.

His heart was pounding, his throat was dry, but Doug Garrett did what he said he would do. He and Karla and his brother were captured by the police wire as they chatted breezily about the murders and about a plan to kill the potentially dangerous witnesses. As cops monitored the hidden recorder in waiting units outside, Karla made unsuspecting confessions of her guilt. She added a grim insight as to why she had turned her murderous fury on Deborah Thornton. "Because she was there," Karla said.

Doug Garrett steered the conversation to another topic the cops had asked him to bring up: Had the vicious murders been sexually arousing to Karla?

"Well, hell, yes!" Karla responded as the tape whirred on.

Within minutes, armed with a warrant, Houston police stormed into the apartment and arrested Karla Tucker and Danny Garrett for the murders they had once again confessed.

The prospective testimony of Douglas Garrett against his brother and sister-in-law touched off a legal wrangle. It centered on Doug Garrett's mental competence to appear as a witness. Mack Arnold produced evidence that Doug Garrett had been a mental patient in the early 1960s. His beliefs now that Karla and Danny were slaves of the devil was evidence that he still suffered from odd delusions, the defense contended. His testimony was allowed. He told jurors he had wrestled painfully over his decision to tell the police what he knew. Finally, he said, the Lord had told him he must. "I can't think of anybody in the world who wants to sit where I'm sitting now," he said from the witness chair.

But he added he was deadly serious about his belief that the person who had counseled Karla and Danny to commit their murders was none other than the arch-fiend king of hell: Satan himself. "I believe they were obsessed with the devil," he testified. "The devil had taken over their minds, bodies, and consciences."

Prosecutor Joe Magliolo praised the courage that Doug and Kerri Garrett and Jimmy Liebrandt had shown by their willingness to help police solve the brutal murders. He helped to soften the hurt he knew they felt about testifying against their family and friends. "They did their job. They did what they had to do," Magliolo said of them. "In everybody's life you have to draw a line sometime . . . and Karla Tucker stepped over that line."

The jury had been out only about an hour when it summoned the bailiff to say they had reached their verdict. As expected, it was guilty.

Now Mack Arnold braced himself for the final, desperate test of his skills. Prosecutor Magliolo had already indicated he would yield no quarter. He would demand that the beautiful brunette die for her crimes.

Mack Arnold took up his theme. Once the jury understood that Karla Tucker had herself been a tragic victim, they could find it in their hearts to understand what had happened and why they need not take the young woman's life to assure it would never happen again.

Dr. Barbara Felkins, a widely respected psychiatrist, took the stand for the defense. She had examined Karla Tucker. In her opinion the defendant had been psychotic at the time of the killings from her heavy use of drugs and alcohol and should not be held responsible for cold-blooded, premeditated murder. "She was in a frenzied state," Dr. Felkins told the jury. "She did not realize that what she was doing was wrong. Karla, basically, throughout her entire adolescence, was never sober."

Influenced by her drug-addicted, prostitute mother, Karla's life was a blurry nightmare of destructive excesses. And the laughing statement that murder had erotically excited her? "Karla told me she was just talking big when she said that," Dr. Felkins told the jury.

Prosecutor Magliolo challenged the psychiatrist's conclusions as inconsistent with important facts testimony had revealed. If the murders had been committed in some psychotic state, in what state of mind had

Karla and Garrett been when they coldly and methodically planned to steal and sell the motorcycle parts from Dean's apartment after removing them to their own place? How had they been cleverly able to obtain the key to Dean's home? Why had Karla told Liebrandt she intended to wear rubber gloves to conceal her fingerprints? Wasn't it true that Karla decided to kill helpless Deborah Thornton because Garrett had carelessly spoken Karla's name during the deadly attack on Dean, and Karla feared that information might be given to police unless Thornton died, too? Finally, the prosecutor demanded, what was the mind-set of Karla Tucker when she coldly tried to arrange for the murders of two other men who knew her awful secret?

Before he placed his final witness on the stand, Mack Arnold spoke to the jury. He said he was now going to call for the testimony of Karla Faye Tucker. "I think Karla would like for the truth to be known in this case," Arnold softly said.

Karla Tucker's sweet face was wet with tears throughout the two hours of her testimony and cross-examination. Step by bloody step, she recounted for the jury the mayhem she had authored in Jerry Lynn Dean's bedroom on that June night. She tumbled out her bleak expectation that mercy should or would be granted her.

"I don't see how anybody could ever be forgiven for something like I've done," she murmured softly. "Sometimes I think that if someone came up to me to do same thing or worse, I still don't think that would be justice to me. Not enough."

Then the child that remained in the twenty-four-year-old street walker talked about the child that had once been. "I started smoking dope when I was eight years old. I was shooting heroin when I was ten."

A friend of her older sister, Kerri, offered the

ten-year-old a ride on the back of his shiny Harley. He showed the gawky, sugar-faced kid how to mainline horse. "It was after that that I started to do every drug that there was," she said.

Her heavy drug use had meant trouble in the Houston grade school she attended. She dropped out with her mother's blessing before completing the seventh grade. Her mom and dad had separated when Karla was twelve. She lived with her dad for a while, then her mom came to take her back.

"I continued to use drugs. I would get strung out and kick . . . strung out and kick. I never really stopped doing drugs completely."

Karla was thirteen when her mother took Kerri and her to an Allman Brothers Band concert. One of the band's roadies couldn't take his leering eyes off the seductive teen who filled out her tight hip-huggers with an already tempting body and studied hooker's walk.

"He took me to a hotel and we partied," she said. The roadie wanted Karla to travel with the band. She pleaded with her mom. Her mother let her go. Her trips were always paid for, but the roadie and others got what they paid for. Karla developed an expensive taste for cocaine.

Karla was still a teenager when she met and married Steven Griffith. "I was fifteen, probably just fixin' to turn sixteen when I moved in to live with Steve. A couple years later we got married. I left him when I was twenty-one and went to work with Kerri full-time hustling."

It was January 1983 when Karla met and fell in love with thirty-seven-year-old loser Danny Garrett. "We met at this doctor's office who would sell you drugs," she remembered. "We started living together after about two weeks."

228

Garrett, a swaggering biker and sometime bartender, enjoyed having the pretty girl at his side. He talked tough about his past criminal exploits and his plans to become a daring bandit. He planned to engineer lightning raids on houses where drugs were dealt and run-down warehouses where they were manufactured. Somehow he never got around to pulling off any of those capers, but Karla believed he would and thought she needed to prove her own toughness to her lover. "I felt like I needed to live up to Danny's standards," she told the jury. "I exaggerated a lot of things to a lot of people because I wanted to fit in with the group I was with," she added.

The murders were a blur to her, she said. "I was shooting more speed than usual. I was pretty wired. I do remember seeing the bodies. I don't remember seeing any blood or any holes. It was not realistic to me. It was like opening a book and reading it and saying, 'I did that.'"

Her father had testified the day before along with her grandmother. Both had pleaded for mercy on Karla's behalf, but she seemed to remain haunted by something her father had reluctantly conceded. If the person on trial were there because she had killed Karla, what would he ask the jury to do? He would want them to render justice, her father sadly acknowledged.

"I've hurt a lot of people," Karla said somberly. "I wish I could take the hurt out of everybody and put it all on myself. I know what I've done, and when I think about it in my own mind, there's no justifying it."

DA Magiolo cross-examined the tearful defendant. "Do I misunderstand you, Miss Tucker, or are you asking this jury to sentence you to death?" he queried.

"I've thought about that myself," Karla replied. "I don't really know what I'm asking."

"Are you trying to get a little sympathy?" the prosecutor honed in.

"No, sir," Karla answered.

During the years she sold herself to men, had she ever had to be a bit of an actress? She said she had.

"Do you think a little bit of that actress is showing here today?" Magliolo demanded.

"No, sir," Karla answered, awkwardly fingering the cheap plastic cross around her neck.

Now it was time for each lawyer to sum up the case for the waiting jurors. Mack Arnold knew that his road led sharply uphill. "There are two Karla Faye Tuckers in this world," Arnold began. "One was a prostitute and dope addict who ran with bikers. She didn't have rules. She lived by theirs. I think there's a different Karla Tucker today. A drug-free Karla Tucker. I'm not asking you to put her back on the street. I'm asking you to give her life in the penitentiary," Arnold pleaded. "Don't give up on Karla Tucker."

DA Magliolo argued just as dramatically that the young woman deserved to die. "Life in prison is not a deterrent. What deters people from committing crimes is the threat of giving up their own lives," the prosecutor told the jury. "She sentenced herself to death when she took that pickax and put it in Jerry Lynn Dean and his friend. Her sole purpose was to kill them to get another high—to see what it felt like to off someone."

Yes, the DA said, she has admitted her guilt and spoke of remorse, but "she has mixed truth into her testimony to hide her lies."

Magliolo concluded his emotional summation with high theatrics. The tape on which Karla Tucker had confessed her guilt and acknowledged a sexual thrill with each blow of the ax had been cued on Magliolo's instructions to a specific place on that recording.

The DA posed this final question to the jury. "Does Karla Faye Tucker deserve to die?" Then he pressed the button that filled the courtroom with Karla's voice in seeming response to his rhetorical query. "Well, hell, yes!" the jury heard the defendant's drug-slurred voice reply.

"That says it all!" Magliolo snapped as the defendant's answer echoed in the courtroom's ears.

The jury that had seemed so cold and hostile to Karla Tucker was torn. They agonized as they struggled to decide if she should live or die.

It was nearly five o'clock on the afternoon of Thursday, April 26, when they returned after three hours of soul-searching deliberation to reveal to a packed courtroom what fate they had decided. Their decree was death. But it had shaken some of the deepest bedrock of their souls.

Prosecutor Joe Magliolo spoke for the panel after they had been discharged. "They said they tried everything they could to find something mitigating enough to give her life. They just thought the case was so bad they did what they had to even though they didn't want to. But I don't think that if the jury was going to do justice, they could have done anything else," the DA added.

Mack Arnold said his client, whom the courts had appointed him to defend, broke down after she was taken back to her cell to await transport to death row, but he added that the verdict had not surprised her and that she had thanked him for doing all that he could.

Danny Garrett later received the death penalty for his role in the murders. Karla testified against him.

Two unsuccessful appeals have so far been put forward in the hope that the life of the beautiful young woman might yet be spared. In prison, away from drugs and the streets, she has become, as Mack Arnold predicted, another person. Her haunting look of innocence has rallied many to the cause of saving and redeeming her gone-wrong life. "I think she reminds people of their own kids who could have gone just as wrong except for good parenting, luck, and the grace of God," Joe Magliolo conjectures today.

Some of Magliolo's close friends and colleagues have joined the efforts to have Karla's death sentence commuted. Some have told him he should visit Karla in prison and get to know the person she is now. Those friends know how important it would be if the man who obtained the sentence of death for Karla Tucker might have a change of heart and add his voice to theirs.

"I've told them that I am willing to talk to Karla, but I'm honestly doubtful that would ever change my mind," Magliolo, now an assistant U.S. district attorney, says today. "I have no doubt that she may have changed in the years since I won her conviction. I hope she has.

"But there are two people who aren't ever going to get the chance to change their lives, are they? Karla Tucker murdered them. I sent that Karla Tucker to prison with a death sentence. No change in her can ever change what she did," the former county prosecutor says.

"I don't think it harms her cause that she is a very attractive woman. I know how sweet she can appear to be. I saw it during the trial. I can't imagine that has diminished. But I have to ask myself this," he adds. "If Karla Tucker were some big, hulking brute who had committed the same kinds of crimes, would there be as much concern and sympathy being shown and all of these efforts to set aside an honest verdict determined by people who heard the facts and saw the defendant? I honestly don't think so.

"I know Karla Tucker looks like the girl next door, but I wouldn't have wanted her living in the house next to mine," he added.

11

Sabrina Butler

THE YOUNG BLACK WOMAN'S EYES WERE WIDE WITH
fright, her exhausted breathing coming in torn gasps
as she rushed through the emergency room doors at
Columbus, Mississippi's Golden Triangle Medical
Center. The small wrapped bundle she carried in her
arms and clutched in panicked desperation to her
breast held the lifeless remains of her nine-month-old
son.

Skilled and sympathetic hands worked in a fury
over the child, but there was nothing the trauma team
at the medical center could do. Tiny Walter Dean
Butler had been dead on arrival.

Now it had come time to talk to the mother, to
console her as best they could, to offer some calming
sedation if needed. Then they would try and determine what might have so tragically stolen the life of
Sabrina Butler's infant son.

It was difficult at times like these to obtain a
completely coherent scenario from a parent. The
shock was still too brutal and overwhelming, the
wracking grief too molten, the crushing guilt too
painful. The horror that had brought them there was
too incomprehensible. But there was a protocol, intru-

sive as it was. There were questions that the law required be asked, forms the same laws mandated be filled out.

There had been someone with Sabrina Butler upon her arrival. Whomever that had been had left, the young night resident observed. He sat in the waiting room in a chair opposite the mother and placed a clipboard on his knee. "I'm afraid the news we have to tell you is not good," he said. "Your little boy didn't make it . . . I'm very sorry."

He watched the woman closely, noting her nearly expressionless demeanor. He asked if she could tell him the events that led up to bringing the child to the emergency room. He listened patiently, imagining how he might be feeling if that had been his own child—sweet, still warm, gone forever on a sterile ER gurney, glided noiselessly to the cold autopsy room to await the probing of the state medical examiner's sharp, passionless knife.

"When I got home, the baby-sitter said he hadn't been breathing right . . . She gave him some kids' aspirin . . . I don't know, maybe he's allergic to that. When I went in, he had just stopped breathing all together . . . I didn't know what to do . . . We just got over here as fast as we could," Sabrina Butler said in a rush. "Oh . . . my sweet little baby . . . My sweet little man," she added.

"Did your babysitter say anything about your child having an accident . . . a fall . . . a serious one?" the intern interjected.

"No . . . no, I didn't think to ask her. When he wasn't breathing I just had a friend get us right over here. Why? Was Walter hurt in some way? I didn't know about that . . . I didn't know anything about that," the young mother said in another oddly cool rush of words.

The emergency room physician found himself staring hard, unable to take his eyes from the woman who had just realized a mother's most terrifying nightmare. Outside of that first frantic dash into the trauma center, she seemed to him remarkably composed through the harrowing ordeal. He had just come in with still-fresh frustration and anguish from laboring over the tiny child in the desperate hope that the trauma team might somehow coax a wonderful saving breath of life from the infant. In the course of that futile attempt, the child's small body had been stripped of its ragged shirt and soiled diaper and moved about in several positions. The doctor had been shocked at the fleeting observations he had made in those chaotic moments. Walter Dean Butler was a child who had suffered serious injuries that night and, from clinical appearances, on other nights, too. He was certain of one thing. The child had not died from an aspirin overdose. That would have been a kind death, and Walter Dean Butler's death had been anything but kind.

The resident's eyes moved back to the sheaf of forms he had just filled in with the information provided by Sabrina Butler.

She was nineteen. She had been married but was separated. There was another child, Danny, almost five now. He didn't live with her presently. He was with the mother of his dad, but he would be coming back to live with her soon, Sabrina said, now that she had an apartment and could take care of him. Her social worker said it could be any day now. She lived in apartment 7 in a nice brick building at 1600 27th Street North over by Morningside, but a better area.

The resident knew the neighborhood as well as he wanted to. He knew it was a troubled place. Many of the bloody horrors that rolled into the emergency room where he worked were the sad export of that north-side neighborhood. Tragic things could happen to a child there in that tumble-down and drug-blighted warren of subsidized rents and broken, fatherless families.

"Mrs. Butler, we'd like you to stay here for a little while," the night resident said. "We're required to notify the authorities when a child is brought in with injuries. The police will be here in a few minutes. They have some routine questions they need to ask you."

The Columbus police department beat car that answered the medical center's request for police investigation of the baby's death arrived not long after the call was made. Enroute, one of the patrolmen had begun to fill out their own report form with some of the sketchy details provided by the dispatcher. He noted the date and time of the original call: twelve-fifty-eight A.M., April 12, 1989.

The patrol cops took a statement from Sabrina Butler that expanded somewhat on the details she had provided to the emergency room staff. She had remembered now that on the wild drive to the hospital she had tried to get the boy's heart beating again by pounding on his chest with her closed fist. She had seen it done on television she said, maybe on the program "911." It hadn't worked though, as hard as she had tried. And she was worried she might hurt the baby with her frantic efforts.

Sabrina Butler was told she could go home. Someone else would probably want to talk to her tomorrow. The cops told her to try to get a good night's rest. She said she would.

The patrol officers needed the child's admission sheet and treatment chart to complete their report. It had gone down to the morgue with the little victim. The night resident who walked with them down there pulled back the sheets that covered the tiny form on the gurney.

"Jesus Christ!" one of them said. "What the hell happened to this baby?" He quickly looked away.

"That's what we want to know," the somber doctor said as he gently tucked the child in again for his last good night.

"Go call the bureau," one of the cops said to his still-silent patrol partner. "I think George Bass is on tonight. He has to see this."

"I don't want to . . . not ever again." Sergeant George Bass, a fifteen-year veteran of the Columbus police department, came within minutes to take his own painful look at the battered child.

He told the patrol to head for the brick apartment on 27th Street North and bring the teenage mother down to headquarters. "I'm not letting this wait until morning," he told them. "I want some answers right now."

George Bass didn't like the answers he got.

"What she told me about how the baby received the injuries just didn't add up right," Bass recalled. "There was this almost hostile attitude on her part. She had said the child had been in the care of a baby-sitter, so how could I expect her to know anything that might have happened. She hadn't been there. How was she supposed to know?

"Wouldn't you have taken the baby-sitter along with you to the hospital if that had been your child? Who else could have better told the doctors how the baby was acting that night? And if there had been some accident that had hurt your nine-month-old baby, wouldn't you be demanding details from the baby-sitter? I know I would have.

"Some parts of her story had already changed. And there was this almost unbelievable air of detachment about her, almost as if it were someone else's child who was dead, not hers," Bass added.

"I let her go home then, but I had a very bad feeling about things. Going down for the autopsy on the baby didn't make me feel any better. I can tell you that. I knew I was going to want to talk to Sabrina Butler again, real soon, once we had more medical information in our hands," the veteran cop said.

George Bass wanted to look away. But he didn't as the stark, too-revealing brilliant light above the autopsy table was positioned by Dr. Rickey Hicks to permit the best illumination for his grim task. The final heart-wrenching photos that would be snapped of Walter Dean Butler were taken by a pathology technician.

Dr. Hicks spoke a steady stream of gross observations regarding the small cadaver beneath his gloved hands. There was severe abdominal trauma visible. The infant had apparently been struck powerful blows to that area. Numerous areas of prior trauma injury to the arms and legs were noted. An X ray was taken of the child's left arm, which had appeared on gross examination to have been previously fractured.

Dr. Hicks continued to speak into the overhead microphone as he picked up the instrument with which he would make his basic postmortem incisions to reveal internal organs and to obtain tissue samples for microscopic analysis.

"The small intestine has been perforated," he noted. There was evidence of hemorrhage and a widespread diffusion of peritonitis. Prolapse of the anus was observed, but evidence of intestinal protrusion through that orifice that had been earlier noted by the trauma team had apparently receded.

Dr. Rickey Hicks was a dad himself. His cool voice did not betray what he was feeling about the sad little life now splayed open beneath his skilled knife. He knew that what his trained eyes had uncovered that early morning would be called into evidence some day soon. The tight feeling in his throat as he thought of his own kids would never register on the autopsy room's quietly whirring listener and keeper of the dark secrets of death.

Sergeant George Bass had made his own notes as the procedure moved to completion. He had what he had come for. Now he wanted the team assigned to the case overnight to talk again to the mother.

Sabrina Butler's previous two statements had been typed up and signed by her. That was the method Chief of Detectives Pete Bowen had made standard procedure. "Always let them say whatever they want to say . . . the truth . . . a lie, it doesn't matter. Then you start in to comparing them. It's amazing how poor the human memory can be when someone is trying to deceive you. They leave all kinds of footprints behind. When you start following them, you generally arrive at the truth," Bowen says.

Some of the truth had begun to emerge. When Sabrina Butler had been brought to headquarters for a third session of questioning, she was unable to provide the name of the person who supposedly had been watching her child that night. There had not been one.

Interrogators now asked how the baby could possibly have suffered the kinds of injuries he had.

Sabrina Butler's coolness failed. She cast her eyes down. "He was crying and crying. He wouldn't stop. I hit him in the stomach. I didn't mean to hurt him," she said in a barely audible murmur.

Her statement was typed. The time was noted. It was eleven-fifty P.M. Sabrina Butler was read her rights and charged with first-degree murder.

George Bass exhaled a long pent-up sigh. Sabrina

Butler had confessed her guilt but not in the horrific detail that police were now able to extrapolate from the medical evidence.

The helpless and crying infant had been laid on the floor of the ill-kept apartment and had been stomped on with terrific and brutal force by his enraged mother. The power of the blows had been of such force and velocity that part of the child's intestines had been violently thrust out through his rectum. It could have been hours before the nervous mother had finally rushed the child to the emergency room, long enough for the peritonitis to set in and spread through his body. The pain the child experienced before his death would have been excruciating. Maybe that was why neighbors had complained of the loudness of the stereo in Sabrina Butler's apartment. Maybe that had been the only way to conceal the baby's pitiful cries.

In the days following Sabrina's arrest, Columbus detectives worked the bleak neighborhood they knew as Morningside, near the subsidized tract of modest brick apartments where Sabrina lived. They found their suspect was well known but—in some quarters, at least—not well regarded. A check of county police records also found she'd had scrapes with the law before. Most revealing of all, however, was the allegation by a grandmother of one of Sabrina's illegitimate children. "What we're being told is that this isn't the first time Sabrina Butler is being accused of hurting a child," Bass said as the morning investigation briefing began.

"About a year ago, the welfare people got involved after there was a complaint that she had been seen tossing her older son out of the back of a trailer that was being used to haul some things.

"They took the boy away from her and gave him to his grandmother. The child apparently suffered from permanent brain damage, and there was a pretty big fuss when Sabrina tried to get the welfare people to give the boy back to her. They decided to leave him where he was . . . thank God," Bass told the early-morning gathering.

"Lowndes County had a case against her about a year back, four counts of forgery . . . later a car burglary beef. She got ten years suspended on the forgeries . . . five years probation, and they let her plead to a reduced charge on the auto break-in.

"She was married for a while to Dean Butler, but he's up doing time on some house burglaries, and she has a friend she says comes around to see her named Steve. Doesn't look like he has any involvement in this though.

"I've got the autopsy reports and photos back," Bass added, placing the file that contained them on Chief of Detectives Pete Bowen's desk.

"I'll have a look later," Bowen said, but he knew he wouldn't. "I didn't want to see that little boy. I wanted to keep myself and the investigation on an even keel," he later said. "I'd heard what he looked like. I knew how I would react. I didn't want that reaction to cause us to make any kind of slip as the case got ready for trial. In all the years I've been doing this I could never understand how anyone would want to hurt a child, especially their own child," Bowen, now the community's chief of police, said.

Forrest Allgood, Lowndes County district attorney, found himself staring in mute horror at the autopsy pictures that had just been placed on his desk by the investigative team. Finally, he slowly inserted them back into the brown envelope in which they had been kept. "My God," he sighed. "He looks like a little gladiator. He looks like he's been fighting for all of his little life."

Grim faces nodded in agreement in Allgood's silent office.

"The medical examiner said he'd seen that much evidence of abuse on a child of maybe ten years old . . . but never on a baby," Sergeant Bass said.

"Babies and old people . . . there just doesn't seem to be anyone to look out for them, and they can't defend themselves," Allgood sighed as the meeting prepared to recess.

"There were never any charges filed in the incident with her other boy, but Mary Butler, the grandmother, says she wants to testify about what she knows. Can you get any of that evidence in?" Bass queried the DA.

"You can bet your life I'm going to try," Allgood responded. "If I can't tell a jury that this woman should never again be allowed to have a child in her care, they might as well shut down every damn courtroom in Mississippi. They wouldn't mean anything anymore, anyway," he added.

The charges Allgood drew up against the teenage mother were based on new state statute that made abuse that led to the death of a child a crime punishable by death.

A court appointment, based on rotation, had given Sabrina Butler one of the ablest defense attorneys in the state. A former football standout at Old Miss, forty-year-old Lee Sudduth was now a formidable 315-pound, six-foot-three giant with a razor-sharp legal mind and a salty irreverence for ordinary courtroom strategy and decorum. Sudduth was mildly shocked but also bemused by Allgood's decision to seek death by lethal injection for his young client.

"This was, at best, a manslaughter case. I don't even know that she was guilty of that. She was willing to plead to that count, however, and I would have let her, given all the circumstances. But there was no way she could have been construed to be guilty under the new child abuse statute," Sudduth recalls from his trophy-lined law office on Columbus's Main Street.

"Forrest Allgood was a new DA and I think he was looking for a hot capital case. I think he believed my client was it. I had to tell him, 'Look, if this woman was anyone other than who she was, a poor black kid who'd had her first baby when she was still a baby herself, you wouldn't be trying to have her put to sleep. You'd take the manslaughter plea. Sabrina Butler never set out to murder her child. There was no cold premeditation involved. There was no first-degree circumstance.'

"I didn't see any way he could back up a consistent pattern of intentional abuse to that child or the other one. Kids get hurt in a lot of ways, and there were other assumptions that could fairly have been drawn about the injuries that caused the baby's death. A prolapsed rectum? Severe constipation can sometimes cause that in a child.

"The so-called evidence of abuse the prosecution wanted to put in was nothing more than hearsay. I don't believe another judge other than Judge Brown would ever have allowed it or a lot of other things that transpired at her trial," Sudduth said. "The whole thing was a very curious legal goin's on," he added in a deep Delta drawl.

It was March 1990 before the case of *the State of Mississippi* v. *Sabrina Butler* made its way into the courtroom of Circuit Court Judge Ernest Brown.

Sudduth's concerns for his client's fate mounted with each day of fresh, heated clashes over procedure and evidence. He felt his defense of the accused teenager had been thrust upon him by a system that now wanted to tie at least one, perhaps both of his hands behind his back.

244

"I applied for an outside psychiatric evaluation of this girl. I wanted the jury to know everything there was to know about her before they made a decision that could end her life. That request was turned down by Judge Brown. He said we could have her evaluated over at the state mental health unit.

"What we did turn up there was horrifying. Here was a child, it was discovered, who'd been the victim of child abuse herself. Her mother taught her how to raise a child. Her mother used to lock Sabrina up in an old empty refrigerator when she annoyed her. She was whipped frequently. She never got past the seventh grade. She had her first child when most little girls were still collecting Barbie dolls. She never had anyone to tell her how to be a mother, how to raise children.

"The prosecution wanted to make this a case about child abuse. Well, I believed they needed to understand how things like that happen.

"Sabrina Butler grew up being disciplined harshly in ways that you or I wouldn't find acceptable, but Sabrina Butler had been the victim herself of violent, cruel punishments, and as awful as they were, she had lived through them. Would she have believed that administering a punishment to a child would result in that child dying? No, she would not. She had no intention ever of causing anything that she could think of as permanent harm to a child.

"Now, can you bring someone to trial in a courtroom where children are imagined to be raised only in some loving, teddy bear world and ignore the fact that there are large segments of our society where that's just a dream, where the realities are sadly otherwise.

"Can you take a poor, uneducated woman and say to her, 'No, we never took the trouble to see that you learned any of these things—we didn't care enough—

245

but now, by God, we're going to bring you into a courtroom and hold you responsible for what you did just the same?'" Sudduth said.

"Justice has to be about fairness. Things that happen need to be examined in a relevant context. The prosecution used up twelve of their challenges to keep qualified black jurors from serving. As it was, we managed to get some blacks on the panel, but how representative that was remained an issue in my mind.

"Some members of the jury wept when they saw pictures of that little boy, and I don't blame them. But there weren't any tears when we showed what Sabrina's childhood had been like.

"We were constantly constrained by rulings from the bench that insisted this was a trial about child abuse, but only the state's narrow understanding of what that meant, not the deeper, stark reality of it."

Allgood had been true to the promises he had made to seek the ultimate penalty. His case to the jury was passionate. The medical evidence was overwhelming.

When Sudduth advanced the notion that the brutal injuries sustained by Walter Dean Butler had come about from a clumsy attempt to administer CPR to the infant, Allgood presented three medical experts who said that version was not remotely consistent with their findings. They said, in fact, it was impossible.

Medical experts stood before the autopsy X rays of the infant's broken arm with a pointer to note the severity of the act that could have resulted in a baby's still pliable bones to be broken.

The previous trauma scars were judged to be admissable as evidence. The mothers of two young black men who had fathered Sabrina's children told the jury she was unstable, angry, inappropriately punitive, and impatient. She was quick to punish her children for innocent, ordinary acts like crying when a diaper needed to be changed, when they were hungry, or just wanted the comfort of someone to hold them.

Most damning of all, she had confessed to police that she had struck the child in anger.

"We were not holding this woman to some incomprehensible standard of conduct in raising her children," Allgood would later say. "No one, no matter what their upbringing, can honestly claim they can't foresee the terrible consequences of inflicting violence on a helpless child. Sabrina Butler didn't grow up on another planet. Her childhood exposed her to many families where love and concern for children was the rule. If she should not on some theory be responsible for her actions, how will society protect any innocent and helpless child? That was at issue here, and it was a tremendously critical issue."

Sudduth chose not to put his client on the stand in her own behalf. He had prepared the young black woman in the pale cotton shift for the somber, unforgiving words he was almost certain would be pronounced when the jury returned to the oak-shaded county courthouse on the old square.

The hulking attorney sat impassively as DA Allgood made his emotional, final argument to the jury. But his pencil flew to life across an ever-present yellow legal pad when Allgood made one particular remark: "Mrs. Butler hasn't told you the whole truth yet," the prosecutor accused.

Whoa there, buddy, you can't say that. Not in any courtroom I've ever been in, Sudduth said to himself in sudden but satisfying surprise. *We're going to appeal the hell out of that one.*

Within hours, Sudduth would hear another unusual decision pronounced in the quiet chambers, this one by Judge Brown. In his final charge to the jury, over

Sudduth's objections, the judge told the jury that they were not allowed to bring back a manslaughter verdict. Their choices were innocent or guilty of murder.

Sudduth's grim prophecy about the trial's outcome was fulfilled. The jury's verdict was guilty, the judge's sentence was death. Lee Sudduth returned to his bear's cave on Main Street and began writing Sabrina Butler's appeal to the Mississippi Supreme Court.

"I'll be damned if that was justice," he snorted. "We're gonna see what we can do about that!"

It was June 1992 when Lee Sudduth and Forrest Allgood presented their uniquely different beliefs about justice for Sabrina Butler before the state's highest tribunal.

In his appeal brief, Sudduth argued thirty-one separate points of legal error he believed had taken place in his client's trial. He argued most vehemently that Judge Brown and Allgood had committed unconstitutional and clearly reversible error by intimating to the jury that Sabrina Butler's failure to take the stand had been some tacit admission of her guilt. Allgood should have known better than to make such an inference. The judge should have declared a mistrial when he did, Sudduth contended.

Sudduth also charged that Judge Brown's refusal to allow the jury to consider an alternative verdict of manslaughter had been a serious procedural error. Several jurors expressed their frustration and unhappiness following the trial that no decision other than life or death had been put before them for consideration. One juror signed a sworn affadavit that said there had been undue pressures placed by other jurors to return a guilty verdict, because the evidence seemed clear the defendant had done what was alleged by the state.

"This case should never have been tried as a capitol offense. The facts were not consistent with the statute that prescribes death as the appropriate punishment," Sudduth pleaded.

The state supreme court deliberated the briefs and oral arguments for three months before handing down their decision.

Sudduth's arguments had prevailed. A new trial was ordered for Sabrina Butler. The opinion handed down was a clear lesson in law. "When an accused exercises his or her constitutional right not to testify, the circuit judge must see that the state makes no direct or indirect comment on this fact," Justice Armis Hawkins wrote in the court's decision.

"The tactical advantage of having the jury wonder why, if the defendant is innocent, he did not testify, is a temptation prosecuting attorneys, especially younger ones, find difficult to resist.

"Allgood had the duty to carefully, very carefully refrain from making any remark that directly or by insinuation focused the jurors' attention or alerted them to the fact that Butler did not take the stand. That was an art he was obligated to master."

Justice Hawkins also defined the role of the presiding judge when circumstances such as those in the Butler case arose. "Though painful, the responsibility and duty of a circuit judge when such a comment is made is to declare a mistrial on the spot," the supreme court justice wrote.

As Sudduth had contended, the court also erred in denying his motion to allow the jury to consider a verdict that allowed a recommendation other than death. The jury should have been told it could return a verdict of manslaughter, the high court ruled.

DA Forrest Allgood was stung by the decision but firm in his belief that he had served the community's —and society's—needs and desires by his vigorous prosecution and his demand for Butler's execution. His remarks to the jury that had resulted in his conviction being overturned had not been intended as the high court had perceived them after Sudduth's skillful arguments.

"I never said Sabrina Butler must be guilty because she didn't testify," the DA said. "She gave three different versions to the police of what had happened that night. What I was arguing was that she hadn't told the truth yet."

"Who was the accused the police were dealing with that night?" Lee Sudduth said. "When she was asked if she understood that she had the right to remain silent, she responded with her understanding of that. She thought it meant you kept quiet until the police said it was okay for you to speak."

There will be a new trial for Sabrina Butler at a date yet to be determined. Lee Sudduth will not represent the young black woman. "I don't believe they want to court-appoint me again. I can't imagine why," he says with a mischievous grin. "I think the supreme court decision was a set of instructions for the prosecution. If they're going to try her again, it ought to be for manslaughter," he says.

"This is a case that needs to be tried again, and it will be," Allgood has vowed. "I wasn't looking for some notch in my belt. I was seeking justice for an innocent baby. That's what this office is here to do. If we can't protect children from crimes like this, what in God's name are any of us doing in this profession? Certainly I can sympathize and understand an unhappy upbringing, but that doesn't erase from someone's heart all understanding of the difference between right and wrong. What happened to that little boy was wrong. It was a crime. . . . a crime that rightfully demanded punishment."

Sergeant George Bass is Lieutenant George Bass now. The case of Sabrina Butler and her tiny son has not left his mind. "People said to me as they read the news about the trial, 'Isn't it a pity the way that little boy died?' " he remembers.

"I thought about that quite a lot and then I started answering this way. It was a bigger pity that she'd ever had the boy and that he went through the hell on earth that he did for nine terrible months of hurt and pain. That was the pity. That all of this was going on, and no one was doing anything about it. Only God and Sabrina Butler know all the things that little baby endured. God might understand it, but I couldn't, and I don't think I ever will. He doesn't tell cops everything they'd like to know," Bass says. "There are a lot of days when I wish He would."

12

=

Judy Goodyear Buenoano

THERE WERE STILL A FEW URGENT MATTERS PAUL DECKER
needed to discuss with the woman in the small, stark
cell over on Q-Wing. Prisoner policy guidelines were
explicit about some of them—simple humanity dictated others.

Paul Decker wished someone had written a book
telling people like himself how best to handle this part
of his job; but he knew there were very few persons
qualified to author it.

Within twenty-four hours the woman in that cell,
Judy Goodyear Buenoano, forty-six, would be
strapped, trembling, into the deadly arms of Florida's
sixty-six-year-old electric chair. A howling, sent-from-
hell 2,500 volts of blue-white death would catapult
her into an uncertain eternity for a gruesome catalog
of crimes against men who had loved her—including
her own nineteen-year-old son. Their deaths at her
hand had earned her the dark sobriquet the "Black
Widow" because of the way she tracked and trapped
her victims in her web.

Paul Decker, forty-one, a psychologist and assistant
superintendent of programs for Florida State Prison,
made his way across the con-sprinkled prison yard

toward the three-story, government-homely, sixtyish building where Q-Wing had been sequestered from the ghoulish curiosity of the general convict population. There, with gentle understanding, Decker would answer any question the auburn-haired grandmother might wish to ask about the cold, implacable ritual that would end her life. He would be businesslike but considerate as he assisted the doomed woman in the last decisions she would make on earth.

Decker's calm, competent approach to those anxious final hours was guided by an axiom that a crusty Southern warden had decreed a dozen years earlier when the Supreme Court paved the way to resume capital punishment.

"We promise you there won't be any surprises," Decker told death row's transient citizens as their end neared. "All we ask in return is that there are no surprises from you."

Decker remembered saying that to a prior occupant of the tiny cell where Judy Buenoano now sat. Serial killer Ted Bundy had been hard to gauge during his stay on "Q." The prison official wondered if the middle-aged grandmother had been told the celebrated slayer of pretty young women had exited the same cell, walked the same scant thirty feet, and entered the same macabre execution chamber that was—while cruelly nearby—mercifully out of sight of the six cubicles that made up death row on Q-Wing.

A team of women correctional officers had come to keep the vigil with the woman who was to be the first ever executed by the state of Florida. The team's supervisor said Judy Buenoano's nights had been restless—haunted by the daytime sounds of technicians conducting tests of the antiquated, scarred oak death chair cons called "Old Sparky."

There had been a reason for those tests, and it had made all of the prison's staff uneasy, defensive.

Less than two months before, Old Sparky had made ghastly, worldwide headlines when tough-guy cop-killer Jesse Tafero had been seated on its lethal lap. The surge that leaped to claim the condemned man somehow went awry. First crackling, flesh-searing smoke rose from the oval metal skullcap designed to send the massive blast of high-voltage current through Tafero's head. Then a sheet of flames burst out from beneath the device, engulfing the victim's grotesquely contorted face. To the horrified eyes of witnesses, it appeared as though Tafero had been burned to death —slowly. Experts would later testify that Tafero may have received no more than 100 volts. Whatever the voltage, he took an eternity to die while frantic prison authorities scurried to bring the chair up to whining, annihilating full power.

Defense attorneys for half a dozen prisoners on death row—including those representing Judy Good-year Buenoano—had rushed before every available state and federal court decrying what had happened to Tafero as clearly cruel and unusual punishment, forbidden by the Eighth Amendment. They warned that whomever Florida next sent to that defective device would suffer such torture—perhaps even being left in a vegetative state as a result of a similar malfunction.

The state of Florida said it already knew what had caused the incident. Routine procedure called for use of a natural ocean sponge, moistened prior to the execution, to be placed inside the skullcap to help conduct the charge of electricity quickly through the victim. In Tafero's case, a worker had instead chosen a man-made sponge. Lacking the same resilient qualities, it burst into flames when the current reached it.

In all other respects, exhaustive tests had shown, Old Sparky was working as it should. No convict on death row had to fear some grisly accident at the hands of the state's executioners.

Governor Bob Martinez, out on the campaign stump in Tampa, offered a politician's assurance to citizens who had been appalled by the Tafero execution:

"There's no malfunctioning of the electric chair, and once we get someone to sit there again I guess that will be the best test of it," Martinez quipped.

That person was to be Judy Goodyear Buenoano. No wonder her nights had been troubled, Paul Decker mused as he approached her cell.

The woman in the sheer, blue death-row sack dress greeted Decker politely but did not stop the swift, distracted flight of her long, slim hands across the skein of bright, colored yarn she was expertly gathering into what appeared to be a baby's bonnet.

"For my new grandchild," she said nervously, half-smiling, then quickly returning to her work.

Decker explained the mission that had brought him to her cell. He chose his words carefully, keeping his visit as routine-appearing as he could. He had found it was easier to talk about some things by referring to them in the third person.

"Judy . . . there are some things the rules require me to tell you about . . . and then there are some other things you might want to know about. . . . I'm here to answer any of your questions about carrying out the warrant. . . .

"There is the question of remains," he then said gently.

"About some aspects of that we have no control. . . . They are taken up to Gainesville to the state medical examiner before they're released. . . . But after that prisoners are free to express their own wishes. . . . A parent, a relative, a friend, a lawyer can be designated to receive them and follow funeral instructions a prisoner requests.

"That is a matter we always try to resolve ahead of time. . . . If it isn't taken care of, the law doesn't give us much in the way of options. . . . Burial takes place over in the convict cemetery at Union Prison. . . . I'm told it's a nice enough service . . . but . . ."

Judy Buenoano's pale face and downcast eyes told Decker his effort was not going as well as he had hoped. He had performed the same services for many others on their way to death in the chair, but they had all been men. They wanted to know the smallest detail so they could swagger and tease guards and other inmates on the row with their macho attitude.

"How much of my hair do they have to shave? . . . I don't want to look bad for my old lady when they ship me out of here," they would say with bravado.

"Am I going to mess myself? . . . Are they going to put me in a diaper or something? Jesus, I don't want to stink. . . ."

"Will they give me a drink . . . or a shot or something . . . so I won't look chicken?" tough guys like Tafero had asked. Decker was obliged by the rules to give them a truthful answer:

"No. . . . No drinks, no shot. . . . A prisoner has to have a clear mind when the time comes. . . . It goes all the way back to old English law. . . . The prisoner has to be aware that he is being punished for his crimes. . . ." Decker would reply.

The official turned from his reverie and continued with Judy Buenoano:

"Inmates are free to dispose of their personal property in whatever way they wish, Judy.

"We take that very seriously. We make certain that the instructions are carefully carried out. . . . Books, pieces of artwork prisoners have made—we make certain they go to the person the prisoner has designated.

"All we need is a list. . . . We take care of the rest—you can rely on that," Decker said.

"The prisoner is allowed special visitation the night before the warrant is carried out. They can name the persons they'd like to come. . . . Then there's the special meal. . . . Anything that can be bought in stores around the prison will be cooked to order—lobster, steak, whatever . . . all the prisoner wants. I can write that down for you now . . . if you'd like," Decker said.

"You ready to run through this, Judy?" he asked.

"I don't think I want to do any of this, Mr. Decker. It makes me terribly uncomfortable," the woman answered without lifting her eyes.

"Besides, I don't think I need to do any of this. I think the court is going to give me a stay. I don't think they want to burn a little old grandmother to death. . . ."

Paul Decker sighed, then prepared to take his leave of the suddenly animated woman. There was no reason to throw a black shroud over her desperate hope. In any event, the methodical countdown toward her death would move somberly apace while her lawyers and the staff of the attorney general's office continued Garden of Gethsemane legal arguments right up to the moment of execution at high noon the next day, June 21, 1990.

But then, who could be certain what the courts would decide in the eleventh hour? Even as the condemned woman was walked into the death chamber—head partly shaved, right leg smoothed by a razor, dressed in black trousers and a man's long-sleeved white shirt—the phone on the wall might still ring with news of a last-second reprieve. Judy

Buenoano's bizarre case had been heard on numerous appeals since she had received the death sentence five years earlier.

Paul Decker exchanged smiles with the woman as the heavy steel cell door closed between them. He wondered how they all kept green their hopes for life. After he left, Judy Buenoano neatly placed all the forms he had brought back into the large manila folder. She passed them through the bars to guard commander Marta Villacorta.

"That man is sweet, but he's so serious," Judy said, grinning. "He ought to lighten up a little bit."

The road that had brought Judy Buenoano to the harsh few feet of drab concrete and steel bars on Q-Wing wound its way back to a gaggle of small, dusty, barefoot north Texas towns where she had been born into a hand-to-mouth family of four kids as World War II drew to a close. Judias Welty was still a toddler when her mother died of tuberculosis. Her father was a dim, usually absent figure in her childhood. He gave her to her grandparents to raise.

"It wasn't much of a life," Judias Welty would recall. "When my grandpa died I was only thirteen. My grandma sent me to a foster home."

From there it had been reform school. A streetwise Judy Buenoano graduated from a scrubland girls' correctional camp in 1959, at age sixteen. She had learned a lot.

"I was damn tired of being on the short end of the stick all of my life. I thought I deserved some better things," she would later say.

At seventeen, Judy fell head over heels in love with dark, handsome Air Force Sergeant Art Schultz. Though the two did not marry, they set up a neat, comfortable home near the base, and within a year Judy bubbled over with wonderful news—she was expecting a baby. That joy was tinged with sorrow when the child, a boy they named Michael, was born. He was a paraplegic, doomed to a life of cruel, heavy braces, wheelchairs, and painful years of therapy.

The relationship soured after Michael's birth. Within a year Judy found another good-looking Air Force sergeant—one who was more willing to take on the heavy responsibility of the crippled child she had borne. James Goodyear was a fun-loving, laughing, gentle man whom Judy felt would see that she and her child got some of those better things her hardscrabble life had never included.

Two more kids were born to the Goodyears as Jim continued his military career—a son, James, in 1966, and a daughter, Kimberly, a year later. Judy loved her new life as an Air Force wife. She discovered that she had a good head for business and added to the family income through a variety of ventures. She liked earning money of her own.

In the late 1960s, Jim Goodyear received orders to report for duty at far-off McCoy Air Force Base in Orlando, Florida, where he would continue his specialty with the Strategic Air Command. Judy welcomed the new adventure. Her marriage to Jim had begun to stale. Her independent business ventures— among them a child-care center on Hoffner Avenue, which was prospering—had pulled them apart. She was not that unhappy when James Goodyear was assigned a year's duty in Vietnam in 1970. Perhaps that separation would be the breather their crumbling marriage needed. And if it wasn't, there were plenty of interesting men in bustling Orlando—the town that Disney built.

Connie Lang worked for Judy at the Conway Acres Child Care Center. They had become as close as sisters, she told friends. Before Jim Goodyear had left for Vietnam, Judy had confided that her marriage was no longer happy. Connie Lang confessed that hers was no better. Judy said she'd had a fantasy about how to end a loveless marriage:

"Well, we could solve our problems by lacing their food with arsenic," Judy laughingly told her friend. Connie laughed too.

When Goodyear left for his Asian tour of duty, Connie Lang moved in with Judy to help care for the three kids. Judy continued to make little jokes about poisoning husbands.

The women who had become as close as sisters shared something more than the pleasant home in suburban Gulf Breeze. After deciding to leave her husband, Connie had begun seeing local businessman Bobby Joe Morris. Judy told her friend that she had become very attracted to Morris herself. Connie stepped aside.

Jim Goodyear came home to a tepid welcome in May 1971. He reported to McCoy Jetport Medical Center for a routine physical. Goodyear was found to be fit for duty then, but within months he was a frequent patient at the dispensary, complaining of stomach pains, vomiting, and cramps. Military physicians believed he might have contracted hepatitis. By September 13, Goodyear's condition had taken a turn for the worse. He was admitted to the Naval Training Center Hospital in Orlando; his fever was spiking, chills racked his body. He died three days later. Dr. Ralph Auchenbach listed a painful litany of ailments that had contributed to Jim Goodyear's death: kidney failure, possible pneumonia and other respiratory problems, substantial liver damage, bouts of light-headedness, numbness of the limbs, and finally hallucinations.

Shortly after her husband's death, Judy Goodyear offered some theories of her own about how he had died: "He picked up something in Vietnam. That man was sick when he got off the plane. I think it was a mixup in some of the vaccinations they gave him. He acted like he had the black plague."

Months later, Goodyear's widow made some even stranger remarks to a woman friend.

"I told her I was having some difficulty in my marriage," Mary Owens said, recounting a conversation she had had with Judy Goodyear at a supermarket.

"She told me she knew a way of solving the problem that was much easier than going through a divorce. . . . All I had to do was put arsenic in my husband's food.

"She said if I wanted to do it I could get the poison right there in the store . . . and there was no way anyone would ever find out because arsenic doesn't show up in the body unless they're looking for it," Mrs. Owens remembered.

Judy Goodyear had some other helpful advice for her friend: "You should take out a bunch of life insurance on him before you do it," she said.

There was something else too: it wasn't an undertaking for the faint-hearted.

"You have to have the stomach for it . . . because of how sick it would make him," Goodyear warned her stunned friend. Now afraid of the woman who had been her friend, Mary Owens broke off their formerly pleasant relationship.

Judy Goodyear became a merry widow with the $28,000 in life insurance benefits that came her way with Jim Goodyear's death. She bought a new MG roadster, a glitzy wardrobe. Orlando had become a bit of a bore. She and Bobby Joe Morris moved up to the busy panhandle city of Pensacola. They would live together in a common-law marriage. On a whim, Judy changed her name from Goodyear to Buenoano—its Spanish equivalent, albeit not grammatically correct. She and Bobby Joe opened a swimming-pool-contracting business. It didn't do well. They pulled up stakes and moved to Colorado, where Morris had some business contacts. He did not live to see them prosper. Bobby Joe Morris died of a heart attack not long after the couple arrived out west—at least that was what his doctors concluded on his death certificate.

A tearful Judy and her kids took his body back to Bruton, Alabama, for burial in a family plot. Lodell Morris, the deceased's mother, remembered an odd, out-of-place remark Judy made then. She praised all the fine qualities of Mrs. Morris's son but scathingly denounced her former husband, Jim Goodyear.

"Every time I turned my back he got into bed with some thirteen-year-old girl," she seethed. "He didn't deserve to live."

Judy Buenoano headed back to Pensacola. She had been the beneficiary of a tidy little insurance policy she had taken out on Bobby Joe. It was sufficient to secure a spiffy new 1980 Corvette and to bankroll her newest business venture, Faces and Fingers beauty salon and nail boutique.

Judy Buenoano started living life to the hilt: cars, clothes, jewelry, swanky clubs, grand gestures toward friends. Young Pam Hill remembered just how extravagant those gestures could be. When she awoke from minor surgery, her hospital room was filled with colored balloons, presided over by a plush and expensive four-foot teddy bear.

"I wigged out when I saw this bear on a trapeze! That was Judy—that was the way she was," the girl who had been her occasional baby-sitter recalled.

More than once, Judy Buenoano had confided to friends that raising her crippled son, Michael, had been a heavy cross to bear. He had reached his late teens with no improvement in his condition, and taking him for extensive therapy sessions, changing the bed linens he frequently soiled, and cleaning up the food that dribbled on him as he tried to eat had not been tasks she always performed cheerfully. Judy liked the admiration she received for her determination to keep Michael at home with her rather than in some cold institution, but the truth was that she had always managed to hire someone else to render most of the care the boy needed.

In the summer of 1980 it seemed that Michael's health was rapidly deteriorating. He was suffering almost complete paralysis now, and a rushed admission to a hospital only slightly improved his condition. His weight had dropped from 190 pounds to only 120. He was suffering from cramps, nausea, stomach pains. His mother had taken out a very large insurance policy about a month before. Should her son die of any accidental cause, she would be the beneficiary of more than $100,000. She had not troubled the nineteen-year-old boy with any of the details; in filling out the application, she forged his name and added that of a fictitious witness.

Michael's mother had a surprise for the boy when he was released from the hospital. The two of them would leave the next day for a canoe trip on the tranquil East River. It would be all right, she promised. He could be propped up comfortably in a lawn chair wedged inside the canoe's prow. His awkward and heavy leg braces would pose no special problem. And his mom knew how to handle a canoe.

A pair of fishermen on a shaded bank of the river were the first to hear the woman's hysterical screams. They saw her pound wildly toward the shore, flailing against the shallow water. She sobbed a plea for them to help:

"My son . . . my son . . . he's in the water there . . . somewhere . . . the boat went over . . . a snake fell into the canoe from a tree limb . . . the next thing I knew he'd capsized the boat . . . please . . . please . . . you've got to find him. . . ."

From another party of anglers, Judy Buenoano borrowed a can of cold beer and idly sipped it while rescuers searched the East River for her son.

Judy Buenoano treated herself to another new car after Michael's insurance claim had been settled. She had come to pride herself on being a tough customer when dealing with insurance adjustors. She liked to tell the story of the time a few years back when there had been an unexplained fire at a day care center she owned. Among the items she would demand recovery for were a rather large number of bottles of chic, expensive Chanel No. 5 perfume.

"I told them there had been 150 bottles of the stuff in there . . . The kids all had gotten it for me as Christmas presents. Guess what? They paid off," she said, laughing raucously.

The widow Goodyear Buenoano had found a new love interest: wallpaper and carpet-store proprietor Michael Gentry. They met at a boisterous seaside watering hole that featured nude female mud wrestling. Before long, Gentry had moved in with Judy, James, and Kimberly. Judy expressed concern that Gentry didn't care for himself properly. From now on he would do as she did—take a heavy dose of vitamin C each day. It would do wonders for him. He'd also start enjoying some homemade goodies under her solicitous regime, Judy promised—tasty morsels like his favorite, Waldorf salad, made by the loving hands of Judy herself.

And now that they had decided to live together—just like a family—Judy suggested that Gentry take out a large life insurance policy, with her named as beneficiary. Gentry agreed and obtained coverage of $500,000. The way he had been feeling lately, maybe it wasn't such a bad idea.

"You may think these pills are making you healthier, but they're making me sicker than hell," Gentry told his mate in the early spring of 1983. "What's in these things, anyway?" he pointedly asked.

Gentry had been feeling light-headed, nauseous, sick to his stomach, and cramped. Judy seemed angry.

"You're probably not taking enough of them. You need to double the dosage," she said, shaking several of the capsules from their dark brown jar.

Gentry said he'd take them later. He put them in his briefcase. He had something else on his mind: the excessively high premium due each month on the huge insurance policy. He told Judy they needed to cancel it for the present; he would reinstate it or take out another one later.

"I'll call them today and cancel it," she responded testily. "I wouldn't want it to put you in the poorhouse."

Less than a month later, Michael Gentry suffered a strange brush with death. He had left a downtown restaurant, entered his car, slid behind the wheel, and switched on the ignition. A roar of red-yellow thunder rocked his car—a homemade bomb had been concealed beneath the hood. It was not a very effective device, and Gentry survived.

Michael Gentry brooded over the hair-raising attempt on his life. Who would want to kill him . . . and why, for God's sake? He was, after all, a carpet salesman—not many paid assassins could have him on their list! As Pensacola police investigated the car-bombing, their questions raised yet other questions in his mind. He remembered the vitamin capsules. He had started to accept them daily again from Judy, but later threw them away. Perhaps he still had a few—he remembered placing some in his briefcase one morning.

Pensacola Police Detective Ted Chamberlain

slipped them into a small plastic evidence container and sent them off to the crime lab. The results that came back within a few days seemed to answer Michael Gentry's question about who might want to harm him. Mixed in with the vitamin C capsules were deadly doses of the poison paraformaldehyde. For perhaps one—maybe more—of the two and one-half years Gentry lived with Judy Buenoano, the woman had been systematically trying to kill him. He was still painfully recovering from the cruel wounds he had received in the bombing—portions of his stomach and intestines and bits of his kidney had been blasted away.

That shocking discovery set into motion nearly three years of painstaking investigation by Chamberlain and other Pensacola cops. It took them first to Alabama, where the body of Bobby Joe Morris had lain in shaded slumber.

"His body had enough arsenic in it to do in eleven people," Chamberlain reported back to prosecutors in the Panhandle.

When the coffin of Sergeant James Goodyear was removed from its grave in Chapel Hill Cemetery near Orlando, medical examiners found his near-perfect state of preservation—after more than thirteen years —both remarkable and telltale. Before the advent of modern embalming technology, the chemical arsenic had commonly been used to slow the decay of the dead. There was pathos too as Jim Goodyear's body again saw the light of earth. A withered single rose remained clasped in his hand. A gold wedding band glinted brightly; it had been put there by Judy Goodyear at the beginning of the couple's nine-year marriage.

The "accidental" death by drowning of Michael Goodyear became an open case again. The forged signatures were discovered. A more exhaustive check of the story Judy Buenoano had told at the time was launched. Too much of it didn't make sense. She had said her son had snagged an overhanging tree limb with his fishing line, causing a deadly snake to suddenly drop into the canoe. In his panic, he capsized the boat. How had a boy who could barely manage small movements of his arms shot off a cast of fish line that had struck a tree on a distant bank? And why was Judy's son's body found more than a quarter mile upstream of where she said the tragedy had taken place, rather than downstream, moving with the East River's unchanging current?

A grand jury returned indictments against Judy Buenoano for the murder of her son and the attempted murder of Michael Gentry. Investigations into the cases of James Goodyear and Bobby Joe Morris continued. Her remaining son, James Arthur Goodyear, eighteen, was accused by police of being the person who had planted the bomb in Gentry's car. A jury found him innocent of that charge, but reached another verdict in the cases against his mother. She was convicted and sentenced to life in prison for the drowning death of her crippled teenage son and the attempt to slay Gentry.

Belvin Perry, the prosecutor who won those first convictions against the "Black Widow," as the press now tagged her, drew another analogy to describe Judy: "She brought to mind for me a Venus's-flytrap —you know, the plant that gives off an odor to attract and then closes in on its prey? Well, that's what she did. Once she got men in her web, she was deadly."

With another indictment for the death of James Goodyear almost certainly imminent, and yet another for the murder of Morris possible, Judy Buenoano made certain she retained the hardest-hitting, most effective defense counsel she could find. That turned out to be an old friend, James Johnston—former state senator, power broker, and tough courtroom veteran.

In addition to her upcoming defense, Judy had another task she wanted Johnston to perform. She had become a sizzling media item; book and movie rights to the exclusive story of the life of the Black Widow had to be a lucrative property, she told Johnston.

He had dealt with the brassy widow before. Defending her interests always required a firm hand: "Some of the things she'd tell me, I'd say 'Hey, I'm not going to say that in a court of law. They'd put me in a straitjacket,'" Johnston declared.

Judy Buenoano's trial for the arsenic poisoning of James Goodyear opened on October 21, 1985. A jury panel of ten men and two women was selected to decide her fate. Assistant State Attorney Belvin Perry said the case against the woman was clear, and damning. He would present volumes of scientific evidence that would prove irrefutably that James Goodyear had died after receiving doses of arsenic up to ninety times stronger than that necessary to prove fatal. After hearing testimony that would show the accused had talked about—even advised—friends of the simple use of poison to end a fractured relationship—the jury would have to conclude that was, in fact, how she had ended her marriage to the Air Force noncom.

Defense attorney James Johnston said though there was no denying that his client's husband had been poisoned, the state could not prove that Judy—or anyone else—had deliberately poisoned the dead man. James Goodyear had been in Vietnam; dangerous chemicals had been used there to conduct the war, his work as a mechanic brought him into contact with other hazardous compounds. Johnston promised he would produce expert witnesses who could offer other, just as plausible, theories to explain how Goodyear might have succumbed. Johnston's arguments did not fare well. When Agent Orange, a wartime jungle defoliant, was advanced as a possible cause of death, rebuttal experts pointed out Goodyear would have had to drink twelve undiluted gallons of that toxin to reach the levels found in his exhumed body.

The defendant claimed that all of the witnesses recalling her statements about arsenic either had misunderstood that she was making a little joke or were now lying.

It did not appear to trial buffs in Judge Emerson Thompson's Orange County Circuit courtroom that the real drama in the case would begin until the likely guilty verdict had been returned and opposing counsel joined in the true battle they faced—trying to sway the jury's verdict toward or against death in the electric chair for Judy Buenoano. In that sentencing hearing, both attorneys would be allowed an evidentiary freedom not permitted by the stricter rules of trial.

When that expected verdict had been returned, James Johnston unleashed his first bombshell. Eighteen-year-old Kimberly Goodyear testified that she knew who had poisoned at least one of the victims. Her dead half-brother, Michael, had done it. She had seen him surreptitiously spiking a bottle of medicine used by Bobby Joe Morris when the family had lived in Colorado in the late 1970s. There had been a reason for Michael's plot to kill his common-law stepfather, Kimberly added in a flood of tears: Michael had become a witness to a shocking family secret when he discovered Morris trying to molest Kimberly.

"Michael was going to do something about it. He didn't want me to live with it," the pretty teenager said from the witness stand.

"I swore to Michael I would never tell," she continued, sobbing. "He was helping me out. He was getting the pain off of me.

"This is something I have to live with the rest of my life . . . and now all these people know it," she added, gesturing to a full courtroom.

Prosecutor Perry gently asked the girl why she had never told her mother about the molestations or mentioned it to police during their lengthy investigation.

"You're trying to blame this all on Michael, aren't you?" Perry concluded his cross-examination, turning toward a jury he believed would understand the girl's desperate attempt.

The testimonies about Bobby Joe Morris, about her son's "accidental" drowning and the attempted poisoning of Michael Gentry, were all admissible in the sentencing phase of the Black Widow's trial. Prosecutors and defense led the jury through a maze of dates, times, places, scientific data, and their own interpretations of what all of that meant.

Johnston sharply attacked permitting the jury to hear testimony about those other crimes. "There is not a chance of this lady getting a fair trial," he argued hotly.

His client's conviction for the murder of her own son had been based on "nothing stronger than suspicion," her attorney claimed. The case was a house of circumstantial cards; the state had not ruled out every other reasonable possibility.

"What evidence is there that says Mrs. Goodyear Buenoano tossed him out of the canoe?" Johnston asked. Then he answered: "There is none!"

And of the accusations that she had told others about arsenic poisoning?

"Are we to infer now—from a joke—that a crime

was committed? . . . There is no evidence that a crime has been committed," Johnston said.

"We know that she said she could poison him with arsenic," Judge Thompson said in ruling on a motion to suppress. "And we know that he died of arsenic poisoning."

The jury heard tearful, sometimes defiant testimony from the defendant:

"Didn't you put arsenic in James Goodyear's food and drink?" Prosecutor Perry demanded.

"No!" Judy answered, her face set in outrage.

"I guess he just had bad luck, then?" Perry jabbed.

"That depends on what you mean by luck," the defendant answered.

The Black Widow claimed her trial was a witch-hunt. She had no idea why arsenic was found in the bodies of Goodyear, Morris, even her own son, Michael. If she had, somehow, been the unwitting hand behind it, "it was an accident."

Pressed about another thread that linked her to the deaths of three men and an attempt on the life of a fourth, Judy Buenoano conceded she stood to gain as the beneficiary of life insurance policies on each. In the case of James Goodyear, there had been a lump sum of $28,000—but an additional $70,000 in benefits had been paid to her as a veteran's widow over the fourteen years since his death. When Bobby Joe Morris died, she collected $50,000. The tragic drowning of her son had enriched her by $125,000, she admitted. And she had never canceled the half-million-dollar policy on Gentry. The mention of Michael brought a rush of tears and a weeping denial:

"Why would I kill my own child?" she asked. "I have lived with guilt every day since he died . . . that it was my fault . . . but I didn't murder him. . . . It was an accident."

Belvin Perry thundered the state's opinion of the Black Widow to the jury considering whether to recommend the death penalty:

"Judy Goodyear spun her web," he charged. "While her man was away in Vietnam, she shared his bed with someone else. Then, when he came back, she slowly began to poison him.

"James Goodyear had bad luck, all right. And there sits his bad luck," the prosecutor said, pointing at Judy Buenoano.

"What mercy did she show Sergeant Goodyear as he lay there in that bed dying from her hand? James Goodyear slowly, painfully, left this earth, while his loving wife watched him suffer.

"She showed him no mercy . . . and I submit to you she deserves no mercy," the prosecutor said.

The jury's recommendation was for death by electrocution. They had not been moved by James Johnston's emotional warning that to put her in the chair would be "literally to burn her at the stake."

Before Judge Thompson passed sentence, Judy Buenoano said she wished to address the court:

"I didn't ever kill anybody, Judge Thompson," she began. "I ask the court to spare my life. I just ask you for mercy."

Chained at the waist, ankles, and wrists, she told the jurist she had found God during her years of confinement. She said if her life were spared she wished to spend it working with the prison ministry. She said Christian love of the kind she had been touched by could deter some of the worst evils faced by younger women entering prison life, such as the sin of homosexuality.

Judge Thompson was unmoved by the Black Widow's plea.

"On the day designated, the death warrant authorizing the execution shall be read to you immediately

272

before execution, and you shall then be electrocuted until you are dead," the judge quietly intoned. There was no third-person artifice.

Paul Decker permitted himself a wry grin on the morning of June 21, 1990. At about 8:10, just as Judy had predicted, the phone rang with the news she had so confidently expected: A judge would hear her appeal that she faced a barbaric death were her execution to be carried out in dubiously reliable Old Sparky.

The courts finally ruled that Governor Martinez had been right—Florida's chair was equal to its deadly task. It was proven not long after the Tafero incident by the execution of two other men on death row. By then, however, Judy Buenoano had won other stays, one based on an appeal that had shocked and hurt her old friend James Johnston. The Black Widow argued that Johnston, anticipating a megabucks book-and-movie deal only if his client was sentenced to death, had not fought skillfully or hard enough to save her from that fate. He had not introduced evidence of her sexual abuse as a child or her resulting emotional scars, her new appeals lawyers asserted.

Stung by the charge, Johnston fought back.

"I talked to everyone she ever asked me to talk to," he said sadly. "There just weren't that many people willing to come forward on her behalf."

Within the year, James Johnston would die from the complications of liver cancer. The state defended his integrity and diligence as the appeal wound on through the courts. Johnston could not have profited from any book-movie deal unless Judy Buenoano had given her final consent. Their agreement provided only a lien on the first earnings of the project, were it okayed by the defendant. Florida's supreme court agreed. Johnston had provided competent counsel. Testimony concerning the defendant's unhappy childhood would have been unlikely to have changed the jury's verdict.

Yet another appeal, alleging that Judge Thompson had erred in imposing the death penalty, was also struck down:

"Systematically poisoning one's husband over a period of time and witnessing the effects of the poison is an unusual manner of committing a homicide," the court's rejection said.

"This is a clearly conscienceless, pitiless crime, especially since Goodyear's death did not occur as a result of a single effort, but by virtue of continued efforts of Buenoano. His death was not instantaneous, and the medical descriptions reveal he suffered considerable pain and torture," the court's opinion concluded.

In November 1992, the eleventh Judicial Circuit of the U.S. District Court of Appeals once more issued an indefinite reprieve to the Black Widow. It ordered a lower-court judge to hear more witnesses on one of the numerous appeals still pending and report back with the findings of those hearings.

Two men who have come to know Judy Goodyear Buenoano well are certain much more will yet be heard from the enigmatic grandmother whose path they crossed, whose web touched their lives.

Paul Decker felt mildly chagrined as he watched the woman being prepared for transport from his prison back to the women's facility in downstate Pembroke Pines. She seemed a decidedly different person.

"There wasn't any more 'yes, sir, and no, sir' after the court granted her stay. She went from politely subdued—when I had been with her—to downright demanding as she left. She was telling the guards, in no uncertain terms, how things were going to be done on the trip back. It made me think she had been putting on a show of sweetness for me . . . and I guess I fell for it," Decker recalled.

274

Pensacola Detective Ted Chamberlain, the man who had become the Black Widow's nemesis with his relentless investigation of her crimes, chuckled at a grim rumor that had come back to him from correction officers on Q-Wing.

"She told them she wants to see me six feet under, with worms crawling out of my eyes," the detective said.

"She's a real beauty," he added.